CAMBRIDGE STUDIES IN INTERNAT

G000078931

THE HIERARCHY OF ⟨

Cambridge Studies in International Relations is a joint initiative of Cambridge University Press and the British International Studies Association (BISA). The series will include a wide range of material, from undergraduate textbooks and surveys to research-based monographs and collaborative volumes. The aim of the series is to publish the best new scholarship in International Studies from Europe, North America and the rest of the world.

CAMBRIDGE STUDIES IN INTERNATIONAL RELATIONS

THE HIERARCHY OF STATES

Reform and resistance in the international order

IAN CLARK

Fellow of Selwyn College, Cambridge

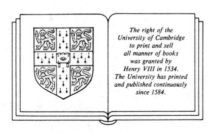

The right of the
University of Cambridge
to print and sell
all manner of books
was granted by
Henry VIII in 1534.
The University has printed
and published continuously
since 1584.

CAMBRIDGE UNIVERSITY PRESS

Cambridge

New York   Port Chester   Melbourne   Sydney

Published by the Press Syndicate of the University of Cambridge
The Pitt Building, Trumpington Street, Cambridge CB2 1RP
40 West 20th Street, New York, NY 10011-4211, USA
10 Stamford Road, Oakleigh, Melbourne 3166, Australia

First published 1989
Reprinted 1991

The hierarchy of states: reform and resistance in the international order
succeeds and replaces *Reform and resistance in the international order*,
published by Cambridge University Press in 1980 (hard covers
0 521 229987; paperback 0 521 29763 X)

Printed in Great Britain at The Bath Press, Avon

British Library cataloguing in publication data

Clark, Ian, 1949 Mar. 14–.
The hierarchy of states: reform and resistance in the international
order. – (Cambridge studies in international relations; 7)
1. Foreign relations, 1815–1990.
I. Title. II. Clark, Ian, 1949 Mar. 14–.
Reform and resistance in international order.
327′.09′034.

Library of Congress cataloguing in publication data

Clark, Ian, 1949–.
The hierarchy of states: reform and resistance in the international
order / Ian Clark.
        p.   cm. – (Cambridge studies in international relations; 7)
Rev. ed. of: Reform and resistance in the international order. 1980
Bibliography.
Includes index.
ISBN 0 521 37252 6. – ISBN 0 521 37861 3 (pbk.)
1. International relations. 2. World politics – 19th century.
3. World politics – 20th century.
I. Clark, Ian, 1949–. Reform and resistance in the international
order. II. Title. III. Series.
JX1315.C57   1989.
327′.09–dc19   89–539 CIP

ISBN 0 521 37252 6 hard covers
ISBN 0 521 37861 3 paperback

CE

To Paula and Steven
who have grown up with this book

CONTENTS

PREFACE

It is now almost a decade since *Reform and Resistance in the International Order* first appeared. My continuing conviction that students of international relations benefit from exposure to the theoretical and historical aspects of the subject, as well as the positive reception accorded the original, encourage me to produce a revised edition. In this, while the overall structure remains similar, completely new chapters have been added, both on international/world order issues and on an introductory survey of change in the international system between 1815 and 1990. The opportunity has been taken to rewrite large sections of the original, essentially to take account of new literature in the field and also to accommodate the twists and turns of superpower relations since the 1970s. My greatest debt remains to the many students I have been privileged to teach over the past fifteen years, most recently to the graduate members of the M. Phil in International Relations course of the University of Cambridge.

INTRODUCTION: THE 'WHIG' AND 'TORY' INTERPRETATIONS

The purpose of this book is to analyse the nature of the hierarchical state system, both in terms of theoretical accounts of its workings and a historical examination of its operational principles since 1815. Its principal focus will be upon the nature of international order and its potential for reform. It seeks to shed some light on the questions raised by Meinecke: 'is this no more than a continual movement to and fro? Or do any organic developments take place here? How far is statecraft timeless, in general, and how far is it changeable and capable of development?'[1] What have been peoples' expectations of the international order and to what extent have they been realised?

These issues will be approached by examining two inter-related dialectics. The first is an intellectual or 'ideological' one between the utopian proponents of reform and the realist advocates of continuing power-political practices. The second is a historical one, involving attempts to implement international order in practice, and is a dialectic between the pursuit of reform and the inherent propensities towards hierarchy and dominance within the system. In terms of this latter, the major issue to emerge is whether it is the hierarchy of states which must be restructured for reform to take place or, alternatively, whether hierarchy is not itself a necessary constituent of international order and a clear demarcation of hierarchical roles evidence of the attainment of reform.

The terms of the ideological dialectic have been much wider than those of the historical: while the intellectual exploration of the issues of international order has encompassed not only reforms within the current international order but also the transformation of the current state system to incorporate world order concerns, in practice the historical dialectic has been confined to attempts to develop regulatory diplomatic procedures and, even more narrowly, to a 'toing and froing' between concert and balance practices among the Great Powers themselves. Nonetheless, although much more wide-ranging

1

in its intent, the intellectual speculation about the potentiality for reform of the international order helps us to understand both the impulse to reform, and its limited impact, in the actual conduct of international relations. Taking both the ideological and the historical dimensions collectively, we may accordingly distinguish a 'whig' and a 'tory' interpretation of international history, the former of which is conspicuously progressive and the latter cyclical when not actually regressive.

The historical survey will trace the evolution of the international order since 1815 and there may be significance attached to that year from whichever perspective it is viewed. One of the conspicuous features of the post-Napoleonic settlement was that it, in Holbraad's words, 'introduced divisions in the hierarchy of states more marked than those that had existed before'.[2] This can either be viewed positively as the commencement of a more conscious phase in the Great Power management of the international system, or negatively as the final *de jure* recognition of the inequalities that had always existed *de facto* in the balance of power system. After all, a system of states organised in terms of disparities in power had been intrinsically a hierarchical arrangement: to bestow legitimacy upon this situation was simply to draw additional attention to this characteristic of the state system. Paradoxically, however, the more formal articulation of a hierarchical order, associated with the concert system, has frequently been regarded as an early and significant effort consciously to reform the international order. To that extent, both utopians and realists have seen virtue, albeit for different reasons, in a hierarchy of states.

The description of the state system as hierarchical should not be understood in too precise a sense. Waltz has used the term to define a structural ordering principle of a political system and, in this sense, it is to be contrasted with an anarchic order.[3] The present work employs the term in the less specialised sense of meaning a social arrangement characterised by stratification in which, like the angels, there are orders of power and glory and the society is classified in successively subordinate grades. This hierarchy is commonly assigned in terms of politico-strategic power, yielding the traditional groupings of Great Powers, medium powers, and small powers. It may equally be described in economic terms, yielding the stratification into first, third and fourth worlds. Outside a statist perspective, it may be analysed in terms of centres or cores, semi-peripheries, and peripheries. Its key theme is that disparities in capability are reflected, more or less formally, in the decision making of the society of states. In this sense, although Waltz's dichotomy between anarchy and hierarchy can be

2

understood, the description of the state system as hierarchical in this book is not intended to deny its 'self-help' anarchical characteristics: hierarchy, thus viewed, collectivises decision making within the rank of Great Powers while retaining the anarchical form of politics as between that rank and the others. From the viewpoint of the smaller states, power politics is in no way diminished.

In the survey of historical efforts to reform international order since 1815, the limited scope of attempts to redesign the international order will be made apparent. Indeed, so narrow are the confines within which this has been attempted that it becomes almost misleading to speak of 'reform of the international order'. At the very most, there have been attempts to have the Great Powers subscribe to limited 'group norms' in terms of which the Powers might conduct their management of the international system; actual efforts to reform the system do not seem to have gone beyond this limited goal and, even here, as will be seen, success has been sporadic and largely non-cumulative. In fact, therefore, when we speak of historical attempts to reform the international order, we should perhaps more accurately refer to attempts to implement certain fairly minimal 'regulatory' mechanisms.[4]

One is struck, therefore, both by the magnitude of the reaction against the prevailing international order, at times when it has experienced dramatic crises, as also by the minimal impact of this on the actual practices of international diplomacy. Hinsley accurately conveys this rich ambivalence:

> At the end of every war since the end of the eighteenth century, as had never been the case before, the leading states made a concerted effort, each one more radical than the last, to reconstruct the system on lines that would enable them, or so they believed, to avoid a further war . . . These initiatives are as characteristic and distinctive of the operation of the system as are the dynamics of its wars. So is the fact that they all came to nothing.[5]

How are we to account for the disparity between the intellectual speculation about reform and the limited achievements of historical practice? In a discussion of the concept of international order, one writer distinguishes between two main approaches to understanding that term.[6] He considers order, first, as 'process' and, secondly, as 'substance'. According to this distinction, order in the first sense

> is essentially formal in character. To satisfy this criterion a society does not have to achieve certain substantive goals or standards. Instead, the emphasis is on means rather than ends, on the manner of behaviour rather than its content, on the mode rather than the quality of life.

3

Order, in the second sense,

> is a matter not of form but of substance. It is not enough, the
> argument runs, for things to be done in an ordered way. It is also
> necessary that what is done should be such as to merit the word
> orderly. The essence or the effect of action is what counts not the
> existence of recognised processes for its execution.

It would be misleading to assert that the ideological debate has been
about order as substance whereas the history has been about order as
process: clearly, world government could be regarded as either a
substantive end or as a processual means and to that extent the
distinction must break down. However, with this caveat in mind,
there does seem to be some point in saying that in the history of
practical attempts to reform international order, the focus has not gone
beyond that of diplomatic 'processes' in an attempt to develop
improved regulative systems. In contrast, the corpus of international-
order theorising is very much concerned with the substantive goal of
creating conditions for the 'good life' for individual human beings.

How then would we describe the 'whig' and the 'tory' interpretations of international history? The whig interpretation has two principal facets: these are, first, a conviction that progress is possible and
that it has in fact occurred and, secondly, a belief that the present is the
culmination of history and that the past can be understood as sequential stages in the process of arrival at this destination. The essentials of
such a historical perspective were long since admirably set out, and
criticised, by Herbert Butterfield, who argued that the whig historians
had an over-riding tendency 'to emphasise certain principles of
progress in the past and to produce a story which is the ratification if
not the glorification of the present'.[7] He summarised in these words:

> The total result of this method is to impose a certain form upon the
> whole historical story, and to produce a scheme of general history
> which is bound to converge beautifully upon the present – all
> demonstrating throughout the ages the working of an obvious
> principle of progress.[8]

This is not the place to enter upon a lengthy exegesis of the notion of
progress and what it might mean in relation to international order, but
a few comments are required. Progress has been defined as 'irreversible ameliorative change'.[9] The central question is, of course, what
would constitute improvement or amelioration in the context of a
discussion of international order? Some might set their sights low and
aim for little more than the 'humanising' of power-political processes;
some might measure progress in relation to the transcendence of the

present state system and its replacement by some form of centralised authority; others again might think of international order in full-blown terms as an idealised world order in which all human values are realised.

How then can a whig interpretation of progress in international relations, or its tory refutation, be substantiated? One source has suggested that theories of political progress can be grouped in five categories, each of which provides a different 'end-goal' or yardstick in terms of which the occurrence of progress, or its absence, might be measured. These are listed as being: (1) a trend towards control over man's selfish or 'unsocial' nature; (2) a trend towards larger and larger political units; (3) a trend towards rational efficiency in social and political organisation; (4) an advance towards greater equality; (5) an advance towards greater freedom.[10] Each of these would clearly be problematic in any political context and, collectively, they are certainly so if an attempt is made to apply them to a discussion of international relations, as a cursory glance would readily indicate. The state, to the extent that it represents a 'general' interest may be thought to realise the first goal of controlling man's unsocial nature but it is itself the expression of a 'particular' interest within an international framework. As regards the second point, it is not clear whether, or in what sense, a trend towards larger political units is in itself a desirable goal or whether, in an international context, the trend towards a global political community should be encouraged merely as a contribution to the third goal, that of rational efficiency. If the latter, the argument is far from self-evidently valid. This third, in turn, begs all kinds of questions about rationality and about the place of efficiency in the scale of human values. As for the last two, the tensions between the ideals of equality and freedom have often been noted and these are aggravated at the international level where, to make the most obvious point, the equality of the lesser states can only be secured by curtailing the freedom of the larger ones. In any event, some international-order theorists would deny that the application of principles of equality is desirable in international relations and would subscribe to the view that, in an otherwise anarchical milieu, hierarchy serves the international community better than equality.

The terms in which 'progressive' change within the international order has been affirmed and denied are, at best, uncertain and far from clear. Nonetheless, it is around these opposed interpretations that the whig and the tory schools have congregated.

The essentials of the whig interpretation have already been suggested but may be pulled together at this point. It is a progressive doctrine and argues that successive phases of international order reveal an improvement on the stage that preceded it: the League of Nations was an improvement upon the Concert of Europe and the United Nations was likewise an improvement upon the League. Similarly, the democratic context in which foreign policy is now conducted represents an improvement upon the aristocratic context of yore and the present international order is itself preferable for that reason. Moreover, the significant aspect of international political life is not the number, and the intensity, of the wars it has experienced but rather the progressive articulation of human revulsion against these wars. There may be profound disparities in standards of living between rich and poor sectors of the globe but the problem is accepted as a responsibility of the international community to a hitherto unprecedented extent. In these various ways, the international order of today is assumed to be an improvement upon the international order of 1815.

The second strand of the whig interpretation is its tendency to read history 'backwards'. What is important is the present and our interest in past international practices exists only to the extent that they explain how the present situation was reached. As Hinsley has observed 'vast efforts have been made, innumerable books have flowed, from the wish to cite Dubois or Dante, Cruce or Sully, as forerunners of the League of Nations or United Europe or the United Nations experiment'.[11] Or, as it has been expressed in one whiggish sentiment, 'the United Nations is the present manifestation of the natural legacy, passed from one generation to the next, of the continuous search for the warless world of peace and security'.[12]

According to the whig view of international history, the modern is the goal and we study history to understand the progressive unfolding of the design immanent within the historical process itself. A clear example of such reasoning can be found in the following passage, written at a time when it was difficult to maintain faith in a progressive account of the world:

> The free people of the earth are today in a situation in which there is no survival for them except as United Nations. The crisis-situation is a result of historical development of the dynamism of the forces of democracy, industrial technology, and nationalism, which in mutual support and conflict have shaped the background out of which the crisis grew. But in their historical texture the possible solution of the crisis is delineated. Democracy, technology, nationalism, all point toward harmonization in the United Nations.[13]

The same author quotes the text of the resolution, for a Declaration of the Federation of the World, adopted by the Senate of the state of

North Carolina in 1941 which is a classic statement of the whig profession of faith:

> Just as feudalism served its purpose in human history and was superseded by nationalism, so has nationalism reached its apogee in this generation and yielded its hegemony in the body politic to internationalism. It is better for the world to be ruled by an international sovereignty of reason, social justice and peace than by diverse national sovereignties organically incapable of preventing their own dissolution by conquest.[14]

It may be worth pointing out that there are some striking resemblances between the whig interpreters of international order and the early school of 'modernisation' theory which played such a conspicuous part within the American political-science fraternity in the early 1960s. To the latter, the 'developing' countries of the third world were to the modern democratic state what the primitive international political system was to the one which has progressively unfolded over the past century or so. As one critic has said of the modernisation school:

> Political modernity is representative democracy, and the practical achievement of the democratic ideal has reached its highest point in the United States of America. The process of modernisation, in less advanced areas of the world, is therefore very simply to be understood as one of 'transition' in which backward polities will grow increasingly to resemble the American model.[15]

In these terms, and according to the whig perspective, the international polity is but a 'developing' system writ large.

The tory interpretation stands in stark contrast to the foregoing account. The characteristic features of international political life are the same now as they were several centuries ago: in contrast to the emphasis upon progress, the tory belabours the theme of constancy or, if in a black mood, even gives expression to a regressive view of the world.

The spirit of the tory view is well captured in the following denunciation of the idealist vision of international politics, a speech delivered at Glasgow University by F. E. Smith, First Earl of Birkenhead, in 1923:

> For as long a time as the records of history have been preserved human societies passed through a ceaseless process of evolution and adjustment. This process has been sometimes pacific, but more often it has resulted from warlike disturbance. The strength of different nations, measured in terms of arms, varies from century to century. The world continues to offer glittering prizes to those who have stout hearts and sharp swords; it is therefore extremely improbable that

the experience of future ages will differ in any material respect from that which has happened since the twilight of the human race.[16]

Where there are signs of change and of improvement, the tory remains convinced that this is only at the level of appearance. Underneath, the reality remains the same. Thus, as one tory has argued, when the international system of the twentieth century replaced the balance of power with a formal regulatory mechanism in the shape of a universal international organisation, all this did was to create 'power politics in disguise'.[17]

The tory interpretation has yet another twist which makes its judgement even more depressing and yields the note of regression in some of its pronouncements. The point is that, in the tory assessment, attempts to improve upon a balance system, as a form of regulatory device, not only do not realise the expectations of the whigs but can in fact be positively harmful – they lead not only to power politics in disguise but indeed to a hamstrung and inefficacious brand of power politics which leaves us with the worst of both worlds. Thus it was Hedley Bull's considered opinion that 'the attempt to apply the Grotian or solidarist formula has had the consequence not merely that the attempt to construct a superior world order is unsuccessful, but also that classical devices for the maintenance of order are weakened or undermined'.[18] In terms of this perspective, the tragedy of the inter-war period is explained not only by the failure of the League of Nations but by its hindering of the balance tactics which might otherwise have secured a fragile peace.

This is not to suggest that there is no middle ground between the two interpretations. On the contrary, most analysts prefer the safer ground in between to either of the two extremes so far presented. Inis Claude might be taken as representative of the 'agnostic' position, which sees an essential ambivalence in virtually all developments in the field of international order:

> Certainly there is no guarantee that international organisation will be successful. It is easy to exaggerate the progress that has been made; supporters of international organisation are often tempted to take too seriously the ostensible gains that exist only on paper ... But it is equally easy – and perilous – to adopt a pessimism which refuses to recognise the advances that have been made and denies the hypothesis that a meaningful opportunity exists for gradual taming of power, harmonizing of interests, and building of allegiance to the ideal of a world fit for human life.[19]

The framework of the discussion thus far suggests a dualism in the history of thought about international relations, the field dividing into utopians and realists, or whigs and tories. In terms of the potential for reform within the international order, such a dichotomy is warranted. However, once we begin to analyse the characteristic structures and processes of international relations, the traditions of thought proliferate beyond those two central schools. Indeed, as Chapter 2 will seek to demonstrate, the idealist/realist debate is no longer the most significant 'fault-line' within the theory of international relations. The list of traditions or perspectives is seemingly endless, some preferring to categorise the field into liberalism, socialism and realism,[20] others employing terms such as pluralist, realist and structuralist.[21]

The significance of such categorisations is twofold. First, they add new issues to the agenda of order and compel the analyst to step outside the framework of the state system and the traditional concerns of statecraft. A review of the implications of doing so will be attempted in Chapter 2. Secondly, they suggest alternative understandings of the essential nature of international relations and, in focussing attention upon new actors and processes operating outside the framework of states, add to the complexity of any endeavour to reform the system. This in itself helps to explain why the historical record of reform is so much more limited than the scope of intellectual speculation: while theorists have sought for new intellectual frameworks, the diplomats have operated within the old, even when they have sought to reform some of its practices.

The first part of the book is an elaboration of the whig and tory ideologies in relation to international order and its potential for reform. Moreover, it singles out two philosophers of the eighteenth century as representatives of the two streams of thought, Kant being presented as the whig and Rousseau, however unlikely, as the tory. It is fitting that the book should focus upon two writers who expressed their thoughts upon reforming the international order on the eve of the period when the study takes up its historical narrative. It has been said that 'whoever studies contemporary international relations cannot avoid hearing, behind the clash of interests and ideologies, a kind of permanent dialogue between Rousseau and Kant'.[22] To the extent that this is so, this book seeks to continue the dialogue and in its survey of the history of international order since 1815, and attempts to reform it, to suggest which of the two might be having the better of the argument.

PART 1

THE IDEOLOGY OF INTERNATIONAL ORDER

1 ORDER AND INTERNATIONAL RELATIONS

The enquiry should begin by asking how states combine to produce a situation in international relations that we would term international order? Obviously, at one level, this is primarily a descriptive task. It involves looking at the history of international relations and discovering how international order has been created. This will be done in the latter half of the book. Equally obviously, this can only provide a partial answer, because it is necessary first of all to arrive at some conception of what is meant by international order. Moreover, such a conception is almost inevitably going to be a prescriptive one embodying certain value preferences, for the simple reason that order itself is not normatively neutral: it carries with it certain connotations and these may not be acceptable to all people. What is order for the policeman may not be order for the anarchist. What is order for the bourgeoisie may not be order for a revolutionary proletariat. What is order for the Great Powers may not be order for the small. What is order for the satisfied states may well not be order for the dissatisfied. Order, in other words, is normally a set of particular, masquerading as a set of general, preferences.

The book will be concerned with certain mechanisms devised, and certain norms of behaviour developed, in an effort to manage the relations between states. The mechanisms and behavioural patterns with which we will be particularly concerned include the following: the Concert of Europe, alliance systems, the League of Nations, the United Nations, bipolar alliance structures, nuclear deterrence, crisis management, detente, spheres of influence, the economic components of international order and finally the re-emergence of a system with features resembling the more traditional balance of power. Intuitively we can appreciate that these various devices and mechanisms are in some way related to the pattern of international order. In fact, for the most part they are to be viewed as means towards the creation of international order. The question remains –

what kind of international order? Do various order-producing systems, in fact, create different types of international order? In other words what, in a prescriptive sense, do we think the main elements of international order should be and how is this order to be attained? From this it can be seen that it is of major importance for arriving at a conception of international order that we should look at the historical pattern of efforts in this direction and examine their various consequences.

Generally speaking, we can divide approaches to international order into two categories. The distinction is implicit in the division made by two authors, seeing order as having two components: first, how can the likelihood of international violence be reduced; secondly, how can tolerable conditions of worldwide economic welfare, social justice and ecological stability be created?[1] In other words, how can a warless and a more just international order be achieved? Hedley Bull makes a similar distinction when he differentiates between 'minimum' and 'optimum' international order.[2] The historical survey of attempts to reform the international system will, for the most part, be discussing order in the former sense because attempts to redesign international order, in practice, have had enough difficulty in coping with the first problem without tackling the others. Nonetheless, theoretically, it is important to investigate the degree of compatibility between these two elements.

The utility of approaching the problem of order from this twofold perspective is that it draws our attention to the fact that under many of the conditions inherent in international politics, there may be an irreconcilable contradiction between the two conceptions. A warless world may not only not be a just one, it may in fact prevent the creation of a just one, as the prevention of violence may obstruct desirable change. In the last analysis the question of international order must be approached by reconciling these two facets of the problem.

If we now move on to study the means by which conflicts of interest between states are resolved, this can be done conveniently by outlining two processes for resolution, the power model and the authority model. The first can be described as the unbridled interplay of opposing forces in which the capabilities of the contestants will determine the outcome. The second can be characterised as the pursuit of decision-making procedures, the legitimacy of which would be recognised by each of the constituent units. All international political practice can be encompassed within these two extremes and a major point of interest for the student of international politics is, which tendency is uppermost or, historically speaking, how have the two tendencies been combined?

How then are decisions made within the international political system? First, the various practices that would fall within the first, the power model, can be reviewed. Here we can distinguish a continuum of practices that begins with diplomacy and bargaining and ends with outright violence. Diplomacy and bargaining are to international relations what the free market is to economics. Every state sets out to obtain the best deal for itself and its success or lack of it in this effort is largely determined by the resources that it commands. Given the characteristic features of the international system, this is perhaps its most distinctive political technique. Since no authority is in a position to arbitrate between two competing states, or to impose a decision upon them, the political process is essentially a test of wills and capabilities.

Another international instrument which would clearly be embraced within the power model is the actual use of force. This surely is the conclusive evidence for the essentially power-based nature of the international political process. In the absence of common political authority, and if states cannot be persuaded to conciliate for pruden- tial reasons, then ultimately force must be the arbiter between compet- ing states. In fact, starting from the premise of the decentralised or anarchic nature of international life, and of the prominent place that this accords to violence as the *ultima ratio*, some people have argued that the subject matter of international relations is no more and no less than the study of war. This view should not be accepted. The study of war is certainly an extremely important part of the discipline but it is not coextensive with the field of international relations as a whole. The area of study centres on the consequences of the type of political organisation into which the world is arranged. War is undoubtedly the most dramatic of these consequences – it is the extreme manifestation of the decentralised nature of the international political system. It is by no means the only such consequence because, although it might be the ultimate form of conflict resolution, it is not the only such technique that has been developed.

Diplomacy, bargaining and war have been mentioned as belonging within the power model of international politics. But there is yet another practice that should be included within this category and that is the tacit use of force, which can be employed by states that have a preponderance of power. This can be illustrated with an example. There is good reason for thinking that there has emerged a serious, if not absolute, conflict of interest between the industrialised countries of the northern hemisphere and the developing countries of the third world – the rich and the poor nations. There are at least three ways in which this conflict could be resolved. On the model of a domestic political system, there could be political activity on the part of the poor states in order to obtain a redistribution of income within the system as a whole. Clearly no political authority exists at the moment that would effect such a redistribution. The second method would be the use of violence on the part of the poor states to force such a redistribution, something that is not as yet a very strong possibility. There is a third means by which this conflict of interest can be resolved and this is the way in which it is, in fact, being resolved at the moment. This is for the conflict to be resolved in the interests of the stronger party. The economic status quo at the moment favours the industrialised countries and they can maintain it by doing nothing at all because their position is backed up by tacit force. The point is this: decisions at the international level are sometimes made by the application of force and the eruption of violence, but we should not be blind to the many decisions, or non-decisions, that are made by those more powerful parties who do not actually have to employ their force but can keep it tacitly in the background.

These are some aspects of international relations that fall within the power model. But there is another side to the story, which should not be ignored. If the basic fact of international life is its decentralised political structure, then what we should be looking at is not only the logical consequences of this fact (the prevalence of war) but the steps that have been taken to try to counteract or overcome this fact of decentralisation. This entails the whole history of efforts to establish norms, procedures, techniques and institutions that might compensate for the absence of a supreme decision-making body within the international system. It is the search for these that constitutes the most interesting theme of modern international history, as is the manner in which the search has been combined with the practices that have been described as falling within the power model. It is the tension, the conflict, the uneasy harmony between the power and the authority models of politics that provide the fascination in the study of international relations.

There are some persistent themes in this diplomatic story. At one level, the history of the period from 1815 can be seen as a series of attempts to instil a measure of order into international life. In the first half of the nineteenth century this was done by a combination of the techniques of the balance of power with those of the Concert of Europe. In the second half of the century, there was a reversion to the

16

techniques of the balance of power expressed in a highly formalised system of alliances. In the period 1919–39, the powers employed the new diplomatic device of the League of Nations coupled with traditional means for the assurance of national security. In the period after 1945, order has been maintained, formally by the United Nations, informally and more effectively by a balance between two highly integrated and antagonistic blocs.

In a sense then, at this level, the story appears almost as a continuing effort on the part of states to divest themselves of their more basic nature and to organise international life around some more lofty ideal. At this level, the story is then one of varying degrees of failure.

Such a judgement may, however, be tempered. From which perspective – chronological or cultural – are we to pass judgement upon the evolving international order and upon the condition of the present order? How are we to assess the attainment of progress or its absence as demonstrated in the history of international relations?

The question of perspective is worth dwelling upon. Let us consider, first, the chronological perspective. In attempting to measure the degree and direction of change within the international polity since 1815, which time-span is the appropriate one? Certainly, we can agree that some historical perspective is necessary in order to visualise elements of both continuity and change. As Stanley Hoffmann has reminded us, berating studies that focus exclusively on the present:

> Because we have an inadequate basis for comparison, we are tempted to exaggerate either continuity with a past that we know badly, or the radical originality of the present, depending on whether we are more struck by the features we deem permanent, or with those we do not believe existed before. And yet a more rigorous examination of the past might reveal that what we sense as new really is not, and that some of the 'traditional' features are far more complex than we think.[3]

Agreement that a historical perspective is needed does not, unfortunately, lead to agreement as to *which* is appropriate. In this study, we will seek for patterns of international order within the 1815–1990 period. Could this time frame be over-restrictive? If we consider a book such as Bozeman's *Politics and Culture in International History*, the fact is impressed upon us that the modern European state system, with its principal characteristics, is only one variant form of organisation in the relationships between individual cultures and political systems.[4] Consequently, to look for minor modifications in patterns of international order within a short period of the modern state system (even when the system is, as now, writ large) may be to do violence to a genuinely world-historic perspective and blind us to the realisation that there are alternative systems of order between peoples, apart from the modification of rules and norms within a clearly established and continuing system.

Secondly, in passing judgement upon the need for change, and the degree of its attainment, we have also to give consideration to the question of which perspective – cultural or geographical – is the appropriate one. To adapt a worn aphorism, where one stands in one's assessment of the current international order will depend crucially upon where one sits. To make only the most obvious of points, in the words of Oran Young, 'it is hardly surprising that those who live in wealthy countries tend to be more complacent about the performance of the international polity than those who live in poor countries'.[5] International orders are not neutral in their consequences for national societies; some states benefit more than others from the prevailing international arrangements. It follows, therefore, that we cannot expect consensus upon the need for reform or about the direction reform should take. As Richard Falk has expressed it 'the unevenness of the struggle for global reform – what is right for most Latin American, Asian, and African countries is not the same as what is right for the Trilateral countries of Japan, Western Europe, or North America, or for the Soviet Bloc countries – makes it impossible to provide global generalizations'.[6]

Culturally, it is probably also true that the dominant institutions and characteristics of present international order are more likely to be mistaken as the only form of order by Europeans, or westerners generally, because that order is mainly their creation, the fruit of a predominantly western political tradition. Bozeman has articulated this perspective at some length and may be quoted in this context:

> The complex framework of international organizations that spans the world today may thus be viewed as the logical culmination of the political history of the West. As a nonterritorial power structure it . . . recalls the traditions set by the great medieval concerts. As an international extension of the modern democratic state it incorporates the values that have governed European and American societies in recent centuries.[7]

Bearing these caveats in mind, how might we then assess the present international order and the extent of change or progress since 1815? Overall, it is difficult to detect any major restructuring of the operative principles of international politics. To put it in its simplest terms, a Talleyrand or Metternich reincarnated at the present time would have little difficulty in mastering the rules of the international political game. As one analyst has argued:

The dramatic changes that have occurred in world society in the last few decades have not included among them such a revolutionary transformation of the international political structure ... The state system – the ultimate cause of war – remains. The problem of security is still present. The role of force and the threat of it have thus not been eliminated. Strategic considerations and the traditional meaning of power still have relevance.[8]

Clearly, therefore, the system of international relations continues to be a system of interaction between sovereign, independent states and at this level, the international order has evidently not been reformed in any meaningful way. Indeed, some would have it that the persistence of this system ensures that no substantial reform can ever take place. This is the thrust of von Geusau's complaint:

In structural and organizational terms the European concept of the sovereign national state offers no perspectives on world order. The system of diplomacy built upon this concept has proved to be a barrier to, instead of a channel for, world order. Diplomatic representation promotes attitudes of defending abstract and divisive national interests, when concern for human suffering and protection of life would have been necessary ... it is concerned with the status and prestige of an abstract entity, rather than the hunger, the torture or the fear of real men.[9]

Even if the system, in structural terms, has not changed it would nonetheless be possible for some of its norms to have developed and to have demonstrated progress, whether in content or in degree of general acceptance. Can we demonstrate significant changes in the nature of these norms? Little evidence is forthcoming in support of such a proposition. When we recall that the system of nuclear deterrence is an important component of the present international order, and when one analyst can specify the ground-rules of the 'nuclear regime' as being those of 'anarchy', 'equilibrium' and 'hierarchy',[10] we can be forgiven for assuming that the essentials of the balance system remain with us. In fact, implicit in the many studies seeking to correlate system stability with the degree of system polarity is a logic of numbers equally applicable to the post-1945 period as it is to the eighteenth and nineteenth centuries. Such logic must surely be based on the assumption that basic norms have not changed throughout this period, even though there have been changes in the number of 'poles' and major changes in the nature of military technology?[11]

Others would argue even that, in terms of cooperative international norms, far from there being progress since 1815, there has been observable regress. Luard makes precisely such a point when he refers to the eclipse of concert norms in the current international situation. He draws the comparison between nineteenth-century international politics and present practices and reaches the following judgement. 'For all the concern of nationalism to build powerful and independent states, the collective principle established by the Concert meant that states became more accountable to others for their behaviour than ever before: they were indeed more so than they are today.'[12]

Thus far, we have been mainly concerned with the political apparatus and decision-making norms of international society. What deserves to be pointed out is that the economic dimensions of international order are becoming a focus of increasing attention and that any assessment of progress in relation to the evolution of the international system would be inadequate if it did not take into account its economic aspects. In part, this is so because of the new-found awareness of the interaction of the global system's political and economic structures and the realisation that the differential impact of various international orders is nowhere more apparent than in the distribution of economic benefits. It follows, therefore, that the 1970s' calls for a new international economic order, based as they were upon the view of the integral union between power-political influence and prevailing economic structures, have broadened out the agenda of international-order reform and that this, as in other areas, has partially been in response to the poor performance of the current order as a means of economic distribution. If we therefore incorporate this economic dimension into our conception of the evolving international order, we would be led to a correspondingly pessimistic judgement. Oran Young, while arriving at an otherwise generally favourable assessment of the performance of the international polity, concedes that it is open to censure on this score at least:

> Many inequalities in the international polity have exhibited a marked tendency to become more extreme rather than less extreme during modern times. With respect to material wealth, for example, this trend has been dramatic over the last hundred years. Thus, it is not possible to sound an optimistic note in this realm by suggesting that there is at least a trend toward greater equality in the distribution of values.[13]

In other words, if equality is one of our measures of progress, then in relation to the international economic order, which can scarcely be separated from the workings of the whole, progress has thus far remained elusive.

The central preoccupation of most of the attempts at creating international order has been the role of force in international politics. In fact, the major approaches to developing international order can be classified according to the attitude that they hold to the question of force in international affairs. From this perspective, we can construct a threefold category of approaches to creating what has been called 'minimum' international order on the basis of the relationship between the mechanism and force. The three categories of international order would accordingly be the following: (1) international order through the recognition of the role of force and through its utilisation; (2) international order through placing constraints on the use of force; (3) and finally, international order through the eventual rejection of the special place which force has in international relations. Each of these will be elaborated in turn.

(1) First, we may consider those theories that recognise the use of force and seek to utilise it for the creation of order. Here two schools of thought can be specified, although the second one should, perhaps, more accurately be regarded as a specific manifestation of the first. What is being referred to here is the school of thought associated with the balance of power. There are two aspects of this doctrine that are relevant to the problem of international order. The first is that the doctrine accepts the state unit and its proclivity to employ violence as the realistic basis upon which order must be created. What is meant by order according to this theory is such things as equilibrium or stability. Threats to order would be attempts to overthrow the system and create preponderance. In other words, this theory seeks not to change the fact of the power potential of the individual states but rather to use this fact in the pursuit of order. No attempt is made to curb the power potential of the individual states. Rather the power of the one is turned against that of the other, thereby producing equilibrium. It is in this sense that balance of power recognises the realities of the situation and attempts not to change them but to utilise them for its own ends.

The second feature of balance of power to be considered is its attitude to the use of force. The point here is that although for the most part balance of power as theory can be regarded as a means to international order through conflict control, the theory nonetheless makes allowance for violence. This is to say that within the framework of balance of power, order and violence are not entirely incompatible. On the contrary, as a last resort, violence may be the only means of maintaining order. Since order is defined in terms of the stability and the preservation of the state system, a threat to this system can be met by violence and this response would be regarded as order-producing rather than order-destroying. It can, therefore, be seen that balance of

21

power is the theory which seeks least to change the reality of international politics; although order for the most part is produced by controlled force-manipulation, in certain circumstances order can be preserved by direct force-utilisation.

The second school of thought in this section is the school of nuclear deterrence and, as was said, this is merely a subset of the general balance-of-power school. A major difference between the two, however, is that although the former permits force-manipulation in the interest of order, it would nonetheless normally regard force-utilisation in the nuclear sense as incompatible with order. Otherwise the positions are very similar. The argument of the strategists would run as follows. In nuclear deterrence we have a system that displays all the realistic merits of the balance of power but removes from the balance of power its one serious defect. It makes realistic use of force by accepting its existence but seeks to neutralise it by balancing force against force. This much traditional balance of power also did. But the additional virtue of deterrence is that this neutralisation is so strong that no attempt to disrupt the balance is ever likely to occur. For this reason, there will never be any need to maintain equilibrium by violent means. Order is therefore maintained by a protracted stalemate. Thus emerges the paradox that nuclear weapons, the greatest single threat to the continuation of the human species, are regarded by many as the best possible guarantee of peace and order currently available to the actors in the international system.

It is at this point that there is a danger of the classification, herein presented, breaking down. We have placed nuclear deterrence within the category where the fact of force is recognised and utilised. At the same time, we can see that it might also fit into the second category of the placing of constraints on the use of force because the nature of the weapons is surely a powerful constraint in its own right. Nonetheless, the order that is produced is, just as in the balance-of-power situation, the product of the natural interplay of forces rather than the product of deliberate intervention by means of some agreed authoritative procedure. There is no consciously constructed mechanism that would constrain the use of force. To this extent, nuclear deterrence represents a *laissez-faire* situation in which order in the last resort depends on the free interplay of competing forces. To the extent that there are constraints on the use of force built into the system, they are no more than an extension of the cost-benefit analysis of the value of using force that existed in the traditional balance situation as well. There is no constraint of a legal, institutional or physical nature.

(2) Within this second category – of order produced by constraints

on the use of force – should be included such devices as collective security, arms control and the development of international law. What these three mechanisms have in common is a shared realisation that the major problem of order is that of the sovereign right of the state to resort to war, and what each of these devices seeks to do is to place – respectively – an institutional, a physical and a legal constraint on the use of that force. As in the ideas put forward in category one, force is seen to be the basic cause of the problem but while the theories in category one argue that force, in one form or another, is also the solution, those in category two contend that the only solution is to change the rules of the game with respect to the utilisation of violence by states.

According to collective security, the major threat to order is one which would allow the use of violence against the interests of the international community as a whole. For that reason, the balance of power is to be institutionalised. This will have, according to the supporters of the theory, two beneficial results. First, it will make the balance of power more effective and there will be less chance of a preponderant power emerging. Secondly, it will ensure that violence, if used, is always used in a legitimate manner. Since power is vested in the international community, that power will not be abused in the way it has been by individual nation states.

Arms control starts from similar premises, namely that the nature of the international system is such that violent conflicts between states are an inevitable concomitant of the system. It too accepts the system but tries to limit the resulting violence by placing constraints on the capabilities of the states. It does not seek to improve the states or the system within which they operate. So much is this so that the cynics dismiss arms control as the continuation of strategy by other means. Arms control agreements do, nonetheless, seek to limit the competition of states, or at the very least to channel that competition into certain preferred areas.

Arms control, however, suffers from an internal tension, which might best be described in the following manner. We can conceive of war in many ways, Clausewitz's notion of war as a political instrument probably being the most famous. However, two other conceptions might be introduced because they help to illustrate the problems within the arms-control camp. We will label these the pathological and the cataclysmic conceptions of war. The pathological relates, of course, to the study of diseases. What is meant by this is that the relationship between war and international society should be regarded as analogous to the relationship between disease and health.

23

According to this conception, it is assumed that health is the normal condition of the international system: the usual characteristic of the international system is cooperation and non-violent conflict resolution. When a war occurs this represents a disease of the international body politic, an affliction which must be removed so that international society may be restored to its previous condition of health. Evidently, this conception of war incorporates a value judgement within it – that peace is the norm and war constitutes a deviant case. It is also to be regarded as an affliction that is imposed from the outside. This is to say that it is different from the accidental view of war in that war is produced not by man's failings alone but by the intervention, figuratively, of a malevolent Nature. War, like disease, is a scourge of nature and not something that man inflicts upon himself.

Secondly, and employing Rapoport's term,[14] we can conceive of war as a cataclysm. In many respects, this category is virtually identical with the previous one. The idea is that war is regarded as being analogous to a natural disaster of some kind, say a cyclone or an earthquake. Once again, as in the previous instance, this suggests an aberration from the norm and it also suggests an affliction from the outside. Wars, like natural disasters, do not represent a human failing: they are something that nature imposes upon humanity.

Nonetheless, despite the similarities in these two conceptions, there is an important difference in the recommendations they make in relation to war, which arises precisely from their respective analyses of the nature of the problem to be tackled. The pathological view that regards war as a disease follows the medical tradition that diseases are curable. Once their causes have been understood scientifically, remedial action can be taken and international society restored to health. This is clearly not applicable in the case of the cataclysmic interpretation which works on the assumption that no matter how perfect our scientific understanding of natural disasters such as earthquakes, we still cannot cure them. The most that we can do is take preventive action, which will not stop these occurrences but will minimise the damage resulting from them.

This distinction is not just an academic one but one that could have important practical implications. For anyone engaged in devising a country's foreign or defence policy, it naturally makes all the difference in the world whether war can be prevented altogether or whether the best that can be done is to limit the resulting damage. If we start off with the premise shared by both the pathological and the cataclysmic views that war is a scourge, we can agree that we would like to avoid wars and, as has historically been the case, that an important contribution to this end can be made via arms control. But the problem with arms control is that there may be more than one purpose behind it: it may be undertaken with the intention of avoiding war altogether and thus as a complete cure – in accordance with the pathological view; alternatively, an arms-control programme might be pressed with the intention of limiting the amount of damage that would result from a future war. This, then, would be the cataclysmic recommendation that measures be taken to reduce the impact of future disasters.

Unfortunately, these two goals, flowing from different assessments of the problem, can be in conflict with each other. Clearly, if we were to be guided by the second objective of arms control, that of damage limitation in the event of war, this could undermine the first objective, that of preventing war: if an agreement reduces the number of missiles each side has in order to limit future damage, this could have the unfortunate side-effect of actually increasing the likelihood of war breaking out, precisely for the reason that a reduction in anticipated levels of damage in future wars might diminish the fear of war and, to that extent, undercut the deterrence upon which the avoidance of war is based. Efforts to strengthen deterrence by reducing damage-limiting capabilities, on the other hand, could in fact ensure that in the event of war, the maximum amount of damage will be realised.

Lastly, within this second category of imposing constraints upon the use of force, something must be said about international law. It is perhaps a truism but there was virtually no such thing as international law before the sixteenth or seventeenth centuries for the simple reason that there were no independent national units whose relations required regulation by such a body of law. This is one way of saying that international law arose simultaneously with the emergence of the European international system. In turn, this suggests that international law developed simultaneously with the conception of political sovereignty. It required the disintegration of the mediaeval ideal that all Europe constituted a political and religious whole, subject to Emperor and Pope respectively, before there was any felt need to promulgate a body of rules according to which the newly emerging political units of Europe would conduct themselves. In other words, international law was no more than the obverse side of the emerging doctrine of sovereignty.

For that reason, there is a tension within international law because it is, on the one hand, a reinforcement of national sovereignty and, on the other, it is intended to be a constraint upon that sovereignty. This duality can be highlighted by describing a utopian and a realist interpretation of the role of international law.

The essential difference between the two positions may be clarified by the following illustration. Some commentators on the American constitution argue that there are two things to be learned from its study. On the one hand, the constitution contains the basic rules of the game: it describes the respective powers of the various organs of government and lays down the moves that the various players – the presidency, congress, the judiciary – may make. So the most basic function of the constitution is to serve as a rule-book. A study of the constitution also reveals more than this. It not only indicates the rules of the game, but also provides a fairly accurate reflection of the state of play. If one considers the way in which articles of the constitution have been interpreted by the Supreme Court, or the specific amendments to the constitution, this offers some insight into the present distribution of power between the various branches of government – for instance, it might be concluded that the run of play was favouring federal as opposed to state powers, or favouring the executive as against congress. In any case, the point is that the constitution, although it is essentially a rule-book, may also from another angle be regarded as a score-card.

These two perspectives on the constitution capture the essence of the respective positions of the utopian and the realist. For the utopian, international law is a body of rules that govern the processes of international politics. For the realist, international law does little more than reflect the state of international political play. As a case in point, there is the widespread argument that international law has been basically European law, an outgrowth of the European state system. As such, many aspects of it have been found objectionable by the emerging third world states who regard it as an instrument that both reflects and perpetuates the dominant position of the Western powers within international society. For instance, from the point of view of the Australian aboriginal, the international law that permitted Australia to be acquired in the name of the British Crown was not an objective body of rules. It would be seen very much as an instrument that facilitated the realisation of the interests of the dominant powers at the time, the expanding European states.

(3) The third category of minimum international order is the set of solutions that advocates the reform of the system in such a way that the problem of force is solved by making it disappear. This includes the various theories of world government that regard the main obstacle to international order as the anarchy between the individual states and that, consequently, recommend that the only way to remove the anarchy is to destroy the units that produce it, namely the states.

There is an influential tradition of thought, concerned with reform of the state system, that self-consciously employs the model of the domestic political system as the basis for its solution to the problem of international order. It is assumed that government at the national level has been successful in solving the problem of order and that, by extension, we can eliminate war from international life by setting up some form of world government. A lucid description of this approach can be found elsewhere:

> One of the chief intellectual supports of this doctrine is what may be called the domestic analogy, the argument from the experience of individual men in domestic society to the experience of states, according to which the need of individual men to stand in awe of a common power in order to live in peace is a ground for holding that states must do the same. The conditions of an orderly social life, on this view, are the same among states as they are within them: they require that the institutions of domestic society be reproduced on a universal scale.[15]

The argument relies heavily on social-contract imagery. Order is established at the national level by a social contract whereby people submit to a common authority, the better to protect their lives and liberties. Accordingly, just as men used to live in a state of nature, so the states now live in a state of nature *vis-à-vis* each other. The solution, therefore, is a further social contract whereby the states give up their absolute freedom to a common authority.

This approach to issues of international order has a long heritage in Western thought. When it is remembered that Europe throughout the mediaeval period had been regarded as a unity, whether in its religious or its imperial aspects, it is not surprising that those who were witnessing the emergence of a state system dominated by sovereign, independent states should have recalled that earlier period of European unity and should have regarded a supra-national entity as the natural solution to international anarchy and war. If it is true that man never recovers from the shock of leaving the womb, then this seems also to have been the case with the states of Europe.

It is now necessary to address the specific problem of order in international relations. The basic difficulty is that of finding means for effecting political change within the system. In most domestic societies this task is accomplished because there are institutions – such as electoral procedures – that allow for the expression of grievances and thus make the system aware of needs for change and sometimes, although not always, facilitate the initiation of change. The international system obviously does not have any such procedures or

27

institutions that command total authority. The result is that the major deficiency of the international system is its inability as yet to devise any universally acceptable means for permitting peaceful change.

This elementary point has been repeated for the simple reason that the basic condition of international politics relates directly to the problem of the nature of international order and the type of international order that is acceptable. The international system has as yet not managed to devise a universally acceptable means for the peaceful resolution of conflict brought about by change within the system. However, in this chapter we have been considering various international devices and mechanisms that have as their basic premise the doctrine that order is to be attained by either deflecting or constraining or eliminating the element of force in international politics. The major implication of the whole train of thought embodied in these various solutions is that international order is achieved by the control of violent conflict. But if violent change is not to be permitted and the system as yet has not developed institutions for the accommodation of interests on a peaceful basis, how are conflicts of interest, and especially those induced by change, to be effected? Or does order require the complete ossification of the system, one in which no change is possible and order becomes no more than a synonym for the preservation of the *status quo*? Clearly this is neither a realistic nor a desirable alternative. If not, in what way can we arrive at a conception of international order that makes allowance for change in cases where this change is likely to be resisted? This is a problem that is common to all political systems but it is brought out especially clearly in the international case because of the peculiar qualities of that system.

Posing the question in this form should make us aware of the difficulties in the path of a definition of what we have termed minimum international order, because if it is equated with the prevention of violence then we must assume, given that there is not an absolute harmony of interests, that this type of 'negative' order is going to be in the interests of certain sectors of international society and is going to affect adversely the interests of certain other sectors. A moment's reflection on the various mechanisms for promoting order that will be examined in this book would appear to confirm this conclusion.

First of all, consider the balance of power. As its very name implies, this is a system of order that derives its motive force from the fact of power. There is order for those states that are in a position to counterbalance power by power, the Great Powers. Consequently, as Modelski has observed, 'I regard order-keeping as a function assumed and performed in recent historical experience by the great powers and by the diplomatic and strategic complex associated with them.'[16] From the viewpoint of the lesser powers, the order is uncertain, depending upon a volatile balance that they themselves cannot control. At the same time, one virtue of the balance of power is that it does not discriminate against change for its own sake. The only requirement is that change, if it is to be brought about, must be accompanied by adequate power: change comes about as soon as there is a margin of power on its side.

The League of Nations too instituted its own brand of international order. It perpetuated the division into large and small states and although it made concessions to the small states, it would be difficult to deny that it produced an order sustained by, and largely in the interests of, the Great Powers. It was also to produce a striking example of international order being harnessed to the requirements of the existing status quo. The order that was produced at Versailles was one that was overwhelmingly in the interests of the victor nations. It perpetuated a sharp division between the victors and the vanquished, between the 'have' and the 'have not' states. Because of the inbuilt bias of the inter-war international order, this was one that could not adjust peacefully to change.

This example very clearly demonstrates the principle that most international orders have tended to favour the interests of some states at the expense of the others. The best example of this is the situation where the international order has been named after one particular state that has exercised commanding influence over the system as a whole. Thus we have had the so-called Pax Romana, Pax Britannica, and a Pax Americana. The League of Nations was conspicuously a Pax of this nature.

The post-1945 period has not witnessed any striking modifications in this respect. We could point to the United Nations Security Council and say with justification that the order inaugurated in 1945 was one overwhelmingly in favour of the major powers. It imposed a system of collective security in which order would be enforced upon the smaller states if they resorted to violence, but because of the veto the same constraints could not be imposed upon the Great Powers.

Moving outside the ambit of the United Nations and looking at the basic reality of the postwar power configuration, we could say even more precisely that the order that has been established is one dictated by, and in the interests of, the two superpowers. It is they who command the nuclear deterrent that plays such a major role in the maintenance of the present international order. It is in their interest

29

that many regional disputes have been frozen. As the superpowers have become involved in almost all regions of the globe, and usually on competing sides, the solution of regional disputes that would normally have been accomplished by traditional military means has been prevented. It has become too dangerous, in many cases, to have these disputes resolved because it might lead to a confrontation between the superpowers.

There is another sense in which the present international order is one suited to the interests of the superpowers. Most of the conceptions of order that have been considered thus far have been based on an understanding that the state has the monopoly on the legitimate resort to violence within the system. That is to say that central to the very idea of order has been a recognition of the sovereignty of the state in matters of its own jurisdiction. Just how central this notion of state sovereignty and state monopoly of violence has been in the development of the international system can be seen with reference to the numerous complaints that the emergence of transnational terrorist groups as international actors, capable of resorting to large-scale violence, constitutes a major threat to international order. In accordance with the traditional image, only states are entitled to exercise this right of violence.

In essence, then, the problem with the notion of 'minimum' international order is that, in the absence of alternative means of securing change, attempts to predicate order upon the control of violence inevitably introduced disequilibria into the system. More so than anything, it has been the pursuit of order in this sense that has reinforced the hierarchical dimensions of international society since the powerful states are, by definition, best placed to resist any change which adversely affects their interests. What remains problematic is the extent to which such a hierarchy establishes a pattern of order that at least minimally serves the interests of the wider international society.

2 INTERNATIONAL AND WORLD ORDER

PERSPECTIVES ON INTERNATIONAL RELATIONS

Theory, in the field of international relations, is presently in a fragmented condition. If, during the two postwar decades, writers shared certain fundamental analytic perspectives and assumptions, this has become decreasingly so since the 1960s as the menu of theory has become transformed from restricted *table d'hôte* to unlimited *à la carte:*

> There is no longer a consensus on the subjects of inquiry and theorizing. The view that international theory should be organized around the structures and processes of the states system, the activities of the great powers and their decision-makers, particularly as they relate to war and peace, is no longer accepted by a significant number of scholars.[1]

This fragmentation has occurred at a number of distinct levels. In the first place, it has contributed to lack of agreement about the function of theory itself. In consequence, theory performs a variety of tasks, ranging from the clarification of basic concepts (such as war or power), partial theories (which seek to clarify a particular aspect of the field, such as the causes of war or the nature of crises), grand theories which seek to provide an all-encompassing explanation of the dynamics of the international system (such as balance of power) and, finally, 'paradigms' which offer not simply an explanation of how things work but provide a definition of the structures and processes of the very field of international relations itself. As will be demonstrated shortly, it is within this last category that the widest fissures have recently appeared.

Such lack of consensus may evoke scepticism about the necessity or value of the theoretical enterprise. Why should the study of international relations be distracted by digressions into theory if the endeavour is likely to prove bewilderingly varied and ultimately inconclusive? Can we not simply gather the empirical evidence and study the 'facts' as they present themselves?

There are a number of compelling arguments why such a simplistic empiricism is not methodologically possible. First, although the events of international life are real enough, we describe them through language and hence linguistic clarification and systematisation is an inescapable task within the discipline. If the standard vocabulary is reviewed – power, national interest, war, appeasement, intervention, terrorism, stability, order, balance, sovereignty – it becomes immediately apparent that a function of theory is to forge some agreement and consistency in the usage of these terms.

Second, however, these are contested terms not simply because of linguistic carelessness or imprecision but, more radically, because there is lack of agreement about which empirical situations deserve to have these words attached to them. Although seemingly a straightforward empirical procedure, this soon slides into a dialogue involving values and judgements. The difficulty in addressing what constitutes international order has already been discussed and renders impossible the answering of this question by means of historical narrative alone.

Third, the 'facts' are not neutral because they will themselves reflect the questions asked and the methodology employed. Basic theoretical assumptions inescapably direct the line of investigation and determine both where one should look for evidence and also what kind of information is likely to satisfy the enquiries that are made: the types of empirical fish that are caught will depend critically upon the nature of the methodological net that is used. Studies of international order are peculiarly susceptible to this problem.

A number of basic methodological choices confront the analyst. These pertain to the inter-related issues of field, unit and level of analysis. In terms of the first, the basic choice is between a macro- or micro-approach; in terms of the second, there is a need to specify the nature of the actors or 'prime movers' in international relations; in terms of the third, it is possible to break into the action at different levels, each rung on the analytical ladder leading towards greater comprehensiveness. In varying degrees, these choices touch upon central assumptions about the 'individual' or 'structural' nature of behaviour. As has been observed of this problem, 'structuralists assume that human behaviour cannot be understood simply by examining individual motivation and intention, because, when aggregated, human behaviour precipitates structures of which the individuals may be unaware'.[2] Any endeavour to understand the history of diplomatic norms and practices, as well as the wider issues of order that fall outside this statist agenda, requires some appreciation of the determinants of international behaviour along these lines.

Each of these points raises issues, some of which are general to the social sciences and others of which are peculiar to international relations. In the search for explanations, should we focus upon the whole or the parts of the whole? Are the units of action the states themselves, or their representatives, or other non-state entities? Should the field be studied at the level of individual decision makers, at the level of the behaviour of individual states, or at the level of the international system as a whole? For instance, is the Cold War best understood as the product of individual decision making (Stalin's paranoia and the change from Roosevelt to Truman), the character-istics of Soviet and American policy (Soviet expansionist ideology or the exigencies of America's capitalist economy), or of the dynamics of the postwar distribution of power within the international system (the rise of the two peripheral giants and the simultaneous crisis in the traditional European balance of power)?

More profoundly, at issue is the overall paradigm within which these analytical schemes should operate. When one attempts to understand the history of international relations and its present reality, which characteristic structures and processes define the field? Is it the evolution and development of the state system, of the practices of statecraft and of the state's central role in the creation of war and peace? Is it the evolution of the basic needs of humanity, abstracted from the particular political settings in which they have operated and which serve merely as contingent instruments for the attainment of the ends of humankind? If so, to focus on state interaction is to confuse the means and the ends. Finally, should the main theme of 'international' history not be regarded as the evolution, and impact, of a capitalist world economy which has structured the modes of production and exchange and the social relationships which derive from them?

These and other basic paradigms and conceptualisations clamour for the attention of the student of international relations.[3] Pettman has offered us a simple dichotomy in terms of which these perspectives might be categorised:

> We arrive in the global arena at a different idea of social structure in each case: the *pluralist* conceives of a society of states, competing for power but sharing values and institutions, that is, constrained and disposed by a balance of power; the *structuralist* fastens upon the fact of global classes derivative of modern modes of industrial pro-

33

> duction, distribution and exchange . . . And yet, state formation and class formation within world society seem to me to be separable and equally significant processes . . .[4]

This dichotomy has been further elaborated by others into a tripartite scheme:

> The classical state-centric approach persists in its stubborn blindness to anything but diplomatic and military relationships, or 'high politics'. The liberal–pluralist or functional approach, while emphasising other kinds of relationships – most notably economic interdependence – persists in its adherence to concepts or ideologies of progress, modernity and the benign influence of economics on political affairs . . . and the economic structuralists, while pointing to significant patterns of domination in the modern world, usually persist in an economic reductionism . . .[5]

These wider considerations have implications for the specific issues to be explored in this volume. The main theme of the second half of the book is, consequently, the nature of the regulatory mechanisms adopted by the Powers in their inter-relationships and the attempts to 'perfect' these mechanisms. Unfortunately, expressing the objectives of the study even in these minimal terms is not without its own problems because there remains the danger of a further confusion.

The essence of the problem lies in trying to discern the status of these regulatory mechanisms, whether they do actively regulate the behaviour of the Powers or whether they are merely the passive reflections of other processes within the system – in other words, whether we are talking about causes or about consequences. This difficulty has been usefully set out by Waltz:

> In a purely competitive economy, everyone's striving to make a profit drives the profit rate downward. Let the competition continue long enough under static conditions and everyone's profit will be zero. To infer from that condition that everyone, or anyone is seeking to minimise profit . . . would obviously be absurd. And yet in international politics one frequently finds that rules inferred from the results of the interactions of states are prescribed to the actors and are said to be a condition of the system's maintenance.

He later continues:

> The close juxtaposition of states promotes their sameness through the disadvantages that arise from a failure to conform to successful practices. This 'sameness', an effect of the system, is often attributed to the acceptance of so-called rules of state behaviour. A possible effect of action is turned into a necessary cause in the form of a stipulated rule.[6]

Waltz's point, therefore, is that there is a genuine difficulty in discerning which 'rules' or 'norms', if any, are being observed by states and that we cannot simply deduce these rules from the resultant patterns. The problem in distinguishing, and defining, the essential characteristics of these regulatory mechanisms, which are of course nothing if not rules or norms, is as a result especially acute.

The problem is touched upon, if not satisfactorily resolved, in other writings. Keohane and Nye, for instance, discuss the same issue when they present their ideas about 'international regimes', which is alternative terminology for the regulatory mechanisms under review. Their analysis runs as follows:

> International regimes are intermediate factors between the power structure of an international system and the political and economic bargaining that takes place within it. The structure of the system (the distribution of power resources among states) profoundly affects the nature of the regime (the more or less loose set of formal and informal norms, rules and procedures relevant to the system). The regime, in turn, affects and to some extent governs the political bargaining and daily decision making that occurs within the system.[7]

According to this formulation, the regulatory mechanisms that have characterised the international political process occupy an uncertain twilight zone somewhere between underlying power configurations and the resultant political outcomes. However, the problem of what is cause and what is effect remains and the status of these mechanisms continues to be in doubt. A study that seeks to demonstrate the history of international regulatory mechanisms in terms both of their continuities and of their evolution, is thus confronted with the very real problem of adequately capturing these mechanisms and putting them down on paper; like sand, they tend to slip through the fingers. Even where it is possible to define the essential characteristics of a system, and to distinguish it from another, the question remains whether it matters in any case, because it is unclear whether it is the 'international regimes' or the underlying power structure that, in fact, is responsible for most of the regulation that occurs.

In any event, the limited confines within which historical efforts at reforming the international order have been carried out should become abundantly clear. To the extent that international-order reform has been about the 'taming' of power politics, it has been about the minor modification of one process and its partial substitution by another. Order as substance has thus far not exercised the minds or the imagination of the world's statesmen. From this perspective, therefore, the personal preference of Arthur Burns would serve as a fair judgement upon the historical record of order-reform enterprises since 1815:

> The Powers' representatives gathered in 'conversation' with each other do not as a matter of course form a community capable of an approach to the good life. But severally they can contribute to the humanising or to the depraving of the power-political process ... If so, power-political activity should be evaluated in terms of its approach to an end – the 'humanising' of the process itself. From such a conclusion it may be thought possible to construct an ideal humanised world order. I believe that the conclusion is to be avoided, and that acts of statecraft are to be judged by the humane quality of their method and mode, and not by their tendency to produce Utopia.[8]

The field of international relations is therefore fragmented around a number of central issues. It is divided about the level at which international events should be explained and about the determinants of action within this universe. It is divided about the overall perspective on the nature of international structures and processes. It is unclear as to the proper bounds of normative enquiry. These general matters can now be illustrated specifically by means of an enquiry into the proper framework into which our study of order ought to be placed.

FROM INTERNATIONAL TO WORLD ORDER?

To say that order exists is to make a claim about a pattern among a number of units. As such, it is important to establish the nature of the units that are so 'ordered' because the implications for statecraft will vary considerably as between different frameworks. The function of this section will, accordingly, be twofold: first, to establish the theoretical varieties of patterns of order, focussing on different units in each case; secondly, to assess the substantive implications of these theoretical frameworks. This latter will be done by considering three issues on the international political agenda: war, human rights and distributive justice.

The concept of order can be categorised in terms of the entities amongst which the relationship exists and also in terms of the functional or issue area that is deemed central to this condition. On this basis, it could be suggested that theoretical explorations of the idea of order in international relations take a number of forms. For convenience, these will be addressed as follows: charter order, realist order, international economic order, world economic order and world order. Each of these five constitutes a particular model of order and helps us to clarify ideas about the kinds of structures and processes that are deemed to be necessary for the attainment of order. Each also embodies a paradigm about the central core of international relations and draws upon the various conceptualisations of the substance of the field described at the outset of this chapter.

Charter order is embodied in the contemporary doctrine of the state system. One finds it expressed in the Charter of the United Nations, in much of international law, as well as implicitly in the rhetoric of diplomacy. Its point of departure is that order describes a relationship between states. These relations are orderly to the extent that, at best, there is an absence of war between the members of international society or, at least, that in the prosecution of their conflicts the states adhere to certain institutions and practices.

Amongst the working assumptions of this pattern of order are the following. The basic ground rule of international society is the principle of national sovereignty. This constitutes the basis of the claim to membership of international society, derived from the constitutional law of the state itself, insofar as it has no legal superior,[9] but thereafter imposes obligations on the other members of that society. The sovereignty of states gives rise to a claim to legal equality and to respect for this condition even by stronger powers. States enjoy self-determination and domestic jurisdiction and it behoves members of international society not to interfere in the domestic affairs of other states.

In order to give expression to these basic principles, international society has developed a number of institutions and procedures. The order of states is sustained by a variety of international organisations, foremost amongst which is the United Nations itself. It is also supported by a significant corpus of international law which, at the present time, limits the free resort to force by states to instances of self-defence. Various forms of international settlement, of both a political and judicial nature, are available to states through these institutions. Although it is recognised that such a conception of order has been accompanied by increasing regulation of functional areas of international life and, indeed, that greater functional cooperation can greatly strengthen the political architecture of international society, this conception of order is relatively narrow and certainly places the avoidance of war high on its list of priorities.

If the above might be described as the 'dignified' conception of international order, the realist model represents the 'efficient' conception. What this shares with the above is its focus on the relations of states and especially on the realm of politico-security affairs. Of all the conceptions of order, it is the one that most clearly assumes a hierarchical organising principle but, far from attempting to modify the existing reality, seeks consciously to entrench acceptance of this hierarchy as a means of creating order. Its central *motif* is the role of the Great Powers in the management of international society. Order exists when the Great Powers perform the dual tasks of both managing their relations with each other and also imparting a degree of central direction to the workings of the international society as a whole.[10] They perform the former task by creating military balances and by managing their mutual strategic relationship, by codes of crisis management and by the adoption of concert principles defining the scope and limits of their conflicts with each other. They perform the latter task by such mechanisms as unequal alliances, spheres of influence and the control of unruly client states involved in regional conflicts.

If the thrust of the charter model is to tame the existing realities by concealing the disparities of power under a cloak of sovereign equality and by restraining the exercise of force by international due process, the realist model accepts the hierarchy of power and the manipulation of force as the only secure foundation for a durable form of order.

The third model, that of international economic order, is the liberal economic counterpart of the charter conception, with some pinches of realism thrown in for good measure. It is a pluralist conception which takes the state system as its basic framework but, whereas hitherto order has been canvassed essentially in politico-security terms, this model emphasises the balance of economic wellbeing amongst states as the measure of order. The hierarchy with which it is concerned is, therefore, not the hierarchy of military power, but rather the hierarchy of first, third and fourth worlds. Its goal is not simply to achieve restraints on force, either by regulation or manipulation of force, but to secure the economic benefit of all states which participate in the international economic society. While economic disparity is recognised as a source of political revisionism and as a source of potential violence, it is fair to say that this model also places a value on economic mutuality as an end in itself.

The classical expression of this framework was the 1970s programme for a new international economic order. This sought to adjust the international financial and trading regimes in such a way that the less developed states would be less disadvantaged and sought to do so by such devices as adjusting the terms of trade, stabilising commodity prices, regulating the behaviour of multinational corporations and by improving poor country access both to technology and to international financial markets. First world programmes devised to attain similar ends, although sometimes appealing to rich country self-interest in appeasing the discontented, operated within a similar framework of adjustments to the international economic order.[11] Another variant of the same conception, but in the context of North–North, rather than North–South, economic relations was the Trilateralism of the late 1970s or the economic summitry of the 1980s.

In the fourth model, that of world economic order, we move from a pluralist to a structural framework of analysis. Immediately the state ceases to be the focal point of investigation and the pattern of order is to be created around entities other than the state. The hierarchy which exists is a hierarchy of economic exploitation grouped around centres and peripheries and created by the world capitalist system of production and exchange. Such a conception is radical in the twin senses that the analysis is conducted outside the ambit of state structures and also in the sense that the institution of a genuine form of economic order demands not the adjustment of the rules of the existing game but rather the overthrow of an entire economic system which, in the model's terms, inescapably creates economic inequalities. The perspective has been summarised as follows:

> The international order corrupts the economic, political, and cultural development of dependent areas. Rather than whittling away at the edge of liberal orthodoxy, dependency theorists have sought to pulverize the intellectual structure altogether.[12]

Finally, we reach the 'atomic' conception of world order in which order is neither contingent upon relations between states, nor an attribute of economic relations between structured networks, but rather a quality that should be assigned to relations among, and goals of, individual human beings with all other structures eliminated from the picture. It has been described by Nardin:

> The chief alternative to this state-centric conception of international society is one in which the individual person is regarded as the real member of international society and the proper subject of its laws . . . It is based on a conception of human unity that has been part of the Western tradition at least since the time of the Stoics.[13]

In one cut, such a conception destroys the intellectual justification for distinguishing order within domestic society from order within international society. Both are part of a connected effort to realise human values and goals and the measure of order is the extent to which these objectives are realised. Rather than distinguishing between the political philosophy of the state which strives to secure the 'good life' for its citizens and the political philosophy of international relations, in which survival is an acceptable goal, the two become coequal realms. Accordingly, the achievement of order is in proportion to the degree to which human relations, whatever their territorial extent, protect decent standards of human existence and core rights of liberty and justice.

What this elaborate theoretical exercise succeeds in doing is to make us realise that most of the difficult questions about what a reformed international order might look like resolve themselves into questions about the precedence to be assigned to various elements in these varying conceptions of order. This, in turn, is difficult because the conceptions are frequently incompatible in terms of initial assumptions and goals or, at the very least, the attainment of one dimension of order is possible only by the sacrifice of another.

The nature of these choices can be briefly outlined in general terms. They will subsequently be examined in greater detail when the substantial issues of war, human rights and distributive justice are explored.

The first tension to reveal itself is that between some of the elements of charter order and those of world order. In terms of the former, the sovereign states are autonomous and the major precondition of an orderly international life is the mutual respect for noninterference which the states accord to each other. Otherwise expressed, this amounts to a claim that it is the state which is the major bearer of rights and obligations within international society, enjoying as it does both a right to domestic jurisdiction and a concomitant obligation to refrain from intervention in the domestic affairs of other states. This is to be contrasted with the demands of world order in which scheme it is the human beings that are the bearers of rights and duties. Order is deemed to exist only if certain standards of human existence and certain rights are protected.

It is immediately clear that there may well be conflicts between those competing sets of demands. Which conception of order is to be given precedence in the event of a collision between the two as in a case where domestic violation of human rights evokes intervention by the international community? In this instance, either the protection of individual rights is neglected or the autonomy of the state is infringed.

The realist and charter conceptions are equally hostile to each other. It is those very rhetorical principles of the charter ideal such as sovereignty, equality and nonintervention that are most palpably violated by the hierarchical principles of the realist order. The tacit acceptance of the right of Great Powers to special privileges within the international community, such as spheres of influence and the right to 'police' them, denies rights of national self-determination to other members of the community. Poland has been an important element within the realist order since the late eighteenth century but the fate of that country has scarcely been testimony to the vitality of charter principles.

As previously suggested, realist and world order compete with each other as ends and means. For the realist exponents of minimum international order, the structures of hierarchical domination, while unappealing in themselves, provide the essential preconditions of elementary stability upon which a more ambitious programme of world order might be constructed whereas the critics denounce such practices as blocking off any prospect of world order: what is a necessary means to an end in the realist framework is interpreted by world society proponents as a negation of that end.

Cutting across these various goals is also the relative primacy of 'political' and 'economic' conceptions of order. The charter and realist platforms have traditionally emphasised high politics over low whereas the remaining three draw our attention towards the economic realm. In the case of the structuralist world economic order model, economic processes are fundamental and politico-territorial units, as well as the order prevalent between them, merely contingent. One sees the competing pressures at work in such issues as that of the new international economic order. Although presented as a seeming set of economic demands, it was reacted to by some Northern spokesmen as a political programme. It was deemed to be political in the first sense that what was really at stake was political power within the international hierarchy and the attempt to secure for the South a more prominent political voice within the existing regime. Secondly, it was political in the less savoury sense, according to its critics, because Southern leaders simply sought to deflect onto the international economic system what was in fact the shortcomings of their own domestic political structures: disorder was deemed to be a fault of international trading and finance rather than a matter of domestic corruption and inequality.

From the standpoint of the economic structuralists, however, the new international economic order (NIEO) demands were irredeemably conservative because they failed to come to terms with the inevitable consequences of the capitalist economic system. Inequality and exploitation, in their terms, is inextricably a part of the very system itself and, to this extent, a 'reformed international capitalism' is logically and actually impossible. Further integration of the South into the international cycle of trading and finance, as sought by the NIEO, would worsen the South's position rather than improve it.

In summary, what seems to underlie the competing conceptions of order thus far reviewed is the ambivalent nature and status of the state itself. In some conceptions, the state is central to any pattern and is the principal unit of order: in others it is but one form of collective action amongst many or, at the end of the spectrum, a mere epiphenomenon with no independent power of agency of its own. To focus exclusively upon the interactions of territorial states, on this accounting, is to omit half of the texture of the present system created by 'the global consolidation of industrial capitalism'.[14] Finally, the state is ambivalent because it is both a producer and a destroyer of order. It can serve as a bastion to check external threats to human values but it can also be a destroyer itself of those very values. Some states have protected their members from threats of genocide externally: other states have practised genocide internally. Given the diversity of this experience, fitting the state into any conception of order is as difficult in theory as it has been in practice.

THE OBLIGATIONS OF INDIVIDUALS AND STATES

The discipline of international relations has been criticised recently for its tendency to 'consistently eschew all normative argument'.[15] This might have been a reasonable complaint a decade or more ago but scarcely seems an accurate comment at present in the light of the burgeoning literature on expressly normative issues.[16] This development has itself been a reflection of both theory and practice – the intensification of images of an interdependent world, the impact of common ecological problems and recognition that state practice and international law no longer conform to the stereotypical notion of the state as the sole actor and exclusive bearer of entitlements on the world stage.

The general theme pervading this literature is that of the respective rights and duties possessed by individuals *qua* human beings as compared with their rights and duties as members of separate political and territorial communities. In Hoffmann's terminology, are there duties beyond borders or, in that of Linklater, are rights enjoyed as men or as citizens?

The restrictive ethical position is that duties terminate at state boundaries. A moral order can exist only within a stable structure of rights such as is created by the individual state and to cross a border is, metaphorically speaking, to enter a moral void. This doctrine has been termed the morality of states and clearly delineated by Beitz as being

> based on a conception of the world as a community of largely self-sufficient states which interact only in marginal ways. States, not persons, are the subjects of international morality, and the most fundamental rules that regulate their behaviour are supposed to preserve a peaceful order of sovereign states.[17]

As against this, there is a cosmopolitan view that human beings, as members of an extant or incipient universal community of human-kind, have general obligations to each other that are not contingent upon state practice or boundaries. Moreover, either the substructure of increasing international interdependence, or the recent practice of states themselves, can be offered as evidence that human rights and obligations are, in fact, a part of the existing order:

> If we turn to the present century, it seems that the firmness of the idea of international society as a society of states is once again in doubt ... A new cosmopolitanism is intimated in the revival of natural-law thinking represented by such developments as the Nuremberg trials and subsequent efforts to give international protection to human rights.[18]

Let us examine how these general positions are manifested in the recent discussions of war, human rights and distributive justice.

War What is the relationship of war? Are there mutual obligations in that condition? Upon whom does the obligation fall? These are some of the normative issues pertaining to war that have been extensively canvassed in recent years.[19] The subject of war is a pertinent instance of the general theme because if states at war have obligations, when they are engaged in overt violence, it might presumably be thought that states engaged in peaceful relations, *a fortiori*, have obligations to each other. As against this, there is the permissive doctrine of 'war is hell' which argues that in a situation of necessity, with the survival of the state at risk, no obligations can constrain the state's conduct of the war: there can, on this conception, be no moral duty to place in jeopardy the state, as the sole moral constituency.

The practice of war in respect of its conduct delivers a mixed verdict. There have been many unrestrained military campaigns. More significant, perhaps, is the existence of a body of international law, of military codes of individual states and of widespread just war doctrines all of which seek to mitigate the practices of war. This is not the place to discuss all these ramifications but three issues are relevant to the present context. Each, in its own way, demonstrates the mixed

43

condition of the contemporary scene in which state and individual coexist uneasily with each other in our intellectual and legal frameworks.

First, there have been discernible shifts since 1945 in the legal regulation of war. The creation, in the aftermath of the Second World War, of a separate category of war crimes, now entitled crimes against humanity, reflected an acceptance of rights enjoyed by individuals, rather than just by states, and deserving protection through the mechanisms of international law. The corollary of this was further extensions in the area of responsibility for war crimes such that individuals, rather than states alone, could be directly accused and tried on such charges. Both as a bearer of rights or obligations, the individual now occupies a more salient position in the international law of armed conflict than had historically been the case.

Secondly, the respective status of state and individual arises once more in the context of discrimination between the targets of war. That portion of just war doctrine, the *ius in bello*, which concerns itself with the conduct of war (rather than with the reasons for which the war is undertaken) has traditionally sought to specify the legitimate targets of warfare and to suggest that the number of permissible targets is less than the total number of inhabitants of the enemy state. As soon as such a principle of discrimination is introduced, we begin to make distinctions between the state as a whole and categories of individuals, such as combatants, within it.

Thirdly, in the view of some theorists and notably of Walzer, states do not have unlimited entitlement to the prosecution of war, nor do belligerents enjoy *carte blanche* in its conduct precisely because human beings possess fundamental rights and do not lose these rights even in a condition of war. Although wars may commonly be fought for collective ends, pursued as a result of collective decisions and by resort to collective means, this does not override the individual basis of rights which constitutes the foundation upon which restraints in war can be constructed.

Human Rights. The problems of coping with human rights in international relations are usually presented as dilemmas of foreign policy. From this perspective, there may be benefits, as well as costs, in espousing a human rights platform. The benefits may be deemed to be that human rights are the business of foreign policy, that human rights are increasingly enshrined in, and protected by, international conventions and are thus unavoidable in any case, or, more pragmatically, that it might offer a convenient stick with which to beat those countries for which we have some ideological distaste. As against these, the costs are the raising of international emotional temperatures, interference with the pragmatic interests of the state, the risks of reprisal and the evidence that interference in another state's affairs may simply make it more repressive in defence and thereby undermine further those very rights we seek to protect.

Much of this debate is carried on at the level of foreign policy calculation. However, the issues raised by human rights are of more fundamental significance to the conduct of international relations. The nature and protection of human rights within an international setting provides a poignant example of the dilemmas in reconciling the opposed demands of international and world order. How are we to balance the state's insistence upon autonomy against the individual's demand for international protection of rights? Is humanitarian intervention by states a desirable step towards greater global justice or a recipe for international turmoil and disorder? Do we better secure human rights by weakening or strengthening the powers of the individual states?

The attempt to answer these questions brings the discussion back to the central theme. Are there universal standards which apply to human beings in all situations and where does the responsibility lie for ensuring that any such standards are observed? Which is to take priority – the attainment of individual human rights or the maintenance of a viable and stable international order that might itself be undermined by human rights interventionism?

The recent emergence of such issues is less of a novel departure in the history of international thought than a reversion to the earlier frameworks of the late medieval period:

> the Christian theologians who dominated the early phase of international thought derived from their metaphysics of natural law the principles which were in the twentieth century to subvert the logic of statehood by introducing a universal commitment by states to the idea of basic human rights.[20]

There is, to be sure, great uncertainty about the existence, let alone the content, of human rights and about the extent to which a concern about them should be allowed to inform the conduct of foreign policy. Beitz has argued an extreme case that 'the principle of state autonomy ... lacks a coherent moral foundation',[21] and in so doing, at least in principle, leaves the door open to unbridled intervention. Vincent, in more circumspect vein, cautions for a more limited human rights stance but still maintains that there is a bedrock, concerning the right to life, below which rights should not be allowed to fall:

45

Why should we modify the rules of international society, which allow each state to do as it wishes within its own frontiers, so as to admit this basic right which all must acknowledge? Because of a commitment to the value of human life without which the daily round would lose much of its meaning. And if it is a commitment to *human* life, then it is not to be diluted by the mere boundaries which human beings happen to have constructed against each other. This, in my view, is the core of all cosmopolitanist arguments . . .[22]

Distributive Justice. The debate about principles of distributive justice within the international community is but a specific restatement of the more general arguments already rehearsed. Are there obligations beyond borders and, if so, do they extend to issues of economic distribution? What duties do rich countries, or the inhabitants of rich countries, owe to the poorest members of the international community? That the attention of international relations theorists should have turned to such issues was itself an indication of the calamitous impact of maldistribution as it made itself felt in the 1970s and as erstwhile development strategies fell into some disrepute.[23]

A widely discussed argument for distributive justice was that advanced by Beitz.[24] From the facts of global economic interdependence, he concluded that obligations ought properly to be coextensive with the sphere of social interaction. Accordingly, there is no compelling reason why obligations should terminate at national frontiers.[25] From this position, Beitz elaborated the work of John Rawls in such a way that his principles of justice could be made to apply in the international, and not exclusively in the national, sphere:

I shall argue that a strong case can be made on contractarian grounds that persons of diverse citizenship have distributive obligations to one another analogous to those of citizens of the same state. International distributive obligations are founded on justice and not merely on mutual aid.[26]

It is clear that Beitz's proposals are of a purely theoretical kind and do not lend themselves readily to application. Nonetheless, it should be pointed out that his scheme does not amount to a 'back door' form of world government because he is insistent that such obligations need not be institutionalised in political forms:

a cosmpolitan conception of international morality is not equivalent to, nor does it necessarily imply, a political program like those often identified with political universalism, world federation, or 'world order'. It is important to distinguish moral structures from political ones and to recognize that global normative principles might be implemented otherwise than by global institutions conceived on the analogy of the state.[27]

46

This said, it remains unclear, in the absence of such political institutions, how principles of fairness are actually to be implemented.

A more fundamental problem with this extension of justice to the international realm may be, paradoxically, its failure to take due account of the dual international/national aspects of the problem. At this point, we come back to our original theme that order has both international and individual components to it. Merely to address international arrangements, as if the existence of states had no impact upon the distributive process, would evidently be an unsatisfactory manner of proceeding. Economic order, as it relates to conceptions of distributive justice, must therefore deal with both the international and the domestic dimensions of the problem in such a way that individual needs are met. This is a demanding intellectual exercise as has tellingly been pointed out:

> The cynic who has described foreign aid as a device for taking things away from the poor in rich countries and giving them to the rich in poor countries calls attention to a moral dilemma. In a world of 'have' states and 'have not' states, sharing of power would redistribute wealth among *states* with uncertain consequences for global distributive justice so far as it affects the poorest of the poor in a world of *people*. On the other hand, in a world of rich people and poor people effective controls by donor states to assure that the income transferred actually reached the truly needy would leave the presently powerful states as powerful as ever. Because we live both in a world of states and in a world of people, there are no easy answers.[28]

This analysis usefully clarifies two points. First, it demonstrates yet again the inherent tensions between international and world conceptions of order. Secondly, it sheds light on the problems of separating political from economic conceptions of order. If, in the view of the rich countries, concessions on political autonomy must be made by poor states in order to alleviate the economic lot of their inhabitants, then in the view of poor states the best means to improve their economic conditions is by both insisting upon that autonomy and also taking steps to increase political power within the international community. We return to the centrality of the international hierarchy in those disputes: the rich demand the maintenance of the existing power hierarchy as the price of economic 'trickle down' whereas the poor states seek a reformed hierarchy in which their status is improved. It is only the radical world order and world economic order conceptions which see the removal of this hierarchy altogether as a necessary part of the solution.

A proper understanding of order in international relations brings together both the competing perspectives on the nature of the field and also the multitudinous, and often conflictual, values which might be sought within these frameworks. The history of efforts to implement international order scarcely does justice to this rich tapestry. Nonetheless, the setting out of these theoretical issues serves to enrich our understanding of the dilemmas of statecraft and of the trade-offs that need to be arranged so that minimum international order does not obstruct efforts towards a more comprehensive optimum world order, but that neither does the basic security order collapse under the weight of overweening normative ambition.

3 KANT AND THE TRADITION OF OPTIMISM

This chapter and the succeeding one are concerned with the respective traditions of optimism and pessimism in relation to the international order, the former asserting that reform is both necessary and possible and the latter that reform is both unattainable and dangerous. For reasons of convenience, and in accordance with widespread practice, we may refer to these traditions as those of utopianism and realism. By way of caution, however, it should be pointed out that although there is extensive overlap between optimism and pessimism, on the one hand, and utopianism and realism, on the other, the two are not absolutely identical. Optimism reflects a faith that progressive change is possible, whereas utopianism, in its strict sense, pertains to the pursuit of the unattainable ideal. Likewise, pessimism is a denial of the possibility of progress, whereas realism, again in its strict sense, means the harmonious blending of practical activities with an extant reality without necessarily asserting that reality is itself unchanging. Nonetheless, for present purposes, we shall refer to utopianism as the ideological impetus to reform of the international order and to realism as the main source of resistance.

It is, however, important to emphasise that while utopian and realist thought diverge fundamentally as to the possibility of reforming the international order, much utopian argument is located within the same paradigm as realism. Although, as Banks has pointed out, idealism is found in each paradigm, historically its intellectual centre of gravity is within a state system beset by problems of security and war:

> Realists share the state-centric paradigm with the idealists ... Idealism ... is most easily recognisable among those who agree with the realists about the nature of the problems posed by world politics while disagreeing with them about what should be done in response ... idealists proceed to liberal doctrines; for them, power can be tamed.[1]

Idealists and realists part company on the potential for changing the international order but this should not distract us from the intellectual imagery which they have in common as regards the characteristic actors and processes of international relations.

During the 1950s and 1960s, utopian thought, like ideology generally, was deemed to be at an end. Typically, Judith Shklar pronounced that 'the urge to construct grand designs for the political future of mankind is gone', basing her judgement on the ground that 'the last vestiges of utopian faith required for such an enterprise have vanished'.[2] Subsequently, Paul Seabury expressed the view that 'a utopian concern for "world order" as a planned qualitative transformation designed to meet new needs seems to have been washed out ... Prescriptive futurism now seems passé.'[3] In the event, such obituaries turned out to be premature: thought about international-order reform experienced a resurgence since the 1970s, to such an extent that we might be tempted to equate the intellectual mood of this period with the utopian impulse of the post-1918 decade.

This prompts the question: is there anything novel in the form of utopian speculation about international order that emerged in the 1970s or is the phenomenon better understood as part of that longer tradition of reformist thought that has characterised the history of intellectual endeavour ever since the inception of the European states system? Or, to put the question more incisively, can the current genre of utopian writing avoid Hinsley's bitter indictment of twentieth-century 'peace projects', namely that 'every scheme for the elimination of war that men have advocated since 1917 has been nothing but a copy or an elaboration of some seventeenth-century programme – as the seventeenth-century programmes were copies of still earlier schemes'?[4] Are recent ideas concerning international-order reform as totally atavistic as Hinsley suggests, or do they constitute a watershed in this form of intellectual enterprise? This chapter will suggest that, while there is some novelty in recent reformist thought, its most striking attribute is a reversion to a tradition of optimism that is similar to the classical exposition found in Kant's writings on international order.

However, the delimitations of the exercise should first be specified. It is not the intention of this survey to consider the novelty, or otherwise, of recent utopian writing in terms of its 'preferred solutions' or in terms of the details of its 'preferred world orders'. The instrumental aspects of ideas about international-order reform have been classified elsewhere on the basis of three distinct orientations: political–structural, functional and universal–cultural approaches to reform, all of which highlight the particular instrument or process of reform, or focus on the 'end-goal' to be realised.[5] However, this chapter is not concerned with such solutions. Virtually every survey of peace projects or of the history of ideas concerning international-order reform has been preoccupied with the details of these solutions and has been so at the expense of a more general appreciation of the continuities and discontinuities in utopian thought that stem from the structure of their arguments about the need for reform, irrespective of their preferred variant for its attainment. It is with the logical structures of utopian thought that we are concerned and within these confines that the novelty of recent utopian thought will be assessed. In other words, the focus is upon the mainsprings of utopianism, on why it believes that solutions are possible, or, indeed, necessary.

THE NATURE OF UTOPIANISM

What is conveyed by the term 'utopian thought' is also in need of some initial elaboration. In terms of one classification of patterns of thought about the future, the utopian tradition with which we are concerned falls unequivocally into the natural–rational category.[6] Such an approach is, according to Cox, 'founded on the concept of a duality distinguishing the inward nature from the outward appearance of human institutions and events' and one of the lines of inquiry stemming from it is 'the normative task of designing polities consistent with the rational nature of man'.[7] Viewed from this perspective, the focus of intellectual endeavour is upon the seeming inconsistency between a rational calculation of humankind's needs and wants and the irrationality of the international political arrangements presently in place.

More generally, it can be argued that there are four interrelated distinguishing marks of utopianism, four characteristics of such thought which inhere, to a greater or lesser degree, in all its variants. The first of these is a belief in 'progress'. As one writer has expressed it 'the utopian faith asserts that human nature can be understood in terms not of immutable facts but of potentialities which are progressively actualized in the course of history'.[8] Indeed, Hedley Bull has argued that this belief in progress was the defining attribute of the post-1918 generation of 'idealists':

> The distinctive characteristic of these writers was their belief in progress: the belief, in particular, that the system of international relations that had given rise to the First World War was capable of

51

being transformed . . . that . . . it was in fact being transformed; and that their responsibility as students of international relations was to assist this march of progress.[9]

It should be noted that there is a 'praxis' entailed by this position. Theoretical understanding of the shortcomings of the international order is inadequate by itself: it must form the basis of a programme of political activism. The theorist, as such, is not a neutral observer of the historical process but an active participant within it.

Utopians are, therefore, concerned to promote improvement and because of this it might be said that utopian thought is, in the loosest sense of the word, 'revolutionary' or, in Mannheim's phraseology, 'the explosive material for bursting the limits of the existing order'.[10] This is where utopians most obviously part company with the realists. As has been suggested of the liberal interdependence writers of the past two decades, they 'began to recover the concept of progress for the theory of international relations, and encouraged the belief that the purpose of international theory was not to understand "recurrence and repetition" in the international system but to identify and strengthen alternative historical possibilities immanent within it'.[11]

The second element is logically related to the first: it follows from this belief in progress that utopians share an essentially non-deterministic view of the world. The belief in progress would, in itself, be meaningless were it not predicated upon a similar faith in the efficacy of change through human agency. This faith, in turn, derives from a particular view of the nature of the historical process.[12] Accordingly, the distinctive 'realist' and 'utopian' views of historical motion might be crudely depicted in the following terms: unlike the 'realist', who considers the driving force of history to be located in antecedent causes that push the process along, the utopian makes allowance for the power of the idea of the future that, to some extent, is able to serve as a pole of attraction. Expressed in other words, the realist emphasises the 'supply' side of history (we adapt our needs to what is on offer), whereas the utopian recognises a 'demand' side (political institutions can be tailored to maximise fulfilment of human needs).

The point goes beyond this and raises fundamental issues about the ontological status of 'reality' and about the role of ideas in its construction. According to the utopian view it is precisely because our social and political institutions are a reflection of political values and preferences that ideas of the future can be instrumental in bringing about qualitative change. It is not, as realists would hold, that 'the normative ideas people have are determined by the general structure of the social and political reality', itself 'autonomous', but rather that these structures are reflections of, and changeable by, normative ideas.[13]

The third characteristic of utopian thought is its pervasive rationalism. As one analyst of utopianism has argued, it believes that 'a rational and moral political order can be imposed on the international system' and that 'just as individual men are good and rational, so too states are capable of behaving in a moral and rational manner towards one another'.[14] Indeed, when utopians speak about 'progress', they invariably mean by it the actualisation of mankind's potential for rationality.

The pervasiveness of this belief is easily demonstrated. Perhaps the classic example is to be found in the writings of Norman Angell, early in this century. In *The Great Illusion* (1909) Angell argued that wars were not financially profitable and his messianic message was that it remained only to convince statesmen of this fact in order to liberate mankind from the scourge of war. Likewise, more than a century earlier, Bentham had subscribed to the notion of a rationalist universe: 'Between the interests of nations there is nowhere any real conflict; if they appear repugnant anywhere it is only in proportion as they are misunderstood.'[15] Like Angell, Bentham was convinced that the calamities of international relations were no more than instances in the failure of mutual comprehension.

In this sense, the faith in rationality draws attention to the affinities between utopian thought and the mediaeval natural-law tradition. This tradition assumes that there are objective rules governing the universe and that man, through the use of right reason, can deduce their content. Above all, it was a part of the natural-law tradition that the elements of justice could be objectively known. Accordingly, the post-First World War generation of utopians believed that men, acting rationally, would also be acting in accordance with the dictates of justice: standards of justice were knowable by right reasoning. This came through powerfully in the theoretical underpinnings of the League of Nations. As Lord Robert Cecil, one of the most prominent British sponsors of the League, was to write in condemnation of the old system of the balance of power, to which the League was seen as a corrective, 'there is this fatal objection to the system of international anarchy. It makes justice and right dependent on the fortunes of war.'[16] Now, if war is not to determine what is just, what else can? By implication, Cecil evidently assumed that there is an objective standard of justice to which all men, regardless of nationality, will subscribe. The problem of international relations, for utopians like

53

Cecil, lies in persuading states to adhere to a just international order, not in determining the nature of such an order.

The belief in rationality has its obverse side in the fourth predominant characteristic of utopian thought – the assumption of a natural harmony of interests.[17] Accordingly, the interests of states are taken to be complementary rather than antagonistic and the game of international politics is mixed-motive rather than zero-sum. The 'invisible hand' ensures a happy outcome for everyone because basic interests can be reconciled and are not mutually exclusive. Only, indeed, if such were the case would it be possible for principles of rationality to exercise their sway. Symptomatic of the centrality of this belief to the utopian position were the execrations heaped by the inter-war idealist, Alfred Zimmern, upon the 'wicked theory of the mutual incompatibility of nations'.[18] The real interests of states are in harmony with each other and it is only a misreading, by realist statesmen, of apparent interests which suggests otherwise.

THE KANTIAN TRADITION

For the purposes of the present discussion, it will be argued that Kant is representative of a specific form of utopian thought, and that successive waves of twentieth-century utopian writers have all been heir to this Kantian heritage. It is not intended to provide an elaborate treatment of Kant's analysis of perpetual peace, as this has been adequately done elsewhere[19] but a brief outline of his views is nonetheless necessary in order to establish his utopian credentials.

The starting point for any discussion of Kant's theory of international relations would have to be his definition of the cause of the problem of war. For Kant, the basic cause of international strife is individual human nature. He speaks of 'the depravity of human nature' which 'is exhibited without disguise in the unrestrained relations of the Nations to each other',[20] and also of war as 'requiring no special motive: . . . it appears to be ingrafted on human nature'.[21] The evil consequences of man's nature are, Kant argues, checked at the domestic level by the institution of government but, unfortunately, this only succeeds in displacing the problem:

> What avails it to labour at the arrangement of a Commonwealth as a Civil Constitution regulated by law among individual men? The same unsociableness which forced men to it, becomes again the cause of each Commonwealth assuming the attitude of uncontrolled freedom in its external relations, that is, as one State in relation to other States; and consequently, any one State must expect from any other the

same sort of evils as oppressed individual men and compelled them to enter into a Civil Union regulated by law.[22]

In other words, the attempt to escape anarchy at the individual level merely leads to anarchy at the level of relations between states.

Up to this point, Kant appears to be following the logic of the domestic analogy, setting the scene for an 'international' social contract. However, this is not Kant's solution. Many people wrongly believe that Kant was advocating a form of world government but this is not the case and he is quite explicit on this point. In advocating his league for peace (*foedus pacificum*) as a surrogate for a world governmental authority, Kant insists that this league 'will not aim at the acquisition of any of the political powers of a State'.[23] Gallie is therefore correct to emphasise Kant's position that 'the idea of coercion, to sustain an international order, is both logically and practically an absurdity',[24] in which the rejection of the domestic analogy is implicit and hence that, for Kant, 'there is a fundamental asymmetry between establishing and maintaining a just constitution within a state and in establishing and maintaining a just relationship between states'.[25] This is to say that there is marked discontinuity between the achievement of order within the state and the attainment of order as between the states themselves.

There are various ways in which Kant might be characterised as a utopian. The first prerequisite of utopian thinking is, necessarily, a degree of dissatisfaction with the current order of things. Kant quite clearly feels that the state of war between nations is a morally distasteful condition and one that must be improved upon. In addition to their moral reprehensibility, Kant viewed contemporary international relations as mechanically unsound. In his own words 'a lasting Universal Peace on the basis of the so-called Balance of Power in Europe is a mere chimera. It is like the house which was built by an architect so perfectly in accordance with all the laws of equilibrium, that when a sparrow lighted upon it, it immediately fell.'[26]

Kant's dismissal of the present is related to an optimistic faith in the future. It was argued earlier that the stamp of the utopian is the belief in progress and this is unquestionably immanent in the Kantian philosophy:

> I venture to assume that as the human race is continually advancing in civilization and culture as its natural purpose, so it is continually making progress for the better in relation to the moral end of its existence and that this progress, although it may be sometimes interrupted, will never be entirely broken off or stopped.[27]

Such progress is, in fact, guaranteed by the teleology of his philosophy, which sees mankind advancing towards some ultimate goal, and this goal is to be attained through what is basically a dialectical process between man and nature: nature imposes afflictions and hardships upon man and, in overcoming these, man is gradually guided towards his moral destiny. Progress towards perpetual peace is part of nature's grand design and is guaranteed by nature herself.

In holding this belief in progress, Kant clearly rejects a major element of realist thinking, namely the view that we can project from the past into the future and that we must be guided in the future by our experience of the past. In one passage, Kant gives a powerful demonstration of his utopian persuasion:

> This hope of better times, without which an earnest desire to do something conducive to the common well-being would never have warmed the human heart, has always exercised an influence upon the practical conduct of the well-disposed of mankind . . . Arguments from experience against the success of such endeavours, resolved and carried out in hope, are of no avail. For the fact that something has not yet succeeded is no proof that it will never succeed.[28]

Kant, therefore, shares some general utopian predispositions. It remains only to discuss the particular form of his utopianism that has been his most conspicuous legacy to his successors. In its most rudimentary form, the basis of Kant's utopianism, the font of his optimism, is an argument from necessity directly to a solution – that it is necessity itself which ensures the emergence of a solution. As Kant was to express it succinctly, speaking of the adversities of war, 'the very evils which thus arise compel men to find out means against them'.[29] This theme, that progress is created by adversity, is Kant's most distinctive refrain, as the following passages from the *Idea for a Universal History* demonstrate:

> Nature has accordingly again used the unsociableness of men, and even of great societies and political bodies, her creatures of this kind, as a means to work out through their mutual antagonism a condition of rest and security. She works through wars, through the strain of never relaxed preparation for them and through the necessity which every state is at last compelled to feel within itself, even in the midst of peace, to begin some imperfect efforts to carry out her purpose.
>
> However visionary this idea may appear to be . . . it is nevertheless the inevitable issue of the necessity in which men involve one another. For this necessity must compel the Nations to the very resolution . . . to which the savage in his uncivilized state, was so unwillingly compelled. . . . All wars are, accordingly, so many attempts . . . to bring about new relations between the Nations: and

by destruction or at least dismemberment of them all to form new political corporations.

> By the expenditure of all the resources of the Commonwealth in military preparations against each other, by the devastations occasioned by war, and still more by the necessity of holding themselves continually in readiness for it, the full development of the capacities are undoubtedly retarded in their progress; but, on the other hand, the very evils which thus arise, compel men to find out means against them.[30]

It should also be pointed out that, even if nowhere explicitly stated by Kant, it is at least implicit in the logic of his argument that if necessity fathers its own solution, then by extension, an intensified necessity holds out even greater prospects for beneficial transformation. In essence, the structure of the Kantian argument is as follows: adversity forces man to overcome it; the greater the adversity – the more pressing the need to resolve a problem – the greater the expectation that men will behave rationally and take the appropriate steps towards meeting the emergency. 'Only as war becomes patently more destructive and more costly', Gallie observes, 'will men be moved to take the first difficult steps towards a permanent peace'.[31] In fairness, however, it has to be recalled that Kant's optimism is finally tempered. He is blind neither to the long process of change nor to its reversibility:

> The result is a hypothetical interpretation of human history and destiny which does nothing to flatter mankind, yet provides a framework in which Reason's high demands upon men make sense, without offering them either respite or assurance of success.[32]

Such a qualification is necessary to remind us, that while it is nature's design to effect progress through trial and tribulation, the final responsibility for such improvement lies with humanity and cannot be evaded.

THE TWENTIETH-CENTURY 'NEO-KANTIANS'

It is this optimistic Kantian paradox that good will come out of adversity that best characterises twentieth-century thought about international-order reform. That this is so, and that the argument rests upon an apparent paradox, has been attested by several analysts. Niebuhr for instance, has criticised latter-day utopians on the grounds that 'virtually all arguments for world government rest upon the simple presupposition that the desirability of world order proves the attainability of world government'.[33] Likewise, Louis Beres provides a perfect example of Kantian reasoning in the context of current utopian prognoses. He argues that the success of current forms of inter-nationalism 'is apt to depend significantly upon the perceived urgency of the developing planetary crisis' and then proceeds to highlight

> the seemingly contradictory argument that the appearance of a most desirable system of world order would require an increasing proxi-mity to a most undesirable one. Doesn't this demonstrate a strikingly illogical . . . sort of reasoning? After all, can it be argued plausibly that to improve the world we must first bring it ever closer to the very configurations of global calamity we seek to avert?[34]

This neatly places current utopians within the Kantian tradition. However, to broaden out the argument, it may be contended that all three successive waves of twentieth-century utopian writing have conformed to the Kantian mould. These three successive waves that can be distinguished are: the post-1918 generation of utopians; the utopian reaction to the nuclear revolution; and, thirdly, the utopian reaction of recent years to a perceived 'planetary' crisis.[35] The per-vasive influence of Kantian reasoning in each of these phases can be amply demonstrated.

As regards the post-1918 utopians, it can be argued that the case for the League of Nations was based on no more certain foundation than the necessity of avoiding a repetition of the disaster of the 1914–18 war. The optimism that the League could, in fact, induce a change for the better in standards of international behaviour was explicitly connected with the magnitude of destruction in the First World War, which convinced some utopians that it was a disaster of the necessary Kantian proportions to evince fundamental change in human conduct. Nowhere was this kind of logic employed more clearly than in the utterances of Woodrow Wilson himself who argued directly from necessity to success when he stated of the League that 'if it won't work, it must be made to work'.[36] The structure of this argument has been nicely summarised by E. H. Carr:

> The advocate of a scheme for an international police force or for 'collective security' or for some other project for an international order generally replied to the criticism not by an argument designed to show how and why he thought his plan will work but by a statement that it must be made to work because the consequences of its failure to work would be so disastrous.[37]

The utopian prescriptions of the post-1945 period, and especially those centred upon the impact of nuclear weapons, fall into precisely the same pattern of thought. These writings are too diverse to be considered in any detail but the general tenor of their conclusions make them a part of the neo-Kantian tradition. In fact, the Kantian connection is explicitly made in the title of one such book *Annihilation and Utopia* which directly associates the necessity with the solution.[38] Examples of this logical structure are profuse. Writing in the late 1940s, R. M. Hutchins expounded his faith in world government in the following terms:

> Before the atomic bomb, we could take world government or leave it. We could rely on the long process of evolution to bring world community and world government hand in hand. Any such program today means another war, and another war means the end of civilization. *The slogan of our faith today must be, world government is necessary and therefore possible.*[39]

That this is the principal theme of post-nuclear-weapon utopian writing has been averred by Richard Falk who observes that 'after the atomic explosions at Hiroshima and Nagasaki in World War II, the plea of world order reformers has rested on a claim of alleged necessity. In other words, the argument for reform is backed up by an assertion that the existing system is heading for destruction'.[40] Implicit in such arguments is the adaptation of Kantian logic to suggest that the historical process is now compressed by the dangers of nuclear war: what humanity could previously afford to learn at leisure over a protracted period, must now be reflected in immediate action.

Perhaps the most sophisticated and the most erudite exposition of this line of reasoning is to be found in the writing of Karl Jaspers who considers the view that 'total peril engenders total deliverance. An extreme emergency compels forms of political existence which make not only the bomb but war itself impossible.'[41] Extremity alone can produce the required transformation of people's consciousness and consequently Jaspers concludes that 'what needs increasing is the fear of the people: this should grow to overpowering force, not of blind submissiveness, but of a bright, transforming ethos that will bring forth appropriate statesmen and support their actions'.[42] It is a logic that Niebuhr could not share: 'Undoubtedly fear may be a creative force . . . But the creative power of fear does not increase in proportion to its intensity.'[43] However, even in the act of denying its logic, Niebuhr further affirms the almost universal attraction of post-1945 utopians to the Kantian model.

The third wave of twentieth-century utopian writing is that centred upon fears of some form of ecological or planetary crisis – what we might loosely term the doomsday syndrome. It is not intended to create the impression that all discussions of the perceived 'global crisis' end on a note of strident optimism that declares the emergency will be met but, at the very least, it would be difficult to deny the existence of a widespread sentiment that this 'crisis' has, at last, made the earth ripe for world-order reform.[44] It is certainly this connection which Barbara Ward sought to establish in her popularisation of the concept of 'Space Ship Earth', and it became virtually a hypnotic chant in the writings of the 1970s. Wagar, within earshot of the 'Crack of Doom', issued his injunction that 'we must totalise the search for world order. We must become architects and builders of civilization. Anything less is too little.'[45] Camilleri echoed the cry: 'The very magnitude of the twentieth-century crisis and the structural disorder from which it springs have reinforced the natural predisposition of utopian thinking towards a revolutionary conception of change.'[46] The literature, in finest Kantian style, was soon replete with 'necessities' and 'imperatives'. As G. Hirschfield has expressed it: 'in no century before ours has the need for human unity been so imperative. Indeed, mankind is already unified in a material sense. It is this very fact that renders higher orders of synthesis necessary, if mankind is to survive.'[47] However, probably no one has sounded the Kantian apocalyptic note more effectively than Richard Falk:

> It is possible that the credible threat of catastrophe will generate the will and energy to overcome some bad features of our human existence that we have taken for granted or accepted as unavoidable. I would argue, in fact, that the precariousness of human survival might at last give mankind the opportunity to create a social, economic and political order that would allow human groups to live together under conditions of mutual respect and tolerable dignity.[48]

Falk, be it noted, is not always so optimistic and despite his powerful utopianism, has occasionally shed his Kantian mantle. In one passage, he indeed strikes at the very heart of the Kantian position when he solemnly counsels that 'declarations of ecological emergency' have, in themselves, 'no capacity to induce fundamental world order reform' or, at least, not in a 'progressive' direction.[49] On balance, however, he seems more predisposed towards the alternative view. In fact, the very purpose of his many writings rests on the contrary assumption that such declarations of emergency can play a positive role in world-order reform.

The neo-Kantian role of extremity or disaster has, as was noted above, been a pervasive theme of all utopian writing on world-order reform. It should, however, be pointed out that utopians have been concerned with disaster from two distinct perspectives, both from a retrospective and from a prospective viewpoint. Indeed, it might be contended that in the past century, one of the more noticeable trends in utopian thought has been the shift of emphasis from the former to the latter as a result of which utopian arguments 'from necessity' have tended to focus upon 'previsioned' disasters rather than upon disasters already experienced.

It is an oft-repeated maxim that peace projects and world-order reform proposals have tended to crop up in the immediate aftermath of calamitous wars. As William Penn was to express it in his *Essay on Peace* (1693), mankind cannot 'finally know the comfort of peace but by the smart and penance of the vices of war'.[50] However the 'smart and penance' of war can make its influence felt in two ways, either by direct experience or by an act of creative imagination projected towards the future. It is interesting, therefore, to note Hinsley's observation that 'it was in the last years of the nineteenth century that for the first time in the history of the present European based world civilisation . . . peace proposals were propagated for fear of the danger of war rather than in consequence of its outbreak'.[51] If Hinsley is correct, then we might optimistically judge that there is a learning process at work here. The neo-Kantian argument from future necessities is very similar to the argument from past disasters in the sense that the 'heightened danger' thesis is logically similar to retrospective explanations of interest in peace projects in the aftermath of major wars. The central concept is still that of extremity: what changes is merely our chronological relationship to it. Indeed, it might be contended that this has been the major purpose of recent utopian thought – to make 'anticipated disasters' serve as functional substitutes for 'actual disasters' and so derive the benefits of disasters before they occur. If this can be achieved, it might be taken as a sign of progress. It is for this reason that Jaspers, as was noted above, placed great weight on the creative role of fear – the previsioned dread of nuclear war – since any progress is likely to be achieved only in the shadow of nuclear hostilities and not in their aftermath. If disaster can produce a cathartic effect, it is as well to utilise the threat of it as the actual experience. This was certainly Kant's preference: 'And, at last, after many devastations, overthrows, and even complete international exhaustion of their powers, the nations are driven forward to the goal *which Reason might have well impressed upon them, even without so much sad experience.*'[52]

Returning to the issue of the novelty, or otherwise, of the current utopian position, there would seem to be two other aspects of the question worthy of consideration. The argument thus far has established that most current utopian writing falls within the neo-Kantian tradition because of its emphasis on solutions generated by 'necessity'. Even within this tradition, however, it could be argued that present-day utopian prescriptions differ from those of the past as a result of the specific nature of the threat that they consider is presented to the global order. This argument has at least two strands to it. The first would have it that current global necessities are more likely to issue in international-order reform than previously because of the *source* of the threat to the system. The second maintains that the present crisis will issue in reform because of its specific quality of *terminality*. These arguments will be considered in turn.

Classical 'social contract' or 'domestic analogy' prescriptions for the ills of international anarchy and for overcoming the traditional dilemmas of national military security have always suffered from an inherent tension: that it is with those very states that constitute the source of the threat that cooperation must be entered into in order to eliminate the threat. As Hedley Bull has remarked in connection with this central paradox of the social-contract school:

> The idea of world government by contract involves a dilemma . . . if states are indeed in a Hobbesian state of nature, the contract by means of which they are to emerge from it cannot take place . . . The difficulty . . . is that the description it contains of the actual condition of international relations, and the prescription it provides for its improvement, are inconsistent with one another.[53]

That is to say that the very nature of the issue of military security, because of its inherent zero-sum nature, makes trust between the contracting parties difficult and renders the basis of cooperation tenuous. No utopian prescription has been able to rise above this military security dilemma and this, most analysts would agree, lies at the heart of the repeated historical failures to institute some form of collective security system.

However, it soon becomes apparent that those utopians currently arguing from the basis of a more wide-ranging 'planetary security dilemma' regard this as constituting a major watershed in utopian writing and see it as providing an enhanced prospect for world-order reform. The thrust of the argument here is that the contemporary crisis is not one that has its source in a *competitive game between states* but rather one that has its source in a *cooperative game against nature*. Thus, according to its proponents, the planetary crisis marks a breach with traditional utopian concerns because the danger is located in a different source – nature itself – and this novel dimension to the problem, while bringing with it the prospect of ultimate catastrophe, brings with it also a greater prospect of achieving the reform necessary to avert that disaster. The argument remains within the Kantian mould but not so much on the basis of the extremity of the crisis as on the basis of its source.

That the global environmental crisis is qualitatively different in nature from traditional military security concerns and that there is for that very reason a heightened possibility of its leading to cooperative and constructive international-order reform are propositions that have found widespread support. They underlie virtually all utopian writing of the recent period. The view is perhaps most succinctly expressed in the following quotation: 'The traditional concern of functionalists and others interested in world order systems has been the elimination of war and in this context nationalism has been understandably viewed as a major obstacle. However, when the focus shifts to confronting the environmental crisis national egoism assumes a less threatening dimension.'[54] The same authors explain their reasoning in greater detail, emphasising the inherent difference between 'environmental' security and 'military' security and underlining the cooperation-inducing nature of the former as compared with the cooperation-inhibiting nature of the latter:

> there is the amorphous and unplanned accumulation of environ-
> mental stress, especially in the form of pollution and population
> growth. While engendering definite destabilising consequences,
> their root causes are not traceable to specific conflict producing intent
> on the part of any one country ... Any initiative for cooperation,
> however, will come primarily from the realization on the part of
> individual states of the extent to which their security is threatened in
> the absence of cooperation.[55]

Even such a renowned 'realist' as George Kennan has given expression to the same kind of sentiment, albeit in a less grandiose form, when he argued that cooperation on environmental matters might 'spill over' into, and thereby improve, the international atmosphere generally.[56]

The argument is not as compelling as its seductive simplicity would suggest. As has been argued above, traditionally, supranational solutions have been unattractive because they have required cooperation amongst competitive consumers of security. Is this difficulty overcome by the external-threat imagery of an increasingly malevolent nature? Ostensibly, as Shields and Ott have argued, it should make a difference. However, a moment's reflection suggests that there is no very convincing reason why this should be so. To the extent that the prevailing philosophy of war in the twentieth century has moved away from the Clausewitzian to embrace cataclysmic conceptions, especially under nuclear conditions, it can be argued that war itself (which, in these terms, no one 'wants') has constituted an exogenous threat to the system, equivalent to that of nature, without this leading to international-order reform. Moreover, it is a deceptive imagery to pretend that the 'environmental crisis' is something 'out there' which threatens us all. The environmental or planetary situation is as much a product of state policies as is the danger of war. Moreover, in a competitive economic environment, it is unhelpful to pretend that environmental deterioration is other than the consequence of the pursuit of state interests: as in the sphere of military security, states are inhibited from taking unilateral steps which might yield advantage to their economic competitors. These considerations indicate that the facile distinction between a 'state-engendered' (security) crisis and a 'nature-imposed' (environmental) crisis is simply not tenable.

The response of states to the 'endangered planet' image serves to reinforce this conclusion: if the environmental degradation and 'limits to growth' arguments have had any concrete impact on international politics, then it has surely been to cast states in the roles of competitive consumers of utiles, be they military or welfare/environmental, and, if anything, to intensify the zero-sum nature of *all* international political games, including those of growth and development, as well as the traditional ones of military security.

The last aspect to be considered is whether there is a new force to utopian arguments from necessity because of the 'terminality' of the conditions facing mankind. There is undoubtedly a widespread feeling that this is so, that even if the prospect of disaster has not induced reform in the past, this was because the disaster would be only partial and temporary whereas any future disaster will be total and permanent. The Kantian logic here is that even if the international body politic has not been moved to reform by periodic bouts of influenza, it must nonetheless activate itself when confronted with imminent terminal cancer.

The issue, as posed, is not open to answer. There seems no compelling logical reason why a terminal crisis should possess a greater reform-producing capacity than any other crisis, except in so far as (and this may be a major qualification) the terminality is recognised and acted upon as such. Perception and understanding are, of course, the mainsprings of human action and there is some reason for believing that humans are impressed by the notion of terminality. A good example can be offered from a different, but related, context. In the course of a discussion of Herman Kahn's ideas on nuclear war, Anatole Rapoport makes the following observation:

> Kahn categorically rejects both the idea that the prospect of the horrors of nuclear war has made it 'unthinkable' and the idea that if such a war occurs it will be the 'end of civilization' . . . I believe that the choice of the notation (World War IV, World War V) was meant to dissociate 'World War III' from 'finality'.[57]

If Rapoport's interpretation of Kahn's motivations is substantially correct, one wonders why Kahn should have been perturbed by any glimmer of 'finality'. The apparent explanation must be that Kahn was writing a tract about the continuing utility of the Clausewitzian war-system and, as such, was seeking to counteract revolutionary thinking about nuclear warfare: one can, therefore, only suppose that Kahn was afraid that talk of 'finality' would lead to pusillanimous thinking and, perhaps, induce that very reform of the war-system which Kahn was seeking to prevent.

If we allow this argument, it may be the case that the 'terminality' of the heralded world-order crisis represents a watershed in utopian thought. At the very least, there is reason for suspecting that on the basis of this perceived terminal condition, there has been some reversion, to use Mannheim's terms, from the 'liberal–humanitarian', to an earlier 'chiliastic', tradition of utopian thought.[58] Mannheim distinguishes them as follows:

> The fulfilment of chiliast expectations may occur at any moment. Now with the liberal–humanitarian idea the utopian element received a definite location in the historical process – it is the culmination point of historical evolution. In contrast with the earlier conception of a utopia which was suddenly to break upon the world completely from the outside, this signifies, in the long run, a relative toning down of the notion of sudden historical change.[59]

In these terms recent utopian writings have much in common with the chiliastic tradition.

It has been the argument of this chapter that twentieth-century utopian writings, despite some differences of approach and emphasis, fall overwhelmingly within a broader utopian tradition that may be labelled the neo-Kantian. If we have presently arrived at a watershed in utopian thought, and this is by no means clear, then the most convincing grounds for asserting such a claim seem to derive from the nature of the present 'crisis' that is 'necessitating' reform and especially from its avowed 'terminality'.

In a sense, therefore, the uniqueness of present utopian writings hinges upon the objective existence of this crisis itself – on whether it is as threatening as its utopian analysts claim it to be. If the doomsday prognosis is correct, the perceived necessity becomes more compelling than ever before. If the crisis of today is no more pressing and no more terminal than those of yore, historians may well look back upon the utopianism of a Richard Falk, in two centuries' time, with the same indulgence that we can now look back upon the utopianism of Kant. In the final analysis, we come down to degrees of belief. As Jaspers has observed 'despair and confidence are moods not insights'.[60] If there is anything distinctive about the current genre of international-order writing, it is its sense of urgency. This sentiment may be soundly based; alternatively, it may be no more than a demonstration of the egocentricity of an age that chooses to believe its crises are the culmination or denouement of history – a mood, as commentators have noted, that is especially prone to strike as we approach the end of the millennium. What we do not yet know is whether this utopian mood is also an insight.

4 ROUSSEAU AND THE TRADITION OF DESPAIR

This chapter will be similar in structure to the previous one: it will consist of an outline of the general traits of the realist interpretation of international politics, will demonstrate the development of the attitude of despair within the writings of Jean-Jacques Rousseau, will seek to show how this attitude has been bequeathed to, and elaborated upon by, twentieth-century realists and, finally, will discuss in greater detail some of the key elements embraced within this philosophical perspective. As in the previous chapter, the main concentration will be upon continuities within this particular tradition of thought.

There is, of course, a degree of artificiality in speaking of realist or utopian schools or traditions of thought as, indeed, there is in assuming that we can readily discern a sharp dichotomy between the two. Frequently, writers display hybrid characteristics, which makes it difficult, not to say unproductive, to try to insert them into convenient realist or utopian pigeon-holes. Nonetheless, as long as it is remembered that we are talking at the level of intellectual ideal-types, there is some value in depicting the general characteristics of a realist tradition of thought. As Brian Porter has observed, '"the tradition" then is a device, as the arranging of stars in constellations is a device, for the convenience of the observer ... "Permanent propensities of the political mind" might be a better, though more cumbersome, way of putting it.'[1]

What are the dominant features of a realist understanding of international politics? Most obviously, realism is associated with the fearsome and depressing world of power politics in which states have to be permanently on their guard if life is not to be 'nasty, brutish and short'. It is associated with the imagery of the state as a gladiator engaged in a perpetual combat. As one writer has summarised it, realism entails 'being aware of the grim necessities of communal existence and (of) being able to see that man is prone to fight, to seek power and to pursue his own egotistical ends. Its basic premise is that international relations are anarchic and lawless, and its basic proposition is that all states seek to enhance their own power.'[2]

According to Waltz, an exhaustive listing of the elements of a *Realpolitik* approach would be as follows:

> The ruler's, and later the state's interest provides the spring of action; the necessities of policy arise from the unregulated competition of states; political calculation based on these necessities can discover rational policies; success is the ultimate test of policy, and success is defined as preserving and strengthening the state. Ever since Machiavelli, interest and necessity – and *raison d'état* the phrase that comprehends them – have remained the key concepts of *Realpolitik*.[3]

It can be seen from this quotation that the idea of necessity is as prominent in the realist tradition as it was in the Kantian utopian one but with quite different implications – a point that will be discussed later in the chapter.

More specifically, it can be contended that realist thought is a composite of some six different aspects: some of these, as is to be expected, will simply be the obverse of elements of utopianism considered in the foregoing chapter.

In the first place, it has been argued that one of the main characteristics of utopianism was its belief in the attainability of progress in terms of the realisation of a preferable international order. Utopianism is nothing if not a reformist attitude of mind. What is important for our present study is the fact that realism, as a pessimistic tradition, denies the possibility of progress. For the realist, power politics is the name of the game, always has been and always will be. Accordingly, the parameters of realist thought are set by the boundaries of historical experience and the propositions derived from it depend 'for their validity mainly on historical precedent in the field of state practice'.[4]

As opposed to the linear conception of historical development posited in utopian thinking, the realist conception is a cyclical one. In the words of Hedley Bull,

> As against the belief of the 'idealists' in progress they drew attention to the cyclical or recurrent patterns of international politics. Contrary to the view of the 'idealists' that power politics was a method of conducting international relations that belonged only to the bad old world, they presented power politics as the law of all international life.[5]

Similarly, Nicholas Spykman wrote in 1942 that 'the new order will not differ from the old and international society will continue to operate with the same fundamental power patterns. It will be a world of power politics' and that 'there seems to be no reason to assume or expect that these behaviour patterns of states will suddenly change or disappear'.[6]

This feature of international politics is permanent and since states and statesmen cannot rise above it, there can, therefore, be no significant progress in international life. However, the reasons offered by realists for the non-attainability of progress differ from writer to writer. For some, the belief that wars and violence will always be a feature of international life is grounded upon a theory of human nature – a theory that regards this nature as base, wicked and unchangeable. Since the raw material of politics, namely people themselves, is unchanging, there can be no amelioration of the kind of political order that they produce. Other realists do not have, or do not emphasise, such a gloomy appreciation of human nature. For them, the permanence of the worst features of international political life derives, not from human nature, but from the systemic setting in which states find themselves. As John Herz, the foremost theorist of the 'security dilemma' has noted, 'realist thought is determined by an insight into the overpowering impact of the security factor and the ensuing power-political, oligarchic, authoritarian and similar trends and tendencies in society and politics'.[7] This security dilemma Herz has outlined in the following terms, as a product of the anarchic setting of states:

> Groups or individuals living in such a constellation must be, and usually are, concerned about their security from being attacked, subjected, dominated, or annihilated by other groups and individuals. Striving to attain security from such attack, they are driven to acquire more and more power in order to escape the impact of the power of others. This, in turn, renders the others more insecure and compels them to prepare for the worst. Since none can ever feel entirely secure in such a world of competing units, power competition ensues, and the vicious circle of security and power accumulation is on.[8]

As there is no way of breaking out of this circle, the power political aspects of international life are repetitive and unchanging and attempts to perfect the system are doomed to failure.

Secondly, by comparison with utopians, realists hold a more deterministic view of the historical process and allow correspondingly less scope for the intervention of human agency in the design and implementation of international order. Such order as there is, is in a sense already immanent within the historical process and cannot be grafted onto the system artificially from the outside. As was argued earlier, realists tend to see the historical process driven along by antecedent causes rather than by conscious human design. To that extent, we may seek to understand the process of historical change but not to control it: people tend to be the objects of history, not its subjects.

From this perspective, it is worth pointing out that political realism has undergone a curious metamorphosis and has acquired a nuance which was originally quite alien to it. In its original formulation, the one we tend to associate with the name of Machiavelli, the principles of realism underwrote a political programme that was at once active, interventionist and predicated upon the assumption that much could be achieved by conscious political design and artifact. Although we recognise Machiavelli as the founding father of *Realpolitik*, it is one of the ironies of history that his prince would have to be regarded as the quintessential utopian, the man with the political vision and the *virtu* necessary to implement it. Thus, in its early manifestations, with Hobbes as well as with Machiavelli, realism was to be associated with the active pursuit and creation of political order: only later, and particularly in the context of international order, was realism to emphasise the limitations upon the politician's craft. The statesman whose supreme achievement was the creation of the modern state, was to become impotent when confronted with the chaos prevailing in the global whole.

There no longer is, in Morse's phrase, 'a realist assumption of masterless man'.[9] Realism has, if you will, lost its political nerve: it has moved from a concentration upon goals to an obsession with harmful consequences. At best this leads to complacency in which realists 'succumb to the temptation which Mannheim identified as the hall-mark of conservative thought: the belief in the "here and now" – that Utopia is always "embedded in existing reality"'.[10] At worst, it leads to the paralysis of the political spirit, demonstrated in the admonition of a man who perhaps had more spirit than most: 'men are dangerous not only because they have unlimited appetites and unlimited year-ning for power, but because they are creatures with dreams; and their extravagant dreams turn into nightmares if they seek to realise them in history'.[11]

The third and fourth elements of realism may be dealt with together as they are merely negatives of points already made with reference to utopianism. These were a belief in the power of rationality and, related to this the acceptance of a universal harmony of interests. Both of these would be denied by the realist for reasons that found their classic exposition in E. H. Carr's *The Twenty Years' Crisis*. Rationality alone will be as likely to lead to conflict as to harmony because it will recognise that 'the clash of interests is real and inevitable'. Carr, therefore, urges that 'the reality of conflict be frankly recognised'. Basically, Carr's point was that there are antagonistic national interests and that attempts to assert a universal international interest *per se* are, in consequence, specious. In fact, using a variant of Marx's theory of ideology, Carr argues that all expressions of internationalism are little more than the (conscious or unconscious) rationalisation of the interests of the dominant states within international society. When utopians make appeal to universal standards of justice and claim that it is in the interests of all mankind to observe them, they are, according to Carr, appealing to spurious principles. He, therefore, attacks the residual natural-law elements in the utopian school upon which their belief in rationality and harmony is based. Carr's indictment ran as follows:

> The charge is not that human beings fail to live up to their principles ... What matters is that these supposedly absolute and universal principles were not principles at all but the unconscious reflexions of national policy based on a particular interpretation of national interest ... The bankruptcy of utopianism resides not in its failure to live up to its principles but in the exposure of its inability to provide any absolute and disinterested standard for the conduct of international affairs.[12]

In any case, for the realist, rationality was a two-edged weapon, having within it the potential for good but without any guarantee that this was its only potential. As Niebuhr was to phrase it in his critique of the rationality inherited from the Enlightenment:

> The historical development of freedom was believed to be purely creative partly because it was believed that increased freedom meant increasing rationality; and increasing reason was tantamount to increasing disinterestedness which would overcome both injustice and parochialism ... Unfortunately, the growth of freedom had more ambiguous consequences than the optimists assumed. Reason, despite every refinement, could always become the servant of interest and passion.[13]

Similarly, in a commentary upon Niebuhr's political thought, one writer has noted that part of his legacy was 'a philosophical perspective that assumed the futility of appeals to a "scientific" reason or good will in social affairs and the consequent necessity for a tough-minded use of power in the agonising quest for "relative" justice'.[14]

Fifthly, realism has always made a distinction between individual and state codes of morality in the sense that it does not accept that the

71

statesman should be constrained by everyday ethics. The statesman is a trustee of the national community and, as such, there are special demands upon him that make the application of normal ethical codes inappropriate. Consequently, the conscience of the office is, for the realist, quite different from the conscience of the man and allowance must be made accordingly. It is, after all, in this very sense that *raison d'état* can be appealed to as a justification for otherwise unacceptable activities. It is this point that Thompson makes when he remarks that 'assertions . . . that the only morality is individual morality have to be seen in the light of the differences between the individual and the collectivity and the imperatives to which each must respond'.[15]

Not only does this condition issue in a code of moral practice for the statesman which is different from that of the individual, it also has direct implications for the substance of his statecraft and for the international order that is crafted by means of it. The national leader acts amorally not only because he has a collective responsibility but also because he operates at the interstices of competing national moral claims. This territory is itself a moral void and behaviour cannot be constrained in this area by codes that are inapplicable to it. The obverse of this circumstance is that the statesman's task does not go beyond the creation of an order between states. Intervention in the affairs of other states, based on universalist moral principles, is impermissible precisely because this is a spurious basis for state action. The lack of moral constraint on national action serves more positively also to eliminate moral crusades which might disrupt the stable order of states.

Lastly, and perhaps most decisive of all, realists see states locked in a situation of perpetual competition with each other for the simple reason that they cannot generate enough mutual trust to allow them to escape from this situation. Moreover, in these circumstances, the statesman, according to realist precepts, would be derelict in his duty if he acted upon trust with no assurance of reciprocity on the part of other states. The tragic results that flow from this absence of trust have been summarised by Jervis: 'Because there are no institutions or authorities that can make and enforce international laws, the policies of cooperation that will bring mutual rewards if others cooperate may bring disaster if they do not. Because states are aware of this, anarchy encourages behaviour that leaves all concerned worse off than they could be.'[16] However, nowhere has this situation been better analysed than in Meinecke's classic exposition of the doctrine of *raison d'état*.

> But why is it not possible for the properly-understood interest of the States themselves, co-operating by reason of ethical motives, to

induce them to unite and freely restrict the methods of their power politics, to abide by law and morality, and to develop the institution of International Law and the League of Nations to a full and satisfactory efficiency? Because no one of them will trust another round the corner. Because no one of them believes for certain about any of the others, that it would abide by the agreed limitations in absolutely every instance and without any exception; but on the contrary suspects that in certain instances that other would once again lapse into following his own natural egoism. The first lapse back into evil ways on the part of one state (out of anxiety for its own welfare) and attended by success, would be sufficient to shatter the whole undertaking once again, and destroy the credit of ethical policy. Even if one wished to conduct the foreign policy of one's own state by methods which were not ethically objectionable, one would nevertheless always have to be on one's guard in case one's opponent failed to do so too; and in such a case one would feel oneself released from the moral imperative – whereupon the old, age-old game would then start again from the beginning.[17]

ROUSSEAU AND THE TRADITION OF DESPAIR

In this section, it is proposed to do the same as was done in the discussion of Kant. Briefly, it will outline Rousseau's general discussion of international relations – his conception of the problem and its solution – and, secondly, proceed to a systematic examination of the realist elements within his philosophy. As Kant has been previously associated with a tradition of optimism, so Rousseau will now be located within a general tradition of despair. In other words, Rousseau can be seen as representative of certain features of realist thinking and it is as an illustration of these patterns of thought that he is to be discussed. As with Kant, the point is that these patterns of thought are recurrent and are as conspicuous today as they were two centuries ago.

Man, in the state of nature, is not for Rousseau a warlike creature. He is peaceful and timid, more prone to run away than to fight. Whence, then, does the violence of international relations arise? What is the source of war? War, Rousseau repeatedly asserts, is a social phenomenon, social in the sense that what gives rise to it is the inception of civil society and the resultant nature of the international system. It is the move from the state of nature to civil society that makes man a fighter. As Rousseau puts it 'it is only when he has entered into society with other men that he decides to attack another, and he only becomes a soldier after he has become a citizen. There are no strong natural predispositions to make war.'[18]

73

Why does civil society bring about this change and produce a state of war? For the simple reason that, while it solves one problem of order at the domestic level, it immediately creates another at the international: the institution of the state creates domestic order but initiates international anarchy. In Rousseau's words:

> If the social order were really, as is pretended, the work not of passion but of reason, should we have been so slow to see that, in the shaping of it, either too much or too little, has been done for our happiness? that, each one of us being in the civil state as regards our fellow citizens, but in the state of nature as regards the rest of the world, we have taken all kinds of precautions against private wars only to kindle national wars a thousand times more terrible? and that, in joining a particular group of men, we have really declared ourselves the enemies of the whole race?'[19]

It is in this context that one commentator's point is well made. When we, as we so readily do, compare international society with the state of nature, we should remember that this state of nature is, paradoxically, an artificial one. As Cornelia Navari has commented, 'is not there something very odd about the "state of nature" which constitutes international relations – namely, the fact that it did not always exist? The fact that it was an *established* state of nature which emerged out of something that went before?'[20]

In any case, if this is how Rousseau views the problem of international politics, what is his proposed solution to it? Rousseau argues that, if there is a solution at all, then it lies in a confederation between the states. In other words, he duplicates the logic of the domestic analogy and contends that there must be a second social contract between the states that will remove them from the state of nature in which they find themselves.

Moreover, Rousseau pursues the logic of the domestic analogy to its fullest conclusion in the sense that, if international anarchy is to be overcome, it must be through a confederation 'with teeth'. What Rousseau had in mind was a very strong form of supra-national organisation. Unlike the Kantian proposal, Rousseau's confederation was to have the power of enforcement and there was to be no right of secession from it. Thus, whereas Kant argued that the state should not be subject to law, Rousseau insistently argued the opposite case: 'if there is any way of reconciling these dangerous contradictions, it is to be found only in such a form of federal government as shall unite nations by bonds similar to those which already unite their individual members and place the one no less than the other under the authority of the law.'[21]

Rousseau was arguing that if there was a solution, then such a federation was it. But, of course, he rejects this as a solution on the grounds that there is absolutely no hope of its realisation. As he puts it ironically, all that is needed to establish the federation is the consent of the princes who, unfortunately, 'would resist with all their might any proposal for its creation'. And so, having claimed that there is only one possible solution to the ills of international disorder, Rousseau then goes on to dismiss it as being utterly unattainable.

It is now time to consider the realist elements displayed by Rousseau's assessment of the nature and limitations of international political life. From this perspective, there are six points that have to be made.

First, Rousseau provides, in most poignant fashion, an example of the conviction that the universe is irredeemably irrational. In setting out the case for the creation of his federation, Rousseau insists that it is logically irrefutable. He is at pains to show how the individual princes, as well as international society as a whole, would benefit from such a scheme. In fact, in terms of a rational pursuit of self-interest, Rousseau is convinced that the federation has everything to commend it. Why, then, will the princes never consent to it? At the heart of Rousseau's pessimism is his conviction that men will not act rationally – that even if they are shown where their own best interests lie, they will not behave accordingly. To make this point, Rousseau introduces his distinction between 'real' and 'apparent' interests and believes that states will always pursue their apparent (short-term, selfish) interests at the expense of their real (long-term, enlightened) interests. At the end of his section on the logic of the federation, he concedes that 'this is not, of course, to say that the Sovereigns will adopt this project . . . but only that they would adopt it, if they took counsel of their true interest'.[22] Rousseau plainly suggests that they will not. If any more proof is needed for the contention that he despairs about the rationality of man and the universe, we need only recall his most famous line: 'If, in spite of all this, the project remains unrealised, that is not because it is utopian; it is because men are crazy, and because to be sane in a world of madmen is in itself a kind of madness.'[23] The quotation is significant for two reasons, not only because it reflects Rousseau's despair about human rationality, but also because it is an excellent illustration of his 'realistic' awareness of the role of trust in international affairs.

This leads us on to the second point. To be alone in pursuing rational policies, when other states are not, is a form of madness because, unless a state can trust the rest, then it will be the one to lose out. Standard game-theory situations, such as Prisoner's Dilemma, demonstrate this theme. The point Rousseau is making then is that if the other players are 'mad', there can be no reason to trust their rationality or good faith and, consequently, the only 'sane' course is to act as madly as the others. From a realist point of view, Rousseau's comment is perceptive and shrewd.

If realist thought centres upon this lack of trust and the consequent security dilemmas, Rousseau is an admirable exponent of this turn of mind: 'It is quite true that it would be much better for all men to remain always at peace. But so long as there is no security for this, everyone, having no guarantee that he can avoid war, is anxious to begin it at the moment which suits his own interest.'[24] He elaborates on this theme, returning to his point about sane men in a mad world: 'However salutary it may be in theory to obey the dictates of public spirit, it is certain that, politically and even morally, those dictates are liable to prove fatal to the man who persists in observing them with all the world when no one thinks of observing them towards him.'[25] As with all realist reasoning of this nature, while it is sound advice to give to one state, it becomes self-fulfilling when every state acts in accordance with it because the entire system becomes a vicious self-perpetuating circle.

Rousseau's despair can be taken one stage further: it has been an important article of faith in many of the liberal-utopian-internationalist schools of thought that growing interdependence and knowledge of each other's societies might help to create the basis of trust and understanding between countries, which could, in turn, elevate standards of international diplomacy. Rousseau refutes this line of argument altogether and asserts that interdependence produces conflict and not harmony. As Stanley Hoffmann has written, it is 'one of Rousseau's deepest insights, one that shatters a large part of the liberal vision of world affairs ... (that) interdependence breeds not accommodation and harmony but suspicion and incompatibility'.[26]

Thirdly, it is implicit in most of Rousseau's reasoning that he rejects that strand of utopian thought that sees the perfection of the internal constitutions of states as a path to an improved world order. Whether in its Kantian or Wilsonian formulation, Rousseau rejects this argument because war, we have seen, flows from the nature of the system irrespective of the merits or defects of the individual states. Unlike the drafters of the League of Nations, therefore, Rousseau considers that 'it is not impossible that a Republic, though in itself well-governed, should enter upon an unjust war'.[27]

Fourthly, like all realists, Rousseau perceives within the system an inherent propensity to pursue power. He paints a picture of states, obsessed by power considerations, restlessly striving to improve their relative positions. Accordingly, the pursuit of power is the central dynamic of the international system because the state 'feels weak so long as there are others stronger than itself. Its safety and preservation demand that it makes itself stronger than its neighbours. It cannot increase, foster or exercise its strength except at their expense.'[28]

Fifthly, in his attitude towards international law and towards universal peace principles, Rousseau is the realist without peer. Everything he has said thus far conveys the conviction that states cannot be trusted and that covenants without the sword are but words. This attitude extends to his analysis of international law and universal professions of faith in peace. In fact, on these issues, Rousseau provides a critique that is almost identical to that later developed by E. H. Carr. He dismisses international law on the very same grounds as did Carr:

> As for what is commonly called international law, because its laws lack any sanction, they are unquestionably mere illusions ... the decisions of international law, having no other guarantee than their usefulness to the person who submits to them, are only respected in so far as interest accords with them.[29]

Likewise, in reply to universalist peace sentiments, Rousseau provides the classic realist retort that 'to prove that peace, as a general principle, is a better thing than war is to say nothing to the man who has private reasons for preferring war to peace'.[30]

The sixth point takes us to the essence of Rousseau's despair, the font of his realism. As we have seen, he regards the problems of international life as being inherently insoluble, as a federation will never be adopted. On this basis he may be advanced as an exponent of the philosophy of despair as regards international relations. Probably other words would suffice just as well as 'despair' – a random selection of epithets used by commentators to describe his international political theory includes 'pessimistic', 'hopeless', 'fatalistic', 'gloomy', 'depressing', 'dismal' and 'frightening'. However, despair seems to capture the essentials of Rousseau's moral anguish at the continuance of a state of affairs that he regarded as a moral scandal. It may be objected, and a case could be made out along these lines, that there is very much of the utopian in Rousseau as well – that it is misleading to regard him as an unmitigated realist. Indeed, it could be claimed that while in his 'head' Rousseau is a realist, in his 'heart' he is a utopian. A perfect illustration of this dualism within Rousseau can be found in his Abstract of Saint-Pierre's Project. Rousseau opens in convincing utopian style:

> Never did the mind of man conceive a scheme nobler, more beautiful, or more useful than that of a lasting peace between all the peoples of Europe. Never did a writer better deserve a respectful hearing than he who suggests means for putting that scheme into practice. What man, if he has a spark of goodness, but must feel his heart glow within him at so fair a prospect? Who would not prefer the illusions of a generous spirit, which overleaps all obstacles, to that dry, repulsive reason whose indifference to the welfare of mankind is ever the chief obstacle to all schemes for its attainment?[31]

Having given vent to this utopian outburst, Rousseau's realist *alter ego* quickly reasserts itself: 'In these opening words, I could not refrain from giving way to the feelings which filled my heart. Now let us do our best to reason coolly'.[32]

Surely this reveals both the utopian and the realist elements within Rousseau? We can sympathise with the argument but must finally reject it. The reason for doing so is as follows. If there is to be any distinction between realist and utopian philosophies, it must be on the basis of their views, not about the desirability of international-order reform, but about its attainability. Rousseau's sentiments predispose him to think such reform desirable but he holds out not a shred of hope that it can be attained. This, in itself, suffices to make Rousseau wear the realist mantle.

ROUSSEAU AND TWENTIETH-CENTURY REALISM

Rousseau's brand of realism, just like Kant's utopianism, has found fertile ground for growth in twentieth-century conditions, to such an extent that one analyst has pronounced that 'today's revolutionary system of international politics confirms the sharp and gloomy analysis of Rousseau, whose pessimism was all too easily discounted in the moderate system which died at Sarajevo'.[33]

Why should realism have had such a widespread and dominating intellectual appeal in the twentieth century? Momentously, realism accurately captured the mood of the world political crisis of this age. The radical collapse of the stable European order of the nineteenth century provided the background to this but it was the apparent failure to apply the elementary lessons of power during the inter-war period which led to the system's final demise. If utopianism contributed to the optimism of the 1920s, then the crisis of war set the scene for the intellectual restoration of realism and the doctrines of power.

This occurred most notably in the United States and it should be emphasised that post-Second World War realism has been a peculiarly American doctrinal elaboration. That Americans should have embraced realism so enthusiastically is itself readily intelligible. First, a set of principles for the operation of the international system in which the United States now held primacy was of undoubted appeal to a generation of American leaders facing new world responsibilities. Realism, in this context, served as a convenient guide to policy makers and an acceptable antidote to the traditional idealism, legalism and rejectionism of American foreign policy. Morgenthau saw himself self-consciously as pedagogue to an untutored foreign policy elite and a generation later Henry Kissinger could still remark that 'we in the Nixon Administration felt that our challenge was to educate the American people in the requirements of the balance of power'.[34] Such conceptions had to be instilled from the outside because they were alien to the American tradition. Ultimately, according to Bull, the effort was to fail because 'this exotic, European plant could find no roots in the native soil of the American political tradition'.[35]

Secondly, America's quest for a new diplomacy which would take account of the realities of power was fostered by a distinctive European émigré input. It was to be no coincidence that a generation of leading international relations scholars came from central European backgrounds – Morgenthau, Wolfers, Hoffmann, Knorr and Kissinger – and brought to America a particular legacy. Those who had experienced power at the 'sharp end' of international life impressed upon their American audience that the international community could neglect the harsh realities of power only at its peril.

Of the many aspects of twentieth-century realist thought, three in particular stand out as being part of the tradition of despair bequeathed by Rousseau. The first, above all, bears the imprint of Rousseau's pessimism. It emphasises the unattainability of radical change within the international order and in doing so it goes beyond Rousseau to disparage the very nature of the utopian enterprise and to warn against its inherent dangers. A reading of virtually any twentieth-century exponent of realism would reveal this constant refrain. It constitutes, for example, the very first of Morgenthau's principles of political realism in which he propounds the philosophy that 'politics . . . is governed by objective laws' and that 'the operation of these laws being impervious to our preferences, men will challenge them only at the risk of failure'.[36] Later Morgenthau makes it clear that challenging the laws of power risks not only failure but indeed regression: 'How often have statesmen been motivated by the desire to improve the world, and ended by making it worse?'[37]

This theme, that the attempt consciously to initiate international order will prove to be destructive, constantly recurs in realist writings, especially from the 1930s onwards. One of its earliest proponents was later to write in this vein when he warned that 'the radical sense of the ultimate, which places the status quo of any community under the judgement of an ultimate justice, may be as dangerous as it can be creative'.[38] Likewise, Henry Kissinger, as theorist, has often-times given lugubrious warning of the hazards in pursuing radical changes to the existing order. He assures us that 'the translation into political terms of prophetic visions always falsifies the intentions of their proponents'[39] and is particularly fond of the irony inherent in the fact that 'When you know history, how many tragedies have been touched off by goodwill, you have to admit the tragic elements of existence.'[40]

The second element prevalent in twentieth-century realist thought might be captured in the dictum *si vis pacem para bellum*. This, in itself, is an invocation of Rousseau's logic and gives expression to the idea that in a world populated by 'madmen', it is rational to strive for peace by preparing for war: indeed, this becomes the only 'sane' policy available to national societies. Implicit in this formulation is the assumption that in an imperfect, and imperfectible, world, the most that can be achieved is a form of negative order, in which the worst abuses of power are guarded against. The system, however, cannot move beyond this to the attainment of positive order. The realist doctrine of order is 'negative' in the following sense, clearly revealed in Kissinger's definition of diplomacy as 'the art of restraining the exercise of power'.[41] It sees order as a situation of collective checkmate in which no member of the system is in a position to do damage to the others. Peace is equivalent to equilibrium and it is in the maintenance of this equilibrium, if need be by preparing for war, that peace is secured. Such is the minimum, but also the maximum, programme for the practising statesman. As has been said of Niebuhr's philosophy, clearly testifying to the negative conception of order to which he subscribed, 'in the field of collective behaviour the force of egoistic passion is so strong that the only harmonies possible are those which manage to neutralise a rival force through balances of power, through mutual defences against its inordinate expression'.[42]

To describe the realist conception of international order as negative, in this sense, is not to demean it. Generally speaking, realists do not reify the international order as an end in itself: it is a necessary means to the protection of human values. When it is remembered, as mentioned above, that realism flourished amongst central European *émigrés*, one can see the force of this observation. In the absence of a stable and enduring international structure, power is left unbridled and many human values are violated. On this conception, it is a false antinomy to suppose that international order and human rights are set against each other: without the former there is no solid protection for the latter. Even in this negative sense, the international order can serve moral ends. This much had been realised by Butterfield in whose thought, it has been said, reason of state 'had a strong normative foundation':

> Even while assiduously studying and following the rules of the grammar of power, the statesman should not forget the elementary reason for being of the intricate political and military machinery at his disposal: the achievement of conditions of relative order and stability conducive to the pursuit of the good life by the many individual human beings under his authority.[43]

Nor is the creation of such a negative order a simple task. Although its function is to neutralise power for aggressive purposes, this can best be achieved by diplomatic devices which ensure that the likely abusers of power, the strongest members of the system, feel positively committed to the preservation of the existing equilibrium. The architecture of statecraft must be such that the status quo to be preserved meets the legitimate demands and expectations of the leading powers. This, according to Kissinger, was to be the supreme achievement of the 1815 settlement: 'There existed within the new international order no power so dissatisfied that it did not prefer to seek its remedy within the framework of the Vienna settlement rather than in overturning it ...'[44] It was such a legitimate international order that Kissinger himself was to seek to reconstruct in the early 1970s.

This form of order remains dependent upon the threatened use of force to preserve equilibrium. It was precisely the fear that, in a nuclear context, force could no longer be used to neutralise force that led to anxiety that international order would thereby be undermined. Accordingly, it is not at all surprising that one of the major tasks of post-1945 realism has been the elaboration of strategic doctrines appropriate to the nuclear age in which the 'utility' of military power would be preserved even if its 'usability' had been called into question. In other words, for the sake of international order, the Clausewitzian war system had to be maintained even if technological conditions had changed: the injunction *para bellum* must still have meaning because without it, how can a 'neutralised' order be sustained? Thus Kissinger, in writing his major contribution on the impact of nuclear weaponry, saw the purpose of strategic studies in the following terms: 'In seeking to avoid the horrors of all-out war by outlining an alternative, in developing a concept of limitation that combines firmness with moderation, diplomacy can once more establish a relationship with force even in the nuclear age.'[45] If the prop of order is to be threatened violence, then it follows that the task of the logician of strategy, confronted with nuclear weaponry, is to restore credibility to such threats.

It is also within such a framework that the realist would account for, and justify, the past two decades of arms control between the superpowers. Arms control is a continuation of strategy by other means, not a rejection of it. Although in entering into negotiations and agreements, the superpowers seek to manage the strategic balance and hence preserve stability, they are also acutely sensitive to issues of national advantage and disadvantage: ultimately they must place such concerns above abstract notions of stability. Finally, there can be no such thing as international security in terms of which the value of an agreement might be judged. The sole test of the acceptability of any particular arms control accord is its contribution to the national security of the individual state.

The third dimension of twentieth-century realist thought is a culmination, and a combination, of the other two. It is also the aspect of recent realist thought that has been most frequently misunderstood. It has often been suggested that attempts to integrate 'power' with 'morality' in international politics represent a departure from the pure realist tradition. In one sense, this is true but only if we consider the entire realist tradition to derive from Machiavelli or Hobbes. If, instead, we take Rousseau to be representative of an alternative realist tradition, then the effort to define the place of morality within the realm of international politics, and the resultant despair at the inability to integrate the two adequately, is the twentieth-century realist tradition *par excellence* and not a deviation from it. It is in this specific sense that Rousseau's relevance to the present century is to be appreciated.

There are various ways of making this point. At one level, it has been argued by some that there is a school of realist thought that, while accepting power as a means, rejects it as an ultimate end. Rousseau himself would obviously be encompassed within this approach. Another way of saying this might be that the hypnotic realist chant that 'all politics is power politics' should be heard as a cry of moral anguish and not as a public celebration of the amoralities of *Realpolitik*.[46] No one has provided a more incisive account of the

82

'realities' of international politics than did Rousseau himself; this did not, however, prevent him from deploring what he saw.

It is this despair, that there is a moral realm as well as one of power but an inability to reconcile the two, that is the most characteristic trait of twentieth-century realism. It is manifest in almost every realist analyst of international politics who has made a contribution to the discipline in the last few decades. Nowhere is this better illustrated than in the writings of Reinhold Niebuhr. He was preoccupied by the dualism of human nature and the corresponding potentialities for good and evil displayed within the political universe – with the interplay between the 'light' and the 'dark'. As Thompson has observed 'the heart of Niebuhr's criticism is that modern views of man which stress exclusively either his dignity or his misery are fatuous and irrelevant as they fail to consider the good and evil, the dualism in man's nature'.[47] This duality in man, and the ambivalence of his political enterprises, becomes starker, and its potential consequences more dangerous, with increases in man's power: 'it should have been obvious long before the nuclear age that the mastery over natural forces increased man's power; and that this greater power could be used – and in a sense was bound to be used – destructively as well as creatively'.[48]

Likewise, E. H. Carr, who berated the post-1918 generation of utopians for neglecting the fact of power in international relations, ended up in a moral *impasse* no less agonising than that experienced by Rousseau. Having demolished the utopian edifice, Carr also draws attention to the limitations of realism and urges upon us the classical *via media*, a projected synthesis of the two. Likewise, while he has denied that universal moral principles can be applied to international politics, he nonetheless attempts in *The Twenty Years' Crisis* to find a place for morality as well as for power. He does not succeed and he, no less than his readers, must have been dissatisfied with the compromise at which he arrives. Underneath Carr's preferred solution, one cannot avoid detecting the same despair that strikes one in the pages of Rousseau. Nowhere is Carr's agony better conveyed than in the following passage:

> Having demolished the current utopia with the weapons of realism we still need to build a new utopia of our own which will one day fall to the same weapons. The human will, will continue to seek an escape from the logical consequences of realism in the vision of an international order which, as soon as it crystallises itself into concrete political form, becomes tainted with self-interest and hypocrisy, and must once more be attacked with the instruments of realism.[49]

83

One commentator upon Carr, on the basis of such passages, goes on to argue that 'it is this "vision of an international order", this search for principles, which can give moral meaning and set normative limits to the struggle for power on the international scene, that sets Carr apart from the realist school of thought . . . in its pure form'.[50] The argument depends upon how we define the 'pure form' of realism but, as mentioned above, if we accept Rousseau as a precursor of an equally important tradition of realism, Carr is within its mainstream and need not be 'set apart'.

With Morgenthau, it seems at first that we are back to 'pure' realism. And yet, even in this case, it can be seen that Morgenthau is concerned with the tragedy of international politics and not simply with revelling in *Realpolitik* for its own sake. Walter Lippmann has been quoted as describing Morgenthau as 'the most moral man I know',[51] and Thompson himself refers to 'Morgenthau's essentially tragic view of the course of action open to statesmen'.[52]

Morgenthau perceives the same dilemma that had beset Rousseau, namely that there are certain moral goals to which mankind should aspire but that there are exigencies of international politics in a world of 'crazy' men that render it difficult, if not futile, to try to realise them. Morgenthau himself gave expression to this tension:

> Political realism is aware of the moral significance of political action. It is also aware of the ineluctable tension between the moral command and the requirements of successful political action. And it is unwilling to gloss over and obliterate that tension and thus to obfuscate both the moral and the political issue by making it appear as though the stark facts of politics were morally more satisfying than they actually are, and the moral law less exacting than it actually is.[53]

Finally, in this rapid survey of twentieth-century realism, we can again re-emphasise that its most distinctive refrain has been that of reconciliation between opposites, between power and morality, and a subsequent anguish at its incapacity to perform this task satisfactorily. One such instance of the attempt to achieve a synthesis, or at least an appeal that such a synthesis is necessary, can be found in K. Thompson.[54] In this sense, Rousseau's dilemma, that there should be a solution to the problem of international order but that none is available, still haunts the twentieth-century mind.

If obituaries of utopianism were as common as they were misplaced in the 1960s, so the 1970s witnessed countless intimations of the demise of realism. In the event, they have been equally lacking in prescience as realism has regrouped itself after the paradigmatic attacks of the 1970s and has since sought to recapture the intellectual high ground within the discipline. Foremost in the attempt to do so was Waltz's theoretical statement of 1979[55] around which a revised realist, or neorealist, position has coalesced. Its central theoretical position is the significance of the structure of the international system which requires realist policies by states.[56] Structural realism, as it has been called, represents an endeavour to restate realist theory in a systematic and coherent fashion.[57]

Even with this restatement, however, critics have been concerned with the limited ability of realism to accommodate, or to explain, change.[58] On Waltz's own account, the attributes of the present international system, amongst which anarchy is the most significant, were created in the early modern period and therefore 'change at the structural level seems to have occurred only once in three hundred years . . .'[59]

In response to this, sympathetic critics have suggested that realism has a greater capacity to accommodate change than has been allowed. Hence Keohane, for example, employing realist assumptions, has sought to show that 'the characteristic pessimism of Realism does not necessarily follow'.[60] The creation of institutions and of regimes which go beyond mere power politics is possible, on this account, even assuming states as egoistic, rational actors pursuing self-interest.[61] On his own argument, however, Keohane's point is difficult to assess because the evidence is far from unambiguous. Just as postwar financial and trading regimes could be interpreted either as symptoms of progressive change and institutionalisation, or pessimistically as symptoms of American hegemonic control, so the continuation of regimes, even after the demise of the hegemonic factor, is inconclusive evidence on which to base a theory of progressive change. Others have explained unsettled 'regime' conditions in the 1970s simply as traditional behaviour in that 'as the costs of providing collective goods for the global system increased, the United States retreated to a more narrowly self-interested policy'.[62]

Either way, neorealism, no less than the traditional variant which preceded it, may be said to require for its objective explanatory power a subjective understanding by the actors of the requirements of the system and, to this extent, to be influenced by the role of ideas and values. Thus it has been said that Waltz's work should be read 'as exhortations to policy makers and fellow citizens about how they *ought* to respond to the structure of power'.[63] To this extent, Morgenthau's didactic purpose lives on in contemporary American neorealism or, as phrased by another critic, neorealism 'performs a proselytising function as the advocate of this form of rationality'.[64] The central issue, as to whether states operate in an autonomous sphere, or whether their

85

'necessitous condition' is a construct of values and assumptions, pervades the latest attempts to rehabilitate realism.

REALISM AND NECESSITY

Realism, like utopianism, makes appeal to necessity. And yet, as in the previous chapter, we are forced to consider whether the necessity resides 'in the events' themselves or whether it merely denotes a 'degree of belief'. Again, as with the utopians, there must be a strong suspicion that the necessity that is invoked to bolster the realist case is of the latter kind.

The necessity that figures in the realist account is the demands upon the statesman operating within a world of unchanging power politics. As such, necessity is for the realist a conservative force rather than the revolutionary agent that it has been considered to be by utopians. The necessity that transfuses the realist world is one that binds the statesman to the existing international order because of the dangers of the unknown.

Necessity as the conserver of the power-political mode of operating the international system has been a permanent feature of realist thought, most obviously expressed in its Machiavellian variant. It can perhaps be best demonstrated in terms of the political necessity under which the statesman must function:

> Thus what makes any reform apparently impossible is the profound and pessimistic conviction (rooted in the instincts, and borne out by historical experience) to the effect that it is not possible to improve the character of state activity. The Idealist will always be repeating his demand for such a reform and will always be declaring it to be possible. The responsible and executive statesman ... will always find himself constrained by the pressure of the responsibility he bears for the whole to doubt the possibility of it, and to take up a line of conduct that is in accordance with this doubt.[65]

The statesman, if he wishes to be successful, is compelled to take notice of the laws of power politics and not to stray from them. Thus Kissinger reflects the conservatism of realist necessity when he provides his admonition against attempts at utopia-building: 'The statesman must remain forever suspicious of these efforts, not because he enjoys the pettiness of manipulation, but because he must be prepared for the worst contingency.'[66] He was subsequently to write of the role of the statesman in the same conservative vein:

> his first goal is survival; he feels responsible not only for the best but also for the worst conceivable outcome. His view of human nature is

> wary; he is conscious of many great hopes which have failed, of many good intentions that could not be realised, of selfishness and ambition and violence. He is, therefore, inclined to erect hedges against the possibility that even the most brilliant idea might prove abortive.[67]

We have here a necessity that is quite different from that which functions as the engine of transformation in the utopian dialectic. The realist necessity is one that ensures that statesmen will always play according to the perennial rules of the game. Thus a chapter of one realist tract is entitled significantly 'The Limits of Principle in International Politics: Necessity and the New Balance of Power'.[68]

Some caution is required, however, in our understanding of the sense in which realist necessity acts as a 'conservative' force. This does not mean that realist policies are set implacably against any form of innovation. Indeed, necessity may itself, in the name of realism, require the adoption of 'revolutionary' techniques. This is amply revealed in a telling quotation from Niebuhr about the early development of nuclear weapons: 'No nation will fail to take even the most hazardous adventure into the future, if the alternative of not taking the step means the risk of being subjugated.'[69] The point to be emphasised is that realism is conservative of the general order that prevails in international life, not about the specific modalities by means of which that order is sustained. Thus nuclear weapons, although in technological terms they may be considered revolutionary, are to be used to conserve an order based upon the counterbalancing of force against force.

The argument that realist necessity, no less than the utopian, represents a 'degree of belief' is reinforced when we highlight a central paradox or inconsistency within the heart of realism itself. The paradox is this. On the one hand, realist doctrine asserts a claim to objective understanding of the process of international politics: it is only in terms of such an understanding that the realist can perceive a necessity to which the statesman is bound. Realists, therefore, much more than utopians speak with an air of certitude about politics, because they believe it to be governed by immutable laws, deriving either from human nature itself or from the dynamics of inter-state competition. It is, after all, Morgenthau's proud claim that 'the concept of interest defined as power imposes intellectual discipline upon the observer, infuses rational order into the subject matter of politics, and thus makes the theoretical understanding of politics possible'.[70] Realism is, therefore, closely identified with unshakeable knowledge about how states have behaved and will continue to behave.

On the other hand, it is impossible not to detect, in much realist writing, a radical uncertainty that is itself offered as the justification for cautious and conservative practices in international affairs. It is precisely because he is uncertain as to how other states are going to behave that the statesman must be on his guard and, in Kissinger's terminology, 'prepared for the worst contingency'. Not for nothing is a realist approach to national security affairs associated with 'worst-case' planning – with the idea that national strategy should be predicated upon an assumption that the worst may happen and that states should be prepared for it – and this mentality clearly derives, not from the certitudes of international politics but precisely from its uncertainties. Accordingly, it comes as no surprise to see realists arguing that 'foreign policy is at least three-fourths guesswork'[71] and that 'world politics is an incalculable process'.[72] In the light of this radical uncertainty, the necessity to which realists make appeal becomes increasingly difficult to discover.

Finally, that realism, no less than utopianism, reflects a 'degree of belief' is suggested by the following considerations. The fundamental assumption of realism, the one from which its very name derives, is that there is such a thing as an objectively real world of international politics and that its characteristics are given and knowable. But how can we know what that reality is? How can we be sure that the realists, because of their image of the world, are not the prisoners of their own artificial reality, which they have themselves created? As one writer has expressed it:

> There developed after the Second World War a school of 'political realists' who argued that the facts of aggressiveness and power should be recognised, and that 'idealism' in the form of functional co-operation was misplaced. The 'proof' was war. What the 'political realists' failed to appreciate was that an assumption of aggressiveness, and the organisation of world society into power blocs, would inevitably lead to defensive and aggressive responses that would lead to war. Nothing was 'proved' except that certain policies invoke certain responses. If the intentions of governments were security and peace, then their strategic policies were self-defeating – they brought about just those conditions they were intended to prevent.[73]

The full significance of this suggestion deserves to be pondered. If we push such reasoning to its ultimate conclusion then it leads to no less than the total obliteration of the distinction between realism and utopianism. It becomes uncertain who are the 'realists' and who are the 'utopians' because they are both the creators of an international order based upon an idea of what that order is and what it might be. Indeed, in a sense, it could be argued that it is the realists who are the truly successful utopians because they have created a world after their own image. Could there be any more wonderful tribute to the potency of ideas in human affairs? Lewis Mumford has seized upon this reversion of roles, that it is the realists who are the genuine utopians, and developed the theme in a powerful passage. He deserves to have the last word:

> Utopian idealists who have overestimated the power of the ideal are plainly much more fully in possession of their senses and more closely linked to human realities than the scientific and military 'realists' who have turned the use of absolute weapons into a compulsive ideal . . . The leaders of science, technology, and military affairs who have most despised the function of ideals have actually turned the expansion of their equipment for destruction and extermination into an ultimate ideal. This is utopianism with a vengeance: the nihilistic perfection of nothingness.[74]

PART 2

THE PRACTICE OF
INTERNATIONAL ORDER

5 ORDER AND CHANGE IN THE INTERNATIONAL SYSTEM, 1815–1990

Whether or not there has been progress in the forms of international-order maintenance since 1815, there has undeniably been much change. In scale and substance, as well as in political and technological context, the conduct of international relations is appreciably different from that which prevailed at the beginning of the nineteenth century. Even when the informal norms of the Great Powers suggest continuity, as in their adherence to ideas of balance, these norms are applied in demonstrably altered conditions. Indeed, the core of the debate about change and progress is concerned with whether the altered substance and context of international relations amounts to a qualitative transformation. On this issue, opinions remain divided. In order to facilitate some judgement, this chapter will describe, and assess the significance of, the *macro* change that has occurred over that period. This will permit a more detailed discussion of developments within specific historical periods in the succeeding chapters.

While there has been much change within this period, it should also be emphasised that the early nineteenth century itself represented a point of significant transformation such as to warrant a survey that begins at that date. On the basis of the diplomatic mechanisms established in 1815, the altered relationship between European international relations and the outside world, and the stabilising function of 'buffer' states, one historian has recently proclaimed that 'a prima facie case exists that a profound, durable change occurred in international politics after 1815'.[1] In this sense, while this chapter will trace the evolution of the international system since 1815, the period as a whole has some claim to cohesion, marking it off from the pre-1815 world, which entitles us to treat it as a distinctive era of international relations.

SCOPE

The geographical scope of the international system has expanded significantly since 1815. This process is normally described as representing the globalisation of what had hitherto been an essentially European state system such as to draw in the other continents of the world. This did not occur immediately but as a result of a gradual process extending over most of the period. Arguably, it is as yet incomplete and contemporary prognostications of a 'revolt against the West' constitute evidence that the absorption may yet have enduring effects upon the ultimate character of the system.

To suggest that the European system has been globalised since 1815 is immediately to create a puzzle because it is also accepted that the steady political, economic, military and demographic expansion of Europe had been occurring since the sixteenth century. When we speak of this process of globalisation we must therefore mean something more than Europe's physical extension into new and old continents. At the very least, such globalisation entailed the creation of new centres of political power outside of Europe and the possibility of autonomous action by these states in such a way as both to have implications for European state relations but also to change the style and content of international politics more generally. Such a revolution has unquestionably been wrought during the course of the past century.

As will be suggested later, this has resulted in two seemingly contradictory developments in post-1945 international relations. On the one hand, there has been a geographical extension of the world's political arena and a greater cultural heterogeneity has been introduced into its polity. On the other hand, a process of concentration has occurred whereby the number of dominant centres of political and military power actually diminished. This latter process of shrinkage at the apex of the hierarchy culminated in the early 1960s and has since receded. But for a significant period, the international politics of the postwar world were shaped by the dual effects of *extension* and of *concentration*. The role of the superpowers as external participants in a vast range of regional conflict situations has been the most visible demonstration of this trend. The manner in which the superpower Cold War spilled through Europe and into the Far and Middle East, South and South-East Asia and, if less wholeheartedly, into Africa marks the coming together of this extension and concentration in the postwar international system.

The landmarks in this geographical expansion are reasonably visible and may be interpreted as examples of hierarchical cooption whereby the Great Powers in the existing hierarchy have seen fit to coopt additional members for general or specific purposes. Turkey was coopted by the European powers in 1856. The United States was effectively brought in towards the closure of the century if not earlier. Japan's cooption is perhaps best symbolised in her treaty of 1902 with Britain. However, the process was to go beyond cooption at the top of the hierarchy and was to reveal itself in the expansion of active membership at international diplomatic gatherings. This provides a faithful measure of the declining European hegemony in international affairs. If the Vienna Congress was a wholly European preserve, that at Paris in 1856 brought in the Ottoman Empire, the Hague Conference of 1899 saw the participation of the United States, Mexico, China, Japan, Persia and Siam and the Hague meeting of 1907 included the sixteen Latin American republics besides.[2]

Barraclough undoubtedly goes too far in claiming that by 1905 'the ultimate decisions were no longer made in Europe'.[3] However, he is correct to focus attention on the significance of events in the Far East at the turn of the century. These did not, as he implies, bring about a final and irreversible transition in centres of power and decision making but their importance lies in being a harbinger of a world that was finally to emerge half a century later. In this sense, the Far Eastern crisis of 1895–1905 offers a sneak preview of a future world.

What were the major characteristics of that crisis and what is its significance? Events in the Far East offered a foretaste of independent action by powers outside of Europe in a major series of international developments. If the catalyst for this was the weakened condition of the Chinese empire and a scramble by the powers to ensure no loss of interest in the spoils to their competitors, the period 1895–1905 was nonetheless different from the recently conducted partition of Africa. Not only was China not partitioned, but there was prominent intervention by non-European states. The episode reflected a quickening of Russian interest in the Pacific in general and in north China and Manchuria in particular. It offered a stage for the United States to convert its growing economic and technological muscle into a degree of diplomatic leverage: its stake in the Philippines in 1898, the Hay 'Open Door' notes in relation to China and the hosting of the Portsmouth peace settlement between Russia and Japan in 1905 all bore witness to America's coming of international age. At the same time, Japan's war against China in 1894–5, her alignment with Britain and her symbolic victory over Russia in 1905 testified to an Asiatic presence in the world power structure.

This did not mean that the Europeans stood by impotently. The Triple intervention of 1895 by France, Germany and Russia to overthrow Japan's unilaterally imposed terms upon China, revealed the limits of European tolerance of autonomous settlements in the Far East. It was Germany which was to precipitate the scramble for concessions in China which took place in 1897–8 and in which Britain and France, as well as Russia, were to be the prime participants. Finally, the reversion to concentration on European events in the early twentieth century underlined not the expulsion of Europe from the Far East but rather a voluntary reordering of priorities such that the centrality of European security concerns was fully reasserted.

What remained was a continuing ambiguity about the nature of the relationship between the European and non-European worlds. On the face of it, the First World War seriously eroded Europe's global self-confidence, not to mention her economic capability to sustain such a role. The loss of faith in a superior civilization in the centre found its echo in the periphery where the war had stimulated local industries, as in India and Egypt, had provoked discontent with the heavier hand of war-time 'direct rule' and had issued in new imperial compromises to take account of nationalist disaffection, as well as of the costs to the metropolitan powers of maintaining the imperial edifice.

The war did not, however, at least in the shorter term, signal the end of the European empires. Britain and France's patrimony in the Middle East was expanded and in territorial extent the empires reached their zenith after the war. If there had been shocks to the imperial nerve, there developed also compensatory new programmes for the economic revitalisation of the empires, the more effectively that they might contribute to the economic well-being and political status of the metropole, as in Albert Sarraut's programmes for France's colonies. Moreover, if the responsibilities of the League Mandates system often couched old interests in new rhetoric, the rhetoric was sufficiently potent to provide a new rationale of trusteeship, with considerable appeal on the left of the political spectrum, which militated against any rapid dismantling of the imperial structures.[4]

So little did the inter-war world appear to have changed that the cosy atmosphere of the League at Geneva created a quintessentially European mood for the so-called world organisation. The United States declined to join and for many years the Soviet Union was a social outcast. Japan was to withdraw in the early 1930s after the League's subdued reprimand of its behaviour in Manchuria. The incipient global system of the turn of the century seemed, during this period, to have reverted to an earlier European one in which Britain and France appeared as the centres of world politics. Much of this was, of course, illusory, contingent upon the introversions of the United States and the Soviet Union and the mirage of a Europe fully restored.

The reality was less benign for the Europeans. For France, empire in the Middle East and Indochina was less the badge of greatness in Europe but increasingly an antidote to past humiliation and present insecurity. British strategy throughout the inter-war decades suffered the classic symptoms of imperial over-stretch and its policy in relation to Italy and Germany was constrained by the exposure of its world-wide interests to extra-European marauders, Japan above all. Even if it is superficially attractive to distinguish between a purely European war which broke out in 1939[5] and a Pacific or wider world war which developed during 1940–1,[6] it should never be forgotten that the wider problems of imperial strategy provided the backdrop against which the European crisis was to be handled. Moreover, for at least one of the participants, the Soviet Union, threatened directly by Japan in the East and Germany in the West, such a dichotomy between a European and a world war is patently artificial, as Stalin bought time with his non-aggression pacts in 1939 and 1940.

Fundamental restructuring of the international system, partially deferred, had nevertheless been long underway by 1945. The shaping of the postwar world was therefore to be by a conjunction of long-term tendencies along with the specific and catalytic effects of the war. Again there was to be no precipitate collapse of the European hold on empires and some two decades were required for the major transitions to take place. That said, the core of the old European balance system was effectively destroyed. If the problem for the past two generations had been the containment of German power within and beyond Europe, it was also true that the destruction of German unity had the subsidiary effect of making impossible effective military containment of Europe's other great land power, namely the Soviet Union. A fundamental deficiency in the European balance system, first revealed in 1914 but concealed thereafter, culminated in Europe's partition in the first Cold War decade.

More important for the present theme, however, was that the partition of Europe, perhaps fittingly, was to be a necessary stage in the final creation of the distinctively global system which has emerged since then. It was within this framework that decolonisation was made possible and it was this process that has created the diverse and multicultured context of diplomacy that has characterised international relations since the 1960s. This is the central insight of Walker's almost hyperbolic description:

> The Western way of life, or modernity, has become the West's gift to all humankind . . . On the other hand, much of the substance of recent international politics has centred on the often violent rejection of this process. Resistance to the all-pervasive forces of modernization along Western lines . . . has become a major characteristic of the twentieth century. Concepts of autonomy, nationalism and pluralism have come to challenge the assumed universality of progress towards the 'civilization' of the West.[7]

In this sense the globalisation of the system has had a major impact upon the substance of international relations. It has additionally had a structural effect. If the impact of decolonisation has been to create a new agenda of development, race, and cultural value, then it has also shaped a new hierarchy in which these issues would be politically pursued. The number of states in the international system has expanded threefold over the past half century. The salient point is not however simply the number of states but the number of weaker states in existence. Structurally, the postwar system is, in terms of military and economic capabilities, an extremely unequal one at precisely a time when, formally, equality is more deeply entrenched in the rhetoric of international organisation. 'It is the conjuncture of small size and sovereign equality' Krasner has maintained, 'that makes the postwar international system unique.'[8]

ECONOMY

Although what caused the emergence of a globalised international system was the diffusion of economic and military power and the final integration of new states into the postwar order, the process has throughout been facilitated by technological and economic change. The dramatic development of transport, first by the steam engine both on land and at sea, and then by the internal combustion engine and the development of flight has revolutionised the passage of goods and people. Coupled with this, communications were much improved in the later nineteenth century by the telegraph and more so in the twentieth by the telephone. It is superficial to explain the appearance of an integrated international system simply by the advent of new means of communication but that the facility impinged upon the conduct of diplomacy, both by speeding up the transmission of news about one part of the globe to another and possibly also by limiting the freedom for independent action on the part of the diplomats on the spot, there can be little doubt.

More fundamentally, international relations were to be shaped by the volume and nature of economic exchange. Here, one is immediately confronted by two conflicting views as to the importance that ought properly to be attached to the early nineteenth century as marking a watershed. On the one hand, there is the view of some writers that what was distinctive about the nineteenth century was the emergence of the first fully effective global economic system. As an adjunct of industrialisation itself, and pushed by the activity of Britain, the exploitation of the world's natural resources, the development of world markets for manufactured goods, the development of capital markets and the process of capital export to create economic substructures elsewhere were all carried to remarkably new levels. It is on this basis that one historian has recently insisted that amongst the hallmarks of the nineteenth-century international system was 'the steady and then (after the 1840s) spectacular growth of an international global economy'.[9]

Set against this, there is the 'world systems' view of writers like Wallerstein[10] and the 'development of underdevelopment' view of writers like Frank[11] that there has been an effectively single global capitalist economy, characterised by patterns of capitalist exchange, since the sixteenth century and that whatever may have occurred in the early nineteenth century marks a change of degree only and not a change in kind.

There is much at stake in this debate. At its heart, it concerns the explanation for the process of industrialisation and acceleration of economic activity in Europe and North America and its relationship to the remainder of the 'peripheral' world. According to Frank, it would be a measure of the degree of integration that had already taken place that the core states were in a position to exploit the undeveloped world, thereby rendering it underdeveloped, because of the economic structures already in existence. Accordingly, the economic 'take-off' in the centre was actually *caused* by an integrated global economy already in existence. Alternatively, the effective creation of a dynamic global economy can be seen as the consequence of the dramatic expansion of productive capability in Europe such that, in the words of one analyst, 'quantum jumps in world trade and the emergence of an international economy should be perceived more as the product than the progenitor of industrialization in Western Europe'.[12] Accordingly, Western Europe was the motor, and not simply the beneficiary, of the economic integration taking place:

> Quantum and qualitative leaps forward in international economic relations occurred over the nineteenth century. For that epoch ... the growth and integration of a world economy based upon Western Europe can be observed and measured. For example, between 1800 and 1913 world trade per capita probably multiplied by a factor of 20 ... .Between 1821 and 1915 46 million people crossed the oceans in search of work ... The gross value of capital invested beyond national boundaries increased from just under $1 billion in 1825 to $44 billion by 1913 ... All this movement of commodities, migrants, and capital emanated above all from pronounced declines in the real costs of transporting men and merchandise by land and water.[13]

At any rate, the salient characteristics of an increasingly integrated world economy can be readily documented as far as the period under review is concerned. In particular, the international economy witnessed dramatic expansion in foreign trade, in the development of financial institutions, in the mobility of capital, and in patterns of international settlement and foreign exchange.

There is little denying that the nineteenth century experienced staggering increases in the total volume and value of foreign trade. It rose by 10 per cent annually until mid-century, by which date European states accounted for 70 per cent of total world trade. By mid-century, it was expanding at 60 per cent per annum. Although the rate of increase declined in the 1880s and 1890s under the twin assaults of depression and a return to protectionism, it climbed back to some 45 per cent in the first decade of the twentieth century.[14] Much of the increase, especially in the middle decades of the century, can be accounted for by the lowering of tariffs and also the reduced costs of transportation. Not only were European manufacturers trading amongst themselves, Europe was also sucking in new levels of primary imports. It has been calculated that between 1840 and 1900, exports from South America, Asia and Africa to Western Europe increased ninefold.[15]

Such increase in world trading activity both required, and further stimulated, international financial institutions. During the century, the vast majority of foreign trade was conducted on the basis of bills drawn on the London financial market, and based on sterling. International settlements were also being made on the basis of an increasingly complex system of clearing, continental Europe's deficits with primary producers being financed by its surpluses with Britain and the United States, Britain in turn enjoying a surplus with many primary producers.[16] The foreign exchange system was also increasingly formalised after the 1870s with widespread adoption of the gold standard. 'The thirty years before the first world war', writes one economist, 'saw the establishment and working of an international fixed exchange rate regime, unprecedented in history'.[17]

Finally, the turn of the century was a high point in the mobility of capital. 'If ever a world capital market existed then it was in this period' is one judgement.[18] Britain and France were the dominant capital exporters, France particularly in Europe and increasingly in Eastern Europe. Britain's foreign investments contributed to the opening up of the new frontiers in America, Canada, South America, Southern Africa and Australasia. In the global picture, the much vaunted investment in colonies represented a minuscule proportion of the total overseas investment at this time.

TECHNOLOGY AND WAR

The end of the *ancien régime* was to bring with it, in the words of its recent historian, a transformation in warfare as a result of 'a quantum jump in scale and scope'.[19] The immediate source of this was political change and a new ideology of the state and the citizen's relationship to it, making available unprecedented reserves of man-power. This solved what had hitherto been one of the most potent constraints on the practice of warfare, namely the problem of paying for the armies to go into the field, and resolved one particular puzzle: 'the central mystery of politicized conflict is not why wars took place but how enough men could be found to fight in them'.[20] The French Revolution offered a ready and heady answer to that question.

It seems safe to conclude that the context of international relations had changed in respect of the nature of war by the beginning of the nineteenth century and this was to be an area of rapid and dramatic development throughout the next century and a half. If economic and technological change impinged upon most aspects of social and political life, nowhere did they etch more deeply their effects than in the conduct of war.[21] It can be agreed with Strachan that during the period of revolutionary warfare 'the political and social limitations on warfare were burst asunder by the enormous growth in the power of the state',[22] and it is also the case that the instruments of war both helped to father technological development and were themselves a principal arena in which the technological state could demonstrate its new talents.

By the middle of the nineteenth century, the impact of technology was revealing itself in significant advances in weaponry. The accuracy, range and rate of small arms fire all improved dramatically and it was perhaps the American civil war which gave the first practical demonstration of the new military resources at the disposal of commanders. Simultaneously, the development of the railway significantly altered the ease and speed of supply and reinforcement. Traditionally, strategy and tactics had largely been determined by the simple problems of moving, and supplying, large armies in the field.[23] Now rapid mobilisation and reinforcement became a possibility although it should not be imagined that the railway solved all problems in this respect.[24] Short and relatively successful wars seemed to be the order of the day as Bismarck's wars of the 1860s revealed.

These changes in the nature of war were to percolate through, and in most cases to be rapidly accelerated during, the succeeding century. This chapter cannot hope to document the impressive innovations both in military doctrines and in technology[25] but will concentrate on summarising four areas of importance.

First, the consolidation of large state-organised and, in many cases, state-conscripted armies during the nineteenth century provides a telling insight into the interplay of external and internal political considerations. If organised military power of this nature was increasingly the badge of status in the last third of the century, and if the German example could not be ignored by other states even when it could not be successfully emulated, the social composition of the army reflected the political purpose of the state. Faced with the 'social problem' created by industrialisation and the rapid expansion of an industrial, and potentially disaffected, proletariat, the conservative states of Europe could exploit the nationalism of the age to conscript armies while simultaneously weaning that nationalism away from threatening liberal ideas. If it is true that Bismarck's Germany sought, after 1870, to stabilise the internal and international status quo, it did so by splitting off nationalism from liberalism and the construction of the imperial army was a principal instrument of this purpose. To this extent, the changing face of war was a product of domestic political, as much as external strategic, imperatives.

Secondly, the management of armies was progressively regularised during the course of the nineteenth century. Staff systems were introduced without which 'the mass armies of pre-1914 Europe would have been uncontrollable'.[26] In the longer term, the organisation of such armies, the formation of appropriate military doctrines, ensuring that armies were subject to political direction and control were all to spawn large military-civilian bureaucracies that themselves both reflected, and contributed to, the powers of the state.

Thirdly, this was to be indirectly important in facilitating the state's administration, and encouragement, of scientific and technological research that might have military applications. If one of the salient characteristics of the twentieth century has been the integration of science and technology into the military sphere, and if this has required resources on an unprecedented scale, then the state has become the only organisation capable of funding and administering this task. Illustrative of this general tendency was the story of the development of the military atom during the Second World War where, firstly, ICI attempted to manage Britain's research effort but discovered that even a corporation of this size could not cope with the investment required. Indeed, even Britain itself found the strain of an independent research effort beyond its national resources and had to settle for a combined effort with the United States.[27]

Fourthly, the increasing destructiveness of modern military capabilities has wrought a change on traditional conceptions of the relationship between war and diplomacy and of the role of war in international relations more generally. The pre-1914 attitude to war as a perfectly normal and acceptable regulator of the international system and adjunct of the balance of power has been progressively eroded. Wars have become more costly and potentially destructive to the point where the link between the military means and calculable political objectives has been called into question, especially in the nuclear age. This does not mean that war has become obsolete. Instead, we have witnessed a shift of emphasis away from the use of war as a means of political settlement to the *threatened* use of military instruments in a deterrence relationship. It is unquestionably the case that military deterrence has operated throughout the period since 1815 but since 1945 the organisation of military forces and the development of strategic doctrines for their use have much more deliberately and self-consciously been shaped by deterrence requirements.

It is a moot point whether or not the twin experiences of the two world wars of this century, taken in conjunction with the development of nuclear weapons, have brought about a radical and irreversible change in the function of war in the international system. While the emphasis has shifted to deterrence, it remains paradoxically the case that deterrence continues to be parasitic upon an acceptance of military usage and this possibly serves to qualify the optimistic conclusion of Hinsley:

> The modern international system collapsed on those occasions because states continued to hold the view that they had the legal right to go to war. It also collapsed because states holding this view were

confronted with massive shifts in their relative power which persuaded them in the last resort that war was a reasonable means of
defending or advancing their interests. States hold this view no
longer, and . . . they are unlikely ever again to make this judgment.[28]

Short of such an apocalyptic prognosis, we can assuredly accept that
developments in the means of warfare have impinged upon the
international hierarchy of power. However, it is necessary to be
cautious in assessing this effect. On the one hand, it seems reasonable
to argue that military power has contributed to the process of hierarchical concentration previously discussed and the introduction of
the new term 'superpower' is symbolic of this occurrence. To this
extent, the gap between strongest and weakest in the international
system has manifestly widened in the twentieth century as the fruits
of scientific advance have been brought to bear in the most developed
states. As against this, if the general process of technological diffusion
from developed to undeveloped world has been much less than
development theorists might have foreseen, the process has perhaps
occurred most dynamically in the military sphere, as the third world
has been one of the major consumers, and increasingly also producers, of sophisticated military hardware in the postwar world.

In any event, rash judgements about the extent to which the military
hierarchy of power has determined the distribution of political goods
are probably best avoided. Recent military encounters such as that of
the United States in Vietnam, or of the Soviet Union in Afghanistan,
suggest that disparity in military potential is not, by itself, an assurance of military success. Accordingly, it has been suggested that there
has been a paradoxical disjunction between the postwar military
hierarchy of the power and the fragmentation of imperial relationships:

> Superior military technology was thus not in itself a sufficient
> explanation for the European conquest of the world during the
> centuries of imperial power. The question remains to be answered,
> why this hegemony should have crumbled so rapidly just at the
> moment when the technological superiority was at its most abso-
> lute.[29]

STABILITY

There is a view that for most of the nineteenth century, and
again since 1945, Great Power relations have become stabilised, if not
to the point of eliminating war then certainly to the point of markedly
reducing its incidence. The two world wars, horrendous and costly in

themselves, constitute from this perspective the exceptions rather than a depiction of the general nature of international relationships since 1815.

That the nineteenth century at least seemed to achieve a marked reduction in the casualties inflicted by war is not in doubt, even if some of the particular statistics employed cannot be accepted with much confidence. Schroeder, for example, suggests that 'the ratio of 18th- to 19th-century battlefield deaths per year is somewhere between 7:1 and 8:1.[30] Some general, and some more specific, arguments have been advanced to account for this early-nineteenth-century watershed of stability. Schroeder's own explanation has already been referred to, whereby new diplomatic mechanisms were coupled with environmental changes and resulted in a restrained international system in that 'the 19th-century system inhibited bids for mastery in Europe'.[31]

Another general explanation is that stability is a function of numbers and that the process of concentration of power that has occurred since 1815 has been conducive to stability for this reason. Even so, there are distinct variations on this explanation, some favouring a multipolar balance of five Great Powers to operate a stable balance of power, but others suggesting that the post-1945 bipolar order is the more stable distribution of power. The former position emphasises the virtues of flexibility of alignment in preserving stability, the latter the virtues of certainty which an inflexible opposition of rivals induces. Both, in varying degrees, see benefit in the directorial role of a small number of Great Powers because, like firms, they can more effectively manipulate the market and, like price-fixing, this 'becomes easier the smaller the number of firms involved'.[32]

In turn, this issue creates a division of opinion about the nature of such stability as has characterised the post-1945 order. There are, of course, qualifications that must be entered against any general claim that peace has been preserved since 1945. Just as the nineteenth-century European peace did not represent peace for much of the extra-European world,[33] so the post-1945 peace has been a characteristic of Europe and of the direct relationship between the superpowers, rather than an attribute of the system as a whole. Reasonable estimates suggest that there have been some 150 wars since 1945 producing casualties in the order of 20 million.[34] The Iran–Iraq war which has been fought inconclusively through the 1980s has produced levels of military casualties unmatched since the First World War.

Allowing this, the stability of the European core can either be explained as a function of the postwar distribution of power and the bipolar configuration which was its salient feature or, alternatively, as the specific creation of the new means of warfare, namely, nuclear weapons. On this accounting, it is the balance of terror rather than the logic of numbers that has preserved the central peace since 1945. Either way, the long periods of stability achieved amongst the Great Powers in the nineteenth and twentieth centuries are worthy of note, even if the increasing destructiveness of the wars that have been fought is a safeguard against complacency.

HEGEMONY

Beyond the number of Great Powers that have played a central role in the international system since 1815, there is a body of historical theory which suggests that the working of the system has been critically dependent upon the role played by one central actor – the hegemon – that is responsible for the central direction and maintenance of the institutions of the international order, both political and economic. Such a conception embodies both a theory of continuity, inasmuch as such hegemons are important to the system in different historical settings, but also a theory of change since the rise and fall of hegemonies is a dynamic process.

This provides an alternative perspective upon the significance of the early nineteenth century and upon the extent of common characteristics displayed by international relations since then. What is distinctive about the world of international relations since 1815, viewed from this perspective, is the end of the attempt to establish empire within Europe, or indeed on a global basis, and its replacement by a more sophisticated and non-territorial conception of hegemony. Various developments, principal amongst which was the consolidation of the nation–state, its economic expansion and its integration into a complex world economy, militated against future attempts to create territorial empires within Europe. Napoleon's, accordingly, was the last of the old-style quests to establish mastery in Europe and saw the 'displacement of the cycle of empires by a succession of hegemonies',[35] the most important of which have been those enjoyed by Britain in the nineteenth, and the United States in the twentieth, century.

The hegemon plays the leading role in establishing an institutional environment which is favourable to its own interests (free trade, informal empire) but also accepts costs in being the mainstay of the system (providing financial services, a source of capital, and a pattern of military support). According to this conception, the hegemon is the main beneficiary of the system but also the main provider of externalities to the other members: it receives disproportionate benefits but accepts disproportionate burdens.

The process of hegemonial rise and decline is inherently dynamic. 'In short, the same historical view that justifies creating a hegemonic system', Calleo writes, 'becomes increasingly inconvenient as the hegemony matures. For, as hegemony matures, it also declines'.[36] The dynamic which drives this historical process remorselessly along is provided by the disequilibrium which sets in between the costs and benefits of the hegemonic role:

> These successive dominant states have changed the system, expanding until an equilibrium is reached between the costs and benefits of further change and expansion ... In consequence, there is a tendency for the economic costs of maintaining the international status quo to rise faster than the financial capacity of the dominant power to support its position and the status quo.[37]

In these terms, Britain was the provider of the institutional infrastructure of the mid-nineteenth-century system. It exploited its economic advantage as the leading industrial power to establish a world trading and financial system which was both stable but also advantageous to British interests. This was coupled to a balance of power on the European continent, and British naval supremacy elsewhere, which gave free rein to British commercial and imperial objectives. However, by the later decades of the century, Britain's economic base declined relative to Germany, the Unites States and other European competitors and the imperial overstretch which Britain suffered at the end of the century was a manifestation of her inability to continue to maintain the *Pax Britannica*.[38]

The United States eventually displaced the British hegemony and, during the period of her early post-1945 dominance, established the complex of political, military and economic arrangements which constituted the *Pax Americana*. This, as Keohane has suggested, differed in significant respects from that of its British predecessor in that American economic preeminence was greater than the British had been, was less dependent upon foreign trade and investment and enjoyed its most important economic relationships with its military allies.[39] Structurally, however, the role of the United States has been similar in imparting direction and economic and military support to the postwar liberal economic order and its adjunct security arrangements.

There is now a general consensus that the United States is less capable of performing her hegemonial duties. In the most celebrated recent exposition of this view, the notion of imperial overstretch is elaborated, leading to the conclusion that, as far as Washington is concerned, 'the sum total of the United States global interests and obligations is nowadays far larger than the country's power to defend them all simultaneously'.[40] The choice, for another commentator, is between attempting to rejuvenate America's hegemonial role or 'consciously transforming the global system into a more plural structure'.[41] The optimists, however, contend that some of the cooperative regimes created in the postwar period may well still survive the passing of the original American impetus which brought them into being as these regimes are easier to sustain when already in being than they are to create in the first place.[42]

What is striking about these various discursions on hegemonies in international relations is their emphasis upon dynamic processes within a relatively fixed or static framework. Kennedy's elegant historical overview develops the theme of the restless 'rise and fall' of the Great Powers: to this extent the discussion dwells upon change and transformation driven by the shifts in the relative economic and military capabilities of states. At the same time, from the endless momentum of history, static conclusions can be drawn:

> it has been a common dilemma facing previous 'number-one' countries that even as their relative economic strength is ebbing, the growing foreign challenges to their position have compelled them to allocate more and more of their resources into the military sector, which in turn squeezes out productive investment and, over time, leads to the downward spiral of slower growth . . .[43]

What is happening now to the United States, happened previously to the Habsburgs and to Britain, *despite* the changing context of international relations, and the altered conditions of internal political and economic life that have palpably occurred in the interim. Likewise, Gilpin's analysis highlights the long cycle of hegemonic wars that have characterised international history and vouchsafes that 'it has always been thus and always will be'.[44] The twin *motifs* of relative change in power within a relatively fixed framework of international relations predominate in both accounts.

DIPLOMACY

Finally, the international system has experienced considerable change in the nature and functions of its diplomatic institutions and methods.[45] Whether or not the transformation in style and content of diplomacy has been progressive is a matter of some debate and centres upon the 'vices' of the old diplomacy as against the 'virtues' of the new.

In these terms, what has been abandoned is the old aristocratic forms of diplomacy. Based on common cultural values and shared social standing, this *ancien régime* diplomacy brought in its train a narrow fixation on high politics, an exclusion of the wider public interest, and a disreputable style of secret and machiavellian conduct of diplomatic business. Accordingly, the post-1918 new diplomacy represented a beneficial development of diplomatic practice in that it made it more professional, more publicly accountable, more specialised and hence less prone to the bellicosity of princely advisors.

The reality has, of course, not corresponded precisely with such prescriptions and it is as common to hear the critics who lament the passing of the old style as it is to hear the praises of the new. The ills of twentieth-century diplomacy are often described as being attendant upon that very 'popular' element which was promised as the instrument of a more wholesome and peaceful international society.

The basic institutions of diplomacy, and principally the system of permanent representation in host countries, had already been established by the early sixteenth century and had spread to the rest of Europe from the Italian city–states which had fostered its growth.[46] The reign of Louis XIV in France witnessed further elaboration of diplomatic method and the indelible imprint of France's supremacy was placed on the entire diplomatic system.[47] During the eighteenth century, the aristocratic *esprit de corps* flourished in a setting of shared interest and value and the conduct of business in French lent additional emphasis to the concept of diplomatic community.

Here, as elsewhere, the 1815 settlement was to play a significant role. One of its protocols established the diplomatic hierarchy of forms of representation – the descending rank order being ambassador, envoy, minister resident and chargé d'affaires[48] – and the system of precedence. As in other respects, therefore, the Vienna settlement contributed substantially to the hierarchical ordering of the international community. 'The fussiness and punctilio of precedence may appear humorous in some of their manifestations,' Albrecht-Carrié has written but, 'there was in them a deliberate gauge of power standing, hence their real importance.'[49]

During the succeeding century, a number of developments were to impinge upon the nature of diplomacy and its conduct. By the middle of the nineteenth century, diplomacy began to exploit, if not to be shaped by, the force of nationalism. It also, at least in Britain and France, became exposed to higher levels of parliamentary and media interest which, in turn, could be used to arouse public passion. Above all, diplomacy reflected the technological advances of the era, par-

109

ticularly as regards the speed of communications and travel. This had a number of consequences. It increased the speed of the diplomatic game such that the old-style pre-Crimean war crisis typically lasted several months but in the later nineteenth century it was much shorter.[50] In the long run, it fostered the growth of permanent multilateral diplomatic institutions, rather than purely bilateral contacts, since they were more appropriate to the speed and increasing complexity of international affairs. Unsurprisingly, the last quarter of the nineteenth century saw a proliferation of intergovernmental unions of a functional kind, as well as a host of private international organisations of which the Red Cross was a precursor.[51] Also, it was believed, telegraphic communications diminished the autonomy of the individual ambassador and placed him more readily under the direction of the ministry, although the early first-hand evidence denied that this was so.[52]

The abandonment of the old diplomacy after the First World War did not see the creation of the New Jerusalem. Indeed, to many analysts, the net effect of a democratic style of diplomacy has been regressive: 'Traditional diplomatic standards probably reached their highest level during the century before 1914. Since then they have steadily declined.'[53] What has contributed to this erosion? Wight saw it as the emergence of a revolutionary diplomacy of which espionage, subversion and propaganda were the principal characteristics.[54] Others have traced it to the rejection of traditional diplomatic norms by the major political forces of the twentieth century, such as bolshevism, fascist totalitarianism and third world radicalism. Others see the changing diplomatic framework neutrally as simply a function of the changing context of the increased number of states, greater diversity amongst them and considerable inexperience on the part of new states.[55]

The role of the decolonised Afro-Asian states in contemporary international relations provides a telling illustration of the manner in which change in the geographic scope of the system has materially impinged upon the content and methods of diplomacy. It is not just that the agenda of international relations has in past decades been pushed to take account of issues of race, decolonisation and economic development: more fundamentally, there has been the issue of integrating these states into an essentially European-derived diplomatic framework. Thus Watson has advised that 'we must keep in mind the European origins of present-day diplomacy if we are to see where it has become inadequate and how it can successfully be adapted and in some respects wholly transformed to meet the requirements of its global expansion and of radical change'.[56] Although contemporary diplomacy has grown out of the European system, it is nonetheless different from it.[57] There is not the same political, cultural or economic homogeneity underpinning the diplomatic discourse of today as were present in the early nineteenth century. Accordingly, some of the accepted norms of diplomacy, such as that of immunity, have been severely tested in recent years. This said, it should not be imagined that the non-Western world has been antithetical to the diplomatic order. It is also one of the paradoxes of the present situation, and one which saves us from facile simplifications, that many of the new states have clung tenaciously to the mechanisms of the diplomatic order, seeing within its provisions for noninterference the best safeguard of the independence of their weak states in a hierarchical order dominated by the strong.[58]

These collectively represent the major transitions undergone by the international system since 1815. In each individual area, there is debate as to whether the continuities or the discontinuities are the more striking. Should we be more impressed by the changed context and substance of international relations, or by the constancy of some of the norms for their management? The ensuing historical narrative, arranged into individual periods, is designed to pursue further these questions.

6 FROM BALANCE TO CONCERT, 1815–1854

The interest of students of international relations in the congress system and in the Concert of Europe hinges on an attempt to see these diplomatic techniques in the broad perspective of their contribution to the theory and practice of international relations. That is to say that the questions that mainly concern us are the following: Was there such a thing as the Concert of Europe? Did it survive beyond the period of congress diplomacy in the few years after the 1815 settlement? Upon what principles if any was the Concert based? To what extent was the Concert a novel element in the history of international relations? What is required is an appreciation not only of the historical nature of the European Concert of the nineteenth century but also of the nature of a concert system as one amongst several systems for the management of international relations.

A proper understanding of the Concert is important, both in its own historical terms and because it poses wider questions of interest to the student of international relations. Central to these is the relationship between the Concert and the period of relative peace which prevailed in the first half of the nineteenth century. Was it the Concert which contributed to the maintenance of the stability in the international order which prevailed until the 1850s? Alternatively, was the Concert simply parasitic upon other conditions which made the Concert viable in the first place. According to the former, and optimistic view, the diplomatic modes developed by statesmen can influence the degree of peace and stability in the international system. According to the latter, and pessimistic view, diplomatic innovations like the Concert are most possible when least necessary, because the international environment is in any case benign, and least sustainable when most needed. Was the Concert then a fair weather system unable to cope with international storms?

Viewed in this light, the Concert was a 'negative' factor in post-Vienna international relations, merely a reflection of the things which the Great Powers did not want. Thus seen, it was 'an explicit rejection of the hegemony of one power, of constant warfare and of revolution'.[1] At best, it was only one factor amongst several working for peace; a fuller list included:

> the widespread exhaustion, war-weariness, fear of revolution, and desire for peace produced by a generation of war and upheaval from 1789 to 1815; a moderate peace settlement, a stable balance of power, a system of diplomacy by conference, a Concert of Europe, and other diplomatic devices; the prevalence of monarchical conservative ideology; international cooperation to preserve the existing social order; and prudent skillful statesmanship.[2]

There are two main themes in modern international history, themes that are frequently confused but ought to be kept apart. One is the development of international organisation, the construction of an institutional framework within which independent sovereign states might interact: its focus is upon diplomatic machinery. The other is the assertion of a special managerial role for the Great Powers in the shaping of international order: its focus is upon diplomatic norms. Moreover, it is one of the principal deficiencies of the 'whig' interpretation of international history that it has mistaken the latter process for evidence of the vitality of the former. But not only are the two processes distinct: they are, indeed, in some fundamental sense antagonistic and, far from suggesting a unilinear concept of progress in state behaviour, they may be interpreted – normatively – as symptoms of a duality in historical development in which 'progressive' elements are counterbalanced by 'regressive' ones. If the growth of international organisation is regarded as an expression of the utopian impulse in international affairs, then Great Power management is surely the consummation of realist demands. In actuality, however, the two have become intermingled such that a Great Power role has become a mainstay of international organisation.

Nowhere is this deep-seated confusion more apparent than in scholarly discussion of the Concert of Europe. It is evident in the historical parallels in terms of which commentators explain the Concert, it being depicted as the historical precursor of the League of Nations and of the United Nations. Unfortunately, to describe the European Concert in such a manner is to miss the major significance of the first half of the nineteenth century as a phase in the development of international politics. Rather than see the United Nations as the heritage of Concert experience, we should more minimally see the structure of the Security Council in that role, or, perhaps even more appropriately, the 'conventions of crisis' that some analysts discern in the recent behaviour of the super-powers.[3] This is to say that the significance of the Concert lies in its elaboration of rules of diplomatic conduct for the Great Powers and only tangentially in its contribution to the theory of international organisation. The historian who sees the incipient phase of the Concert, in the shape of the congress system, as occupying 'in man's quest for peace through international conferences and organizations a position which is almost midway between Emeric Cruce's *Nouveau Cynée* (1623) and the United Nations of contemporary fame'[4] is, therefore, well wide of the mark.

The confusion is neatly captured in yet another commentary. The authors of this work argue at one point that 'the Munich Conference of September 1938 can be described as the last great meeting of the old Concert of Europe'.[5] Whatever the historical accuracy of extending the life of the Concert into the twentieth century, the authors are surely correct in perceiving the essence of the Concert to lie in the mode of Great Power management of the international system. Subsequently, however, the same authors obscure the issue by presenting the following summary: 'Taking nineteenth- and twentieth-century inter-national relations as a whole it is evident that the tradition of conference or parliamentary diplomacy is a growing one. The informal Concert of Europe gave way to the League of Nations and that in its turn gave place to the much stronger UN.'[6] Here, once again, the focus has reverted from norms to machinery.

In essence, the significance of the Concert derives from two inter-related ideas. The first of these was the formal assertion of the unique privileges and responsibilities of the Great Powers in the maintenance of international order. The second, made necessary by the first, was that if the special managerial role of the Great Powers was to be recognised, it would be necessary to order more formally the relation-ships between the powers themselves. It is from this dual perspective, as both asserting a special role for the Great Powers and then attempting to mitigate some of the consequences of this, that the unique contribution of the Concert is to be appreciated and its supersession of a crude balance-of-power system to be understood. What this represented was a formalisation of hierarchy as an explicit element within the international order.

These two facets of the Concert system have, indeed, been high-lighted by historians of the period. Of the former facet, Elrod has observed that 'concert diplomacy actively cultivated the conception of the great powers as a unique and special peer group',[7] echoing Albrecht-Carrié's assessment of the rationale of the Concert that 'order could best be maintained by the clear assertion of the right and responsibility of those possessed of power, the Great Powers'.[8] Of the latter aspect, Elrod has likewise drawn attention to the Concert as 'a conceptual norm among the great powers of the proper and permissible aims and methods of international politics',[9] or more simply put, the Concert was a 'group norm'.[10]

Although speaking of a different period, Medlicott is intuitively aware of these two dimensions of the Concert idea. In a comment upon Gladstone's attempted revival of Concert diplomacy later in the century, Medlicott comments that Gladstone did not seem to distinguish between 'the Concert as a tutelage of the great powers over the smaller, and the Concert as a means of preserving the peace of Europe by preventing war between the great powers themselves'.[11] The Concert, therefore, was *of* the powers and *between* the powers. The endeavour to manage the lower hierarchical orders would consolidate the shared interests of the Great Powers and success in such management would reduce the risk of rupture within the Great Power directorate.

Reverting to the above distinction between the Concert as a contribution to the norms of Great Power behaviour and the Concert as a forerunner of international organisations of this century, we discover that such a distinction helps to make sense of the apparently inconsistent judgements of historians upon the Concert in another respect. For some, as will be discussed shortly, the keynote of the Concert was its attempt to formalise international politics, to systematise a spontaneous balance-of-power situation: for others, by contrast, the keynote of the Concert was its informal nature, to the point where its very existence has been called into question. As Holbraad was to put it 'at its best, it might be described as an informal institution; at its worst, as non-existent'.[12]

Some of the resultant confusion is dissipated if we recollect the terms in which the formality or the informality of the Concert is being judged. To those who look to the Concert in terms of a lineage of organisational development – as diplomatic machinery – the Concert is, to be sure, informal, as there was no regularity of meeting and no permanent apparatus. In a more important sense, however, the Concert did formalise rules of Great Power behaviour and, if we look to the Concert for diplomatic norms, rather than diplomatic machinery, the rewards are more obviously tangible. In other words, to characterise, and implicitly to criticise, the Concert as an informal organisation is as true as it is irrelevant because the Concert never aspired to organisational status in our understanding of that word.

Inis Claude is aware of this distinction but, perhaps surprisingly in a

book on the development of international organisations,[13] his refer-
ences to it are implicit rather than explicit. In discussing the Concert,
Claude comments that 'the political conference system ... produced
the prototype of a major organ of modern international organisation –
the executive council of the great powers'.[14] What he fails to stress is
that although the development of modern international organisations
has coincided with the notion of Great Power tutelage, there was no
necessary nexus between them (even if there were strong 'realistic'
reasons for the coincidence) and the history of the former should not
be equated with the history of the latter. The evolution of Great
Power norms of behaviour has, in other words, been a discrete
development, and even if modern international organisations have
chosen to incorporate these norms into a 'major organ', we can
nonetheless imagine Great Power adherence to these norms outside
an organisational setting[15] just as we can imagine international organisations that would not embody these norms.

In attempting to assess the nature and the novelty of the Concert of
Europe, the first question to be answered is whether or not the
diplomatic code established in 1815 was significantly different from
that which had existed prior to 1789. In other words, is it possible to
view the pattern of post-1815 international relations as no more than a
return to the principles which had guided European diplomats in the
years before the French Revolution, principles that had been violated
by the Napoleonic wars? This question may be tackled by trying to
introduce a further distinction, that between the Concert of Europe as
a diplomatic norm and the balance of power as it had operated in
eighteenth-century international relations.

That the Concert was based upon a stable balance of power there
can be little dispute: that it went beyond the practices of a balance
system is not universally agreed. Nonetheless, there are reasons for
believing that a valid distinction can be made between the two.
Schroeder, certainly, is of the opinion that 'what accounted for
European peace after 1815 was rather a system of international order
established upon a balance of power, *but going well beyond it*'.[16]
Likewise, Elrod is convinced, and I think correctly so, that 'the
Concert derived from the common realization of European statesmen
of the Napoleonic era that something new and different must be
devised to mitigate the increasingly chaotic and warlike balance-of-
power system of the previous century'.[17]

At first sight, this is a view that may not commend itself. Most
commentators would agree that the Concert of Europe was in some
important sense linked with the postwar congress system and simi-

larly most historians would be forced to concede that the congress system of diplomacy had its origins in the wartime coalitions brought together to oppose Napoleon. In other words, at first sight, the Concert of Europe seems to derive its historical lineage directly from what was one of the most salient examples of the balance-of-power doctrine in practice. The wars had seen a succession of alliances and coalitions in which the European powers combined to thwart the pretensions of revolutionary and Napoleonic France.

Moreover, the principle of balance that had guided the European powers in their efforts to check French preponderance was visibly carried into the territorial settlement itself. This can be seen in several of its aspects. Most notably it was applied to the provisions that concerned France. Many analysts have drawn attention to the principle, hallowed in balance-of-power doctrine, that deviant states should be restored to their former standing in international society. This principle was certainly observed in relation to France. France was largely restored to her pre-revolutionary boundaries and, although she had to submit to an indemnity and to an occupation army for a short period, she was otherwise readmitted as the traditional French actor on the international stage. To have done otherwise would have placed an artificial constraint on the workings of the balance-of-power mechanism.

The territorial provisions of the Vienna settlement, as they related to France, displayed adherence to the balance principle in another sense. Since France had challenged Europe and attempted to establish predominance, measures were taken to prevent a recurrence of this development. This is clearly illustrated in the alterations to the map of Europe along France's eastern border. In the north, Belgium and Holland were united to pose a more powerful buffer state against any future French expansion. Further south, Prussia's position on the Rhineland was strengthened, again as a check to France. Further south again, the permanent neutralisation of Switzerland was guaranteed by the signatories to the settlement. In the extreme south, Austria's position in Italy was enhanced by the acquisition of Venice.

At least two of the powers were to play critical roles in the preservation of the balance of power created by the settlement. Firstly there was Britain for whom a European balance was an essential precondition of her commercial and imperial expansion. This may have gone beyond self-interest because 'from her island position Britain was able to take a more detached view as to what constituted a reasonable equilibrium'.[18] The other power was the Habsburg Empire which served as a bulwark against France and Russia, but also against the new revisionist force of Prussian nationalism. Accordingly, it has been asserted that 'the Habsburg Empire was vital to the functioning of this complex five-sided checkmate, if only because it seemed to have the greatest interest of all in freezing the 1815 settlement'.[19]

Traditional balance-of-power manoeuvres were characteristic of the Vienna Congress in yet another sense. The most contentious issue to be settled at the Congress was the Polish question. This problem soon produced a clear alignment between the powers. Russia sought to swallow up most of Poland and Prussia was prepared to agree to this provided that she was similarly allowed to incorporate the whole of Saxony. This neither Britain nor Austria could permit. Consequently, France, supposedly the defeated party and not a framer of the settlement, was called into the power struggle and, choosing to support Britain and Austria, was instrumental in forcing both Russia and Prussia to limit their aims.

Was the Concert of Europe no more, then, than the reestablishment of the traditional balance-of-power system? There seems to be some ground for saying so. We have just seen how the balance principle underlay the anti-Napoleonic coalitions and in fact permeated the entire Vienna settlement. And it is equally clear that if the Concert of Europe was anything at all it was the offspring of the very coalition that had produced the Vienna settlement. More specifically, if the Concert of Europe referred to any concrete diplomatic method, it was the one that had its origins in the provisions of the Quadruple Alliance of 1814, reaffirmed in November 1815. As a product of their wartime experience, which (the allies argued) had been successful in managing the war, the European powers agreed in this document to attempt to manage the peace in the post-1815 period. As the sixth article of the Quadruple Alliance stated:

> To facilitate and to secure the execution of the present treaty and to consolidate the connections which at the present moment so closely unite the Four Sovereigns for the happiness of the World, the High Contracting Parties have agreed to renew their meetings at fixed periods ... for the purpose of consulting upon their common interests and for the consideration of the measures which at each of these periods shall be considered the most salutary for the repose and prosperity of Nations and for the maintenance of the peace of Europe.

It was this statement of intent that gave birth to the series of periodic congresses that characterised European diplomatic history for the next few years and, intermittently, throughout most of the century.

While the treaty and the Congress that established the practice of congress diplomacy were themselves to a large extent products of balance-of-power philosophy, it can be argued that the Concert of Europe was something more than the traditional balance-of-power system.

This is not a view that would be shared by everyone. Indeed there are strong historical arguments against it. Carsten Holbraad in his excellent study of British and German ideas on the Concert of Europe has identified a school of thought that he has labelled 'the balance of power' for the simple reason that this school thought of the Concert of Europe solely as an instrument of balance-of-power diplomacy. Nevertheless it can be argued that the main contribution of the Concert of Europe to diplomatic theory and practice was precisely its modifications of the balance of power. This is the very essence of the idea of the Concert of Europe.

The emergence of the European Concert is closely related to, but not identical with, two developments within balance-of-power theory itself. The first of these relates to the process by means of which balance is achieved; the second pertains to the type of equilibrium that is sought.

As regards the first of these developments, balance-of-power theory was already undergoing, late in the eighteenth century, a transformation that would remove from it many of its naturalistic assumptions. The point has been well made by M. Wright:

> The pervasiveness of natural analogues was derived from a tradition of thought which assumed the universality of the Laws of Nature. Human affairs were part of nature and subject to its laws ... the transition from a naturalistic to an artificial conception of the balance of power is a gradual one and to some extent parallels the transition from natural to positive theories of international law.[20]

The balance of power was, in other words, becoming increasingly recognised as a product of human contrivance rather than as a gift of nature and the Concert reflected this development. Wright himself makes this point:

> Although the solidarity and cooperation of the Concert of Europe have often been exaggerated, it recognised, at least in theory, that the balance of power required a more conscious, rational management.[21]

The nature of the equilibrium upon which the Concert was to rest was also different from that which had characterised the eighteenth century: its fundamental concept was, according to Gulick,[22] the coalition rather than the alliance. As Gulick has expressed it, 'this coalition equilibrium, or Concert, became the institutional adjustment of the European state system to the new multiple balance and the inadequacy of the older system of alliance balance'.[23] He elaborates:

> The years 1812–15 are especially meaningful to the student of the balance of power for the further reason that they witnessed the temporary evolution of a coalition equilibrium from the antecedent, eighteenth century system of alliance balance. The wars of the French Revolution and Napoleonic dominion had provided the terrible anvil upon which coalitions were forged; and the statesmen of the great powers attempted to consummate their experience of wartime coalitions by the creation of an automatic coalition which would solve the problem of enforcement for the state system in the postwar period.[24]

This comes close to Schroeder's idea that there was a further modification of balance doctrine after 1815 in practice, if not in intention.[25] It is his claim that the settlement created an elaborate network of intermediary states which served as buffers and spheres of influence. Not only did those small states keep the powers apart and prevent them from fighting each other but, more positively, they 'linked them by giving them something in common to manage'.

But the Concert was to be more than a simple revision of balance doctrine. First, we can agree with the view of Hinsley in his study *Power and the Pursuit of Peace* that the post-Vienna period of international politics was characterised as much by a reaction against traditional balance-of-power politics as by attempts to adhere to the principles of the balance doctrine. If the powers of Europe felt that the balance mechanism was still a necessary element in the proper functioning of the European state system, they no longer seemed so convinced that it was a sufficient principle upon which to order their relations with each other. This should not be overstated. There was not the same moral reaction against power politics in 1815 as was to be demonstrated in 1918. Nonetheless, although the degree was different, the same sentiment was there in embryo. Although the balance of power might preserve the state system, there emerged the beginnings of the feeling that it was not the most efficient way of achieving this end and that perhaps some other mechanism should be relied upon to provide the order thought desirable in the conduct of inter-state relations.

In consequence, the essence of the Concert of Europe was to add an extra embellishment onto the operation of the balance system. Not only should the mechanism operate, but its operations should be sanctioned and legitimised by the European Concert of Great Powers.

How did this work in practice? For the few years subsequent upon the Vienna settlement, and on the precedent established by Vienna itself, the characteristic mode of operation of the European Concert was the Congress. At Vienna, not only was the European balance of power restored but the distribution of power that emerged from the territorial settlement was legitimised by agreement of the powers. Similarly, when in 1818 the allies decided that the occupation army could be withdrawn from France and France fully readmitted to her previous international status by being allowed to join the Quadruple Alliance, these deeds were legitimised by a Congress at Aix-la-Chapelle. The rationale behind the powers' decision to readmit France to full membership of the system was based on traditional European doctrine. As the 1818 protocol itself was to state, 'assuring to France the place that belongs to her in the European system, will bind her more closely to the pacific and benevolent views in which all the sovereigns participate and will thus consolidate the general tranquility'. This is the very essence of Kissinger's notion of a legitimate international order which every great power would have an interest in seeking to sustain. But although the reasoning was traditional, the method employed to achieve this end was novel. France did not just resume her place in Europe as an inevitable fact of nature. Rather she was admitted by a formal act of European diplomacy – the product of a general meeting of the Great Powers.

We can, then, concur with Hinsley in what he considers to be the two main principles of the Concert of Europe – the two principles that give substance to the idea of the Concert of Europe and distinguish it from the diplomatic procedures of other periods of international history. These were:

(1) that the Great Powers had a common responsibility for maintaining the territorial *status quo* of the treaties of 1815 and for solving the international problems that arose in Europe: and

(2) that when the *status quo* had to be modified or a problem had to be settled, changes should not be made unilaterally and gains should not be made without their formal and common consent.[26]

It was this requirement of 'formal and common consent' that most clearly distinguished the Concert of Europe from the simple workings of the balance of power. As has been said, in the immediate post-1815 period, the diplomatic instrument by means of which this formal and common consent was sought was the Congress of the powers.

Of course, there was no unanimity between the powers as to the purpose to which these congresses should be put and clear divisions soon appeared that indicated the internal strains of the system. Moreover, in order to understand these strains, it is first necessary to look at the common interests upon which the powers thought that the Concert of Europe was based.

Here there were divisions from the very beginning, divisions that were to become increasingly conspicuous the more the powers tried to use the congress mechanism in practice. All the powers shared a feeling that it was the duty of the major states of Europe to ensure that international order prevailed on the continent. Unfortunately, they did not share a common conception of what constituted international order.

For Britain, separated by water from continental Europe and with major interests lying outside Europe itself, the main preoccupation in the postwar years was in preserving the territorial settlement of 1815 and the territorial balance of power that this settlement had set out to achieve. In other words, as far as Castlereagh was concerned, international order was precisely that – a problem that began and ended at state frontiers.

Such was not the case for Metternich, the Austrian Chancellor. In common with many leading conservative statesmen of the time, Metternich came increasingly to define international order in terms of internal domestic conditions. Had not the international upheaval of the 1793–1815 period sprung from the internal events in France? In other words, as far as Metternich was concerned, there was no point in preserving simply the structure of the 1815 state system if this structure could in turn be overthrown by domestic upheavals. The powers must concern themselves as much with internal developments within states as with external frontiers.

Metternich's interest did not lie with the state system alone. He was also, as the Austrian Chancellor, concerned with dynastic rights. Consequently he was opposed to revolutions, to constitutionalism, to nationalism, on two main grounds: first, because they represented a threat to international order; and secondly, but perhaps more importantly, because they represented an immediate threat to the Habsburg Empire itself. If any state had reason to fear the principles of the revolution and the emerging principles of nationalism it was the Habsburg Empire, which was vulnerable on every count.

Flowing from these two perceptions of respective national interests, the British and the Austrian, there emerged two views about the functions of international congresses. For Metternich, the states of Europe must act conjointly to stamp out the internal threats to international security. The image that he appealed to was that of a universal conspiracy. Europe should view itself not as divided vertically into states but as divided horizontally into rulers, on the one hand, and revolutionaries on the other. It was the collective duty of all the states to stamp out this revolutionary contagion before it could spread and before it could present another challenge to Europe's international arrangements. In the words of one historian, the monarchs of Europe must hang together if they were not to hang separately. This was the justification for international intervention in internal affairs – precisely the reasoning that was to underlie the interventions in the Russian civil war, following upon 1917.

Again, Europe should not be regarded as having been divided into two rigid camps over this issue. Broadly speaking, there was an alignment of the autocratic powers of the East, Russia, Prussia and Austria on the one hand, and the constitutional powers of the West, Britain and France on the other. However, these were in no sense solid alliances. Despite the Holy Alliance that, ostensibly at least, bound the Eastern powers, Austria and Prussia had a serious conflict of interest over which state should have preponderance in Germany, and Austria and Russia had a serious conflict of interest in the Balkans. Similarly, Britain and France were, throughout the nineteenth century, to find themselves at cross-purposes over Egypt. During the period of the Congress system there was as much common cause between the Anglo-Austrian view of things, as against Russia and France, as any other alignment.[27] The continent was not therefore split into two hard-and-fast ideological camps. Nor were Castlereagh's views basically more liberal than those of Metternich. They were just as conservative, although about slightly different things. This is a point which Carsten Holbraad has made well in his book on *The Concert of Europe*:

> The British conservative idea was about an alliance of great powers established by treaties and formal declarations, not a union of sovereigns founded in common sentiments and interests; about the external freedom of the members of the states system, not the internal condition of the parts of the society of Europe; about the threat of aggression not the danger of revolution. But the essence of the idea was conservative: preservation of the boundaries that the statesmen of 1815 had drawn in an attempt to balance the powers of Europe.

These divisions emerged more starkly in the remaining congresses of the period – those at Troppau, Laibach and Verona, convened to discuss the revolutions in Naples, Sicily and Spain. It is significant that the powers could not at these meetings come to an agreement on joint action to suppress these revolutions; it is a matter of no less consequence, however, that the powers felt it necessary to summon congresses – and, let it be remembered, actually succeeded in convening these congresses – in order to deal with problems that were thought to be important for the peace of Europe. It is this idea, that the individual powers should not take unilateral action on questions important to the whole of the continent, that was the underlying reality of the Concert of Europe and its most distinctive contribution to the functioning of international politics in the nineteenth century.

Perhaps one more point should be made at this juncture. There were two broad reasons why diplomacy by congress or by conference achieved the success that it did at this period. One was undoubtedly that there was no major and urgent issue to be resolved between any two of the major powers. The Great Powers find it easiest to cooperate when they are jointly imposing a settlement on some third party, preferably a smaller state. This is a characteristic of Great Power behaviour as conspicuous in the present day as in the nineteenth century. However, in the case of a direct conflict between the two major powers, cooperation is not so easily achieved. Such a verdict can be found in one survey:

> In practical terms the Concert of Europe could successfully allocate territory from one small or weak state to another. It could also provide the framework for the settlement of crises in which the powers were anxious to reach agreement. But it could not satisfy the territorial ambitions of great powers when these were in conflict with each other.[28]

So, in a sense, the Concert of Europe was, perhaps, not much more than the negative expression of the fact that for the time being the Great Powers of Europe could live with the differences between them. There was no burning issue that cried out for an immediate settlement. But to say this little is perhaps to take too much for granted. To the extent that the Great Powers could tolerate their differences with each other, this may well have been the gift of a benign international environment but it could as easily be testimony to a moderate view of international relations, and a tribute to skilled diplomacy, both of which were key elements in the Concert itself.

There is another reason to which reference has already been made. That the Great Powers were cautious in the post-1815 period, and refrained from pressing their mutual differences to the point of conflict, can be partially explained by the internal condition of the major powers, and of Austria in particular. The French Revolution had taught a lesson that was to be repeated in 1830 and again in 1848, that the social order of Europe was fragile and did not require much to disrupt it. For countries with one eye on the internal situation, this was no time for international adventures.

124

It is this 'negative' view of the Concert that Medlicott has encapsulated in his dictum that 'it was peace that maintained the Concert, and not the Concert that maintained peace'.[29] In consequence, it was the forces operating for peace that created the illusion of a successful Concert and not the Concert that produced stability, a view echoed in Northedge's dismissal of the peace-keeping role of the Concert as working 'quite simply, because the international system as a whole was oriented towards the maintenance of peace at the core'.[30] Elrod is one of the few who regard the Concert in 'positive' terms as an 'essential ingredient of European peace and stability between the Congress of Vienna and the Crimean War'.[31]

What are we to make of these rival interpretations? In a sense the argument is a chicken-and-egg one and, as such, resistant to a satisfactory conclusion: even if the underlying conditions favoured Concert diplomacy, the functioning of the Concert might nonetheless have reinforced the inherent tendencies towards international stability. In any case, there is one important respect in which the answer to that question is immaterial. Even if we accept that the contribution of the Concert to peace-maintenance was minimal, this need not imply that no Concert was in existence nor that our interest in the Concert is thereby diminished: to do so is to assume that the Concert's principal *raison d'être* was peace-maintenance and that our only interest in studying norms of international political behaviour is to determine how they enhance the prospects for peace. But peace and war are more often the byproducts of international activities rather than their proximate goals. To put it in its starkest form: the Concert is of interest primarily as a set of norms associated with the process of Great Power decision making at the international level; whether that process was a peaceful one is of enormous human import but comes second in the order of study.

Another way of making the same point might be to reintroduce the distinction, referred to earlier, between international order as process and international order as substance. The Concert of Europe was a conscious process of regulating Great Power behaviour by requiring that it should be conducted within the terms of the 'formal and common consent' formula. It was, in that sense, a contribution to order, in the sense of an agreed process, if not to the substantive goal of peace.

The main question that remains to be answered is, how long the Concert continued to function as a significant feature of international politics?

As we have so far identified the Concert of Europe closely with the congress system, there is the possibility that the Concert of Europe disappeared with the eclipse of the congress system. Most historians are agreed that the year 1822, in which the Congress of Verona was held, was the last episode in the history of the congress system, as there was no other congress held until 1856 and only one more after that in 1878. Does that mean that the Concert of Europe died a premature death in 1822? This would be a misreading of the situation because although the congress as an international diplomatic instrument disappeared from the scene for over thirty years, the powers did not abandon the practice of legitimising changes to the international order through the mechanism of international procedures, which usually took the form of international conferences.

These conferences bear witness to the continuing concern of the powers to modify the workings of the pure balance-of-power system by making it a cardinal principle that changes in the balance of power, or territorial adjustments likely to have consequences for the balance of power, must receive the formal sanction of the powers and must not occur as unilateral actions.

This clearly happened in the instances of Belgian and Greek independence. The separation of Belgium from Holland was the first major revision of the 1815 settlement and it was achieved by the common consent of the Concert meeting in conference and signing a joint document of guarantee. Similarly, Greece was recognised as an independent state by a European conference. An agreement on the international legal status of the maritime passage of the Bosphorus was likewise achieved in 1841. Once again, it should be made quite clear that there was no great unanimity of the powers on all these questions. Agreements, or compromises, were arrived at only after protracted negotiation. It would be quite wrong to conclude that during this period the European powers provided an outstanding example of harmony and good will. Nothing could be further from the truth. At the same time, they did see fit to adopt a procedure of international legitimisation of change and to moderate their rivalries in order to accommodate such a procedure. And it is important that this fact too should not be ignored. We should not belittle the Concert by mistakenly expecting too much of it in the first place. In the words of one theorist it was a 'practical' rather than a 'purposive' instrumentality. In these terms, it is misleading to regard the Concert as an expression of the 'collective interests and will of the powers'; rather it should more modestly be seen as 'a way of attempting more effectively to secure the conduct of international relations within the limits of the practices comprising the traditions of European international relations'.[32]

If the Concert survived beyond 1822, what then is its date of termination? This is, of course, of more than historical interest. Clearly, one's conception of the essential nature of the Concert must change depending on whether the terminal date is said to be 1822, 1848, 1856, 1878 or 1914. Hinsley is of the opinion that the Concert functioned until 1914 and was then destroyed. Holbraad, too, has traced the evolution of thought on the Concert as far as 1914. Langhorne discovers remnants of Concert diplomacy between 1912–14.[33] There is no reason to doubt that many diplomats and public figures still thought in terms of the Concert of Europe as late as 1914. But, given the principles that lay at the heart of the notion of the Concert of Europe, surely the terminal date must be placed much earlier? It will, therefore, be argued that as a diplomatic instrument having a significant effect on European international relations, the Concert of Europe lasted until the mid-1850s.

It has been suggested that the Concert of Europe was a substantial modification of the balance-of-power system in that, while the aims of the powers involved may have been largely unchanged, the diplomatic procedures they employed were novel, the most important of these being the practice of the international legitimisation of change. Viewed in this light, the pivotal episode in the disappearance of the Concert must necessarily be the Crimean War.

That war was followed by a period, 1859–71, in which the territorial settlement of Vienna was drastically revised. Moreover, this was done unilaterally and by war. The new arrangements were not sanctioned by an international conference or congress. In other words, the map of Europe was redrawn by individual powers without any reference to the 'sense' of a European meeting. If Goodwin is correct in his assessment that 'it was not the Concert that made Europe a reality; rather the Concert was dependent upon it being so'[34] then Europe was no longer a reality after 1856 and the basis of the Concert had been removed. The Concert may, in a sense, have been the victim of its own success. It created an impression of stability which, paradoxically, may have encouraged states to believe that it could be tested without cost. As Jervis has suggested, 'the structure appeared stable enough to permit states to impose a greater strain on it'.[35]

The territorial readjustments being referred to are, of course, those associated with the unifications of Italy and Germany. The Vienna settlement had gone out of its way to ignore the principle of nationality in its territorial redistribution. The unifications scarcely represented the victory of that principle but rather represented the victory of the tactics of *Realpolitik*. In any case, they entailed a drastic revision of the Vienna arrangements, and by means of war. Further, at the end of each war, settlements were imposed in the traditional manner of European diplomacy. If in 1866 Bismarck imposed a lenient treaty upon Austria, this was solely out of regard for future Prussian strategy – out of respect for the balance of power, not out of respect for the Concert of Europe.

If we can agree that the Crimean war is the watershed that separates Concert from non-Concert diplomacy, there still remains some historical puzzle over the precise relationship between the war and the operations of the Concert. However, the apparent gulf between some interpretations may not be as wide as a superficial reading suggests or, at least, the theoretical implications of the contrast in interpretations may not be so very important.

Basically, the accounts of the Crimean war (seen in the context of the Concert) fall into two distinct categories, those that see the war as a product of the Concert's performance and those that see it as evidence of the Concert's breakdown. Hinsley subscribes to the former view: 'Far from being able to prevent the Crimean war, the notion of Europe that underlay the Concert was largely responsible for the fact that the war broke out.'[36] Seen in this light, the war was essentially an attempt to make Russia subscribe to Concert rules in the Near East. This is consistent with Holbraad's interpretation that 'a concert is concerned with maintaining and extending international order rather than with preserving peace'.[37]

Elrod and, to some extent, Schroeder, represent the alternative view. According to Elrod, 'statesmen in key positions failed to exercise self-restraint and refused to honour the rules of the Concert ... The Concert of Europe was the victim. To be sure, remnants of the techniques and assumptions of concert diplomacy endured, but the Concert System itself had been destroyed'.[38] Schroeder's analysis is similar. He contends that 'this destruction of the Concert is the main impact of the Crimean War on the European state system' and makes further elaboration: 'To say that the war destroyed the Concert is only to say that the Concert failed to prevent the war; its collapse was a consequence of its own failure.'[39]

The arguments are similar to those surrounding the outbreak of the First World War: was the war a product of the balance-of-power system or, alternatively, was the war produced by the failure of the balance mechanism? The problem here seems to be basically a definitional one in relation to the purpose of a balance system – whether its primary objective is the preservation of peace or whether it is the maintenance of 'equilibrium', or 'stability' or 'order'. If any of the latter, then it may be necessary to resort to war to secure the ends of the system. Accordingly, the 1914–18 war may be viewed as an attempt to preserve the European balance and, as such, as the vindication of the balance system: alternatively, it may be viewed as the failure of the system to prevent war and, as such, as its negation.

The ambivalence of the relationship between the Concert and the Crimean war is similar in kind. It hinges upon our conception of the Concert and whether, as noted above, we are to consider it a peace-preserving or an order-maintaining device. If the former, then the outbreak of the Crimean war may be taken as *prima facie* evidence of the Concert's failure: if the latter, then there is no inconsistency in arguing that the war was a demonstration of an effective Concert.

Whether we pronounce the patient to have died instantaneously in 1854 or to have hung on in a critical condition until the aftermath of the war, there seems no sound basis for doubting that the body of the Concert was truly cold by the late 1850s. Those who have argued that the Concert continued to function throughout the period of Italian and German unifications do so on grounds that are tenuous where they are not confused.

Albrecht-Carrié, for instance, sees the Concert enduring into the immediate pre-1914 period. Unfortunately, the reasons he provides for this assessment are less than convincing. Of the 1856–71 period, he has this to say:

> The concept of the community of Europe and its orderly functioning through the agency of the Concert was undeniably a reality during the two decades in question. *Nevertheless, the major changes which occurred in this time, the emergence of a united Italy and a similar outcome in Germany, essentially took place without the participation of all Europe . . .* The outcome, the appearance of a united Italy, was tacitly accepted by the rest of Europe *without the formality of her collective sanction.*[40]

The problem with such a formulation is that if we take Albrecht-Carrié's qualifications seriously, one wonders what, substantively, remains of the notion of the Concert, because the aspects that he sees as lacking during the 1856–71 period are precisely those features in terms of which the Concert has been defined. It is tempting, therefore, to point out, as a riposte to Albrecht-Carrié, Medlicott's caustic comment to the effect that 'there was a Concert of Europe when the action of the great powers was concerted, and when it was not there was not'.[41] If less subtle, this nonetheless seems closer to the point.

Albrecht-Carrié's attempts to project the Concert into the post-1870 period are equally strained and depend on an unacceptable degree of equivocation. He insists that the Concert operated after 1870 while

129

conceding that 'the period has a different tone from the preceding part of the century',[42] and later suggests that the alliance system of the pre-1914 era 'while not necessarily a denial of the Concert of Europe, nevertheless has a very different emphasis'.[43] Surely there comes a point where the argument that 'the essence remains even if all visible forms have changed' is detrimental to historical understanding? This is especially so when, as in this case, we are discussing a set of conventions regulating Great Power behaviour, because such conventions exist only to the extent that they are observed: they cannot be honoured in the breach. Accordingly, it can be argued that rather than pretend that the Concert endures but with a 'different tone' and a 'different emphasis', it is more revealing to speak of the Concert's demise and its replacement by something else.

The Concert of Europe, to the extent that it represented a distinctive contribution to international practice, did so by operating as a modification of the balance-of-power system. It can be contended from this that the Concert of Europe did not function in the latter decades of the nineteenth century for the reason that, far from representing a modification of the balance-of-power system, international politics during the period 1870–1914 reverted to the classic traditions of that system, without embellishment and refinement. It is to this period that we must now turn.

7 BALANCE WITHOUT CONCERT, 1856–1914

In the previous chapter, the case was presented that in the second half of the nineteenth century, international relations came to be characterised by a return to pure and simple balance-of-power calculations and this was made the basis of the view that the Concert of Europe ceased to function during this period as, in our definition, the Concert of Europe represented an important departure from balance-of-power policies. In this chapter an attempt will be made to try to demonstrate in what ways the European powers developed a style of international relations that differed appreciably from that which had existed in the first half of the nineteenth century.

This does not mean that there are no continuities between the two periods. On the contrary, there is a striking continuity in terms of the concern about domestic politics and fears of liberalism and nationalism, certainly on the part of the Habsburg and Prussian monarchies. Indeed, paradoxically, historians have suggested that the revolutionary redrawing of the Vienna settlement in mid-century was, itself, ultimately a conservative development with long-term reactionary implications. As suggested by two authors

> Few of them acknowledged that the old order between states had now been sacrificed to maintain the old order within states. Yet there can be no doubt that both Cavour and Bismarck intended the revolutionary characters of their foreign policies to conceal the conservative nature of their domestic policies. The triumph of monarchical conservatism over the forces of liberalism and its compromise with nationalism enabled it to survive into the later nineteenth century.[1]

This, in turn, sets the scene for the *Innenpolitik* school of analysis, which, especially in the context of late nineteenth-century Germany, sees foreign policy as an attempt by an essentially reactionary leadership to overcome domestic political problems. To this extent, at least one of the basic motivations of the Concert period – fear of radical/

131

revolutionary unrest – was to survive throughout the century but to express itself in foreign policies less compatible with the earlier Concert: domestic factors which had earlier sustained the Concert later became potent influences upon international rivalry both within and outside of Europe.

There is need for some caution about terminology. The title of this chapter should not be taken to suggest that there was a balance of power in Europe, in the sense of a distribution of equilibrium, throughout the 1856–1914 period. Manifestly, there were various distributions of power during that period, some more equal than others.[2] For instance, the post-1871 distribution was essentially different from that of 1856–70, if for no other reason than the emergence of a united and powerful Germany at the end of the Franco-Prussian war. Indeed, it is the emergence of Germany that has led historians, like Joll, to refer to a 'new' balance of power after 1870.[3] This can be further refined by distinguishing the loose alignments of the 1870s from the somewhat tighter Germano-centered groupings which emerged between 1879 and 1882.[4] Likewise, other analysts have perceived a further change in the distribution of power after 1900: for Hinsley, the system lapsed into disequilibrium at the turn of the century.[5]

The statement that international politics between the Crimean and 1914–18 wars were characterised by balance can, therefore, clearly not be interpreted as a claim that an unchanging or evenly apportioned distribution of power endured throughout this whole period. The statement relates to something more elementary than this, namely, to the characteristic mode of diplomatic behaviour of the states, and especially of the Great Powers, during this era. Moreover, from this perspective, although Europe experienced substantial war from 1856–71 and then substantial peace from 1871–1914, the argument of this chapter will be that there was an important continuity in the mode of Great Power behaviour such as to mark the international relations of the post-1856 years off from those of the first half of the nineteenth century. To put it in its most basic form, even if there was no noticeable change in the notions of international order that the states hoped to achieve, there was nonetheless a marked transition in relation to ideas about how that order could best be created or maintained, and that transition may best be described as the break-down of Concert diplomacy and the re-emergence of balance strategies.

Such a contention would by no means receive universal assent. Hinsley's position, for instance, appears at first sight to be dia-metrically opposed. He says of the post-1870 period:

It was not solely because of the balance of power, however, that the Powers now reverted to the greater self-restraint of the first half of the nineteenth century. They continued to subscribe to the principles on which a sense of the collectivity of the Powers, of the Concert of Europe, had been based in that earlier period. These principles had survived the recent wars: the continuing tacit acceptance of them was as much the basis of the wide acceptance of the new *status quo* and the common determination to keep the peace after 1871 as was the self-restraint induced by practical considerations arising from the balance of power, though the two factors buttressed each other.[6]

On closer reading, however, it becomes clear that Hinsley's argument for a modified Concert is intended to apply only to the 1870s and, consequently, only to a small portion of our 1856–1914 framework. It none the less serves as a useful reminder that Concert sentiments did endure after 1871, as did the practice of summoning conferences. At the same time, it must also be stressed that this continuity was increasingly overshadowed by a changed, and more sombre, mood.

This has been cogently expressed by M. S. Anderson:

> This atmosphere of intensified international competition . . . meant the end of the concert of Europe as an idea with any effective influence on statesmen. Already weakened by the events of the 1850s and 1860s . . . it had by the 1880s become little more than a phantom, a concept to which lip-service might still sometimes be paid but to which no leader of any state any longer owed a serious allegiance . . . It was impossible to pretend after 1871 that a France and Germany divided by the unhealed sore of Alsace–Lorraine could ever have, at bottom, common objects, at least in Europe. It was difficult to claim, from the 1880s or 1890s onwards, that Russia and the Habsburg Empire, increasingly likely to be divided by conflicting ambitions in the Balkans or Russia and Britain, clearly separated by bitter rivalries in Persia and the Far East, were in a much better position. The dominant characteristic of the diplomacy of the generation which began in the 1870s was the emergence of alliances which divided the major European powers into often competing groups of a closeness and permanence hitherto unknown.[7]

What this seems to describe is, in Gulick's terminology, a reversion from the 'coalition equilibrium' of the early part of the century to a system predicated upon a competitive alliance equilibrium: order is to be sustained less by adherence to agreed Great Power managerial principles and more by unilateral pursuit of a favourable distribution of power. The latter is not a foundation upon which concert diplomacy can successfully be built.

We have seen that at least as late as the Crimean war of 1854, the major European powers showed an inclination to have revisions of the territorial status quo legitimised by some sort of international instrument. However, during the course of the 1850s and 1860s, the map of Europe was radically redrawn without any reference to a European consensus and without the sanction of a multilateral instrument.

From one perspective, it is possible to argue that the fact that this revision was carried out at all was the result of a profound, if temporary, change in the European balance of power. The revolutions of 1848 had undermined any remaining vestiges of the Holy Alliance of the three Eastern states, Russia, Prussia and Austria, and of their capacity to act as a conservative check on developments of a revolutionary or nationalistic nature. Metternich had disappeared from the European scene and Austria no longer functioned as the policeman of Europe. The temporary eclipse of the conservative Eastern powers from their position as arbiter of the fate of Europe was re-emphasised by the impact of the Crimean war on Russia. That war directed Russia's energies into a period of internal reconstruction and during that time, it was less prepared to act as a guardian of the European settlement. The result of all this was that for a short period, the fate of Europe lay mainly in the hands of Louis Napoleon, the new French emperor, who was not averse to territorial revision. It was during those few years of what appeared to be French primacy that the new states of Germany and Italy appeared. As A. J. P. Taylor has expressed this point, 'If Russia was indeed the tyrant of Europe, then the Crimean war was a war of liberation. This liberation delivered Europe first into the hands of Napoleon III then into those of Bismarck.'[8]

Accordingly, the revision of the 1815 settlement that occurred after the middle of the nineteenth century can be explained in terms of the changing distribution of power between those states dedicated to the preservation of the status quo and those prepared to accept change. The claim that after the Crimean war, European international relations returned to the balance-of-power system, asserts more than that there was a change in the distribution of power; additionally, it directs attention to the newly-found autonomy of the states within the European system. There was an increasing feeling that the destiny of each state lay in its own hands rather than in a Concert, and that a state's interests could best be achieved by reliance on its own efforts and energies rather than by reliance on international procedures. The most evident sign that such a change was in fact taking place is, as Hinsley has argued, the return to precise military alliances, the primary purpose of which was to secure the neutrality or the assistance of another power in a projected war. That the powers should have returned to such alliance systems *after* 1870, can be explained largely by the success of such alliances and understandings during the wars that made possible the unified states of Italy and Germany. In these various pacts and alliances, there is a radical departure from the international-conference approach of the first half of the century to one based explicitly on unilateral redistribution of territories and on the engineering of favourable international alignments in order to secure such redistributions. In other words, the ultimate sanction of a territorial change was no longer the voice of the Concert of Europe but rather whether or not there existed a margin of power sufficiently effective to enforce such a redistribution.

The lessons learned by the European statesmen from the experience of the 1850s and 1860s, during which the new states of Italy and Germany made their appearance, were not lost on the post-1870 period. There was, however, to be one important change. The alliances after 1870 were without exception defensive whereas the earlier ones had been offensive. But this change should not conceal a fundamental point of similarity, which was, that the powers still thought that their interests could best be enhanced by bilateral or trilateral alliances rather than by Europe acting in concert. That there was a change from the offensive alliance to the defensive can, in fact, be readily explained by the changed nature of the post–1870 situation. If until the achievement of a German state, Bismarck had been essentially revisionist as far as the European settlement was concerned, after 1870 his diplomacy was aimed at preservation of the newly established status quo. 'Immobility' and 'restraint' were the key objectives of this policy.[9] The defensive alliance was a device appropriate to this more conservative period.

It requires no special insight to realise that balance-of-power principles underlay most of the provisions of these alliances of the last quarter of the century. Significantly, the initiative for the new alliances came from Berlin. Bismarck's fundamental objective was to secure agreements with both Austria and Russia. One was necessary with Austria because their interests seemed to overlap, as both Germany and Austria were central European powers. He needed an alliance with Russia for two reasons. One was to act as a restraining influence on both Russia and Austria and so prevent a clash of these powers in the Balkans. More importantly, if Russia was ignored by Berlin, the chances were that the Austro-German alliance would produce a counterweight in the shape of some agreement between Russia and France. It was to prevent such an eventuality that Bismarck signed his Reinsurance Treaty with Russia. This treaty lapsed in 1890, the year in which Bismarck was dismissed from office and his successor did not believe in taking the same precautions. Within a year or two, Russia and France had entered into negotiations which produced their alliance of 1894, thus presenting Germany with the nightmare which Bismarck had sought to prevent – that of a potential war on two fronts. Europe had therefore split up into two camps: Germany, Austria and Italy, on the one hand, and Russia and France on the other. Britain remained aloof from either grouping. In every sense, this was the classical balance-of-power situation.

It was an age dominated by balance-of-power considerations in yet another sense and this was in the relationship between Europe and the outside world. There are various aspects of this interrelationship that deserve attention: European sources of the imperialist expansion of the powers; extra-European developments as a limiting factor on diplomacy within Europe; and the changing status of Europe as a whole within the global framework. In each aspect, the powers were motivated essentially by calculations deriving from balance-of-power principles rather than from concern with a Concert of Europe.

Most strikingly there was the general European expansion into Africa and Asia in the last quarter of the nineteenth century. It has been the contention of many historians that this development can be adequately explained by reference to the internal balance of the European state system. It is a common characteristic of such explanations that they emphasise the importance of the 'official mind of imperialism' – that is, they see the European governments as positive actors not, as Hobson and Lenin would have it, as mere tools in the hands of some sectional or class interest. Moreover, the European governments, according to this perspective, calculated almost exclusively in terms of national strategy – of preserving or destroying the particular balance that existed between the European powers.

A few examples would help to illustrate this approach. Within the international situation in Europe in the last two decades of the nineteenth century, it seemed that the alignment of the powers was becoming decreasingly flexible and that any attempt to alter the balance in Europe by tampering with the political map of Europe itself could have resulted in a general war. Given this stalemate in Europe, the powers played out their game in Africa and Asia. The classic demonstration of this relationship is perhaps to be found in the partition of Africa. According to this interpretation, the partition was sparked by the somewhat fortuitous British occupation of Egypt in 1882, the consequences of which were to be felt throughout the length of the continent as the powers bartered and bargained for their shares in the territorial carve-up in which, in addition to Britain, the countries of France, Germany, Italy, Portugal and Belgium were the main participants.

The reason why Germany entered the race for colonial possessions has been explained in terms of this balance syndrome. While it has often been argued that, throughout the nineteenth century, Britain, by pursuing a policy of splendid isolation performed the role of the balancer in the European system, from another perspective it can be seen that Britain, far from being a balancing or stabilising element in the situation, was in fact the main destabilising factor. While Britain was not a direct threat to the European equilibrium in the sense of striving for a hegemonic empire within Europe, outside Europe the extent of the British Empire represented a gross imbalance that no other power could rival. It was in order to rectify this balance that Germany, too, sought her place in the sun.

Latterly, however, this interpretation has found less favour with historians who have tended to emphasise the domestic roots of German colonial policy, rather than its source in European diplomacy, at least during the Bismarckian period if not subsequently.[10] Colonial policy, in these terms, had its origins in the quest for domestic, rather than European, equilibrium.

On the other hand, it was a German move in China that was to precipitate in 1898 the scramble for concessions in that country. Germany secured a lease of the Chinese port of Kiaochow and within the year Russia, Britain and France had secured similar concessions. Lord Salisbury the British Prime Minister justified the British acquisition of the lease of Wei hai wei as a response to the Russian lease of Port Arthur, which, he said, 'had materially altered the balance of power'.

That the colonial expansion of the period was related to the European balance, but in the reverse direction, is also suggested by the nature of Anglo-Russian rivalry in Central Asia throughout the nineteenth century. The British in India, in pursuit of their forward policy, had continually pushed outward the northwest frontier, even fighting wars in Afghanistan to counter what was believed to be a Russian threat to India. Simultaneously, the Tsar of Russia had in the course of the 1850s and 1860s enclosed vast areas of Central Asia within the Russian Empire. By the end of the century, the two empires were separated only by a grey area, Persia and Afghanistan, in which the two empires vied with each other to secure political and economic control. In 1907, however, Britain and Russia signed their 'entente', calling a truce in their rivalry in Persia. It is apparent that their reason for doing so was their common need to contain Germany within

137

Europe. In other words, the imperial expansion of Europe in Asia was not only inspired by the dictates of the European balance but was also limited by such considerations. After a century of rivalry in Asia, Britain and Russia came to terms when they realised that their common fear of Germany was stronger than their mutual fear of each other.

The third element in this interrelationship is the decreasing stature of Europe in relation to other emerging Great Powers on the international scene, or, to express the same point slightly differently, the extension or globalisation of the European balance system. Basically the thesis is as follows, as one writer has expressed it.

> As the German attempts in 1914 and 1939 to break through into the ranks of the world powers were to show, Bismarck had created a state sufficiently strong not only to dominate Europe but also to challenge and compete on terms of near-equality with the great extra-European powers . . . from about 1890, the overhauling of Europe by Russia and America . . . was resumed and intensified. Although its victories in 1870 and its rapid industrialisation had raised Germany to a new eminence, it was also, in view of the rising power of the United States and Russia, in a precarious position in the longer term, aware of its great potentialities but aware also that it had a definite time limit within which to exploit its superiority; and this fact imparted an ebullient quality to German policy from the accession of William II in 1888 to the days of Hitler.[11]

In other words, the German attempts to establish hegemony in 1914 and 1939 were more than repeat examples of the numerous historical instances of attempts to achieve preponderance within Europe – they were more than the linear descendants of the exploits of Louis XIV and of Napoleon. In what way did they differ? They differed in that for Germany, in the two world wars, the acquisition of European hegemony was but a stepping-stone to playing an influential role in a future system dominated by large global empires – Britain, Russia, America and Germany. This is the underlying thesis of Fritz Fischer's controversial book on Germany's war aims in the First World War[12] where Fischer seeks to establish that Germany's leaders were influenced by such ideas and sought to create an empire based on Europe and Africa because they saw the future no longer in terms of the old European system of states but in terms of a new system of world states. The Far Eastern crisis at the turn of the century was instructive in this sense that the European Concert was eroded by the activities of the new powers, so much so that it has been suggested that 'the European catastrophe was brought appreciably nearer by the consequences of this meeting between the Concert and newer forces which it could not control'.[13]

In less grandiose terms, there is an obvious sense in which extra-European powers were being called upon to function as adjuncts of a European system that was no longer, as hitherto, sufficient unto itself. This was to be demonstrated most palpably by the American intervention in the 1914–18 war but there were harbingers of this trend in existence before the outbreak of the First World War. Notably, in 1902, Britain called upon the services of Japan to consolidate the former's global position because of the increasing difficulty experienced by Britain of serving as counterpoise to Germany within Europe while also pursuing imperial objectives in the Far East. As has been said elsewhere of the Anglo-Japanese alliance, 'a member of the inner circle of European Great Powers was calling on an Asian state to join the international system in order to redress an imbalance of power at the core of that system'.[14] This step revealed the inappropriateness of 'splendid isolation' in an environment in which the alliance, and no longer the Concert, was the key element of security.[15]

It would be inappropriate at this stage to consider in a serious fashion the origins of the First World War. The literature on this issue is vast and the interpretations are manifold. Some concentrate upon the dynamics of the July crisis and account for the war in terms of a failure of diplomatic management; some stress the global dimensions of Great Power rivalry, and the naval competition between Germany and Great Britain in particular; some dwell upon the European origins of the conflict deriving from the effects of the alliance systems; some look to the longer-term breakdown of the European balance of power which flowed from the new German power established in 1871; others see the war as the inevitable nemesis for the repressive old order that had endured since 1815 but was increasingly unable to come to terms with the new political forces unleashed by industrialisation and rapid economic change.[16] Within these varying interpretations, concentration upon the balance of power is widespread. Geiss, for example, sums up simply in claiming that 'German *Weltpolitik*, the containment policy of the Entente and Germany's refusal to be contained made war inevitable.'[17] Other historians consider diplomacy within Europe to be the decisive source of the war but insist that the style of that diplomacy between 1907 and 1914 itself bore the imprint of the imperialist rivalry of the previous two decades. The mood of realism which prevailed amongst European cabinets had been encouraged by the competitive and bellicose spirit of extra-European confrontation.[18]

The first notion that should be discarded is that the war flowed inevitably from the alliances alone. There is a tendency, having described the European alignments of the 1880s and 1890s – Germany,

Italy and Austria against Russia and France – to read them forward into 1914 and to cite them as the main cause of the war. While this is not entirely without foundation, it suggests a view of international history which is too superficial. The opposing alliances were in no sense rigid unshakeable blocs. The Moroccan crises of 1905 and 1911 and the various Balkan crises of the pre-war period showed that there was sufficient flexibility within these alliances if the statesmen wanted to make use of it. Of these original alliance systems, Italy of course was to defect from the Austro-German camp. Even after the signing of the Anglo-French and Anglo-Russian ententes, there was no guarantee that Britain would enter any war on the side of France and Russia, even if contingency military planning with France was undertaken. Indeed, it seems clear that German calculations were predicated on a belief that Britain would remain neutral, a belief that Britain did little to shake.

Far from the alliances presenting rigid blocs, there were numerous examples of contacts and negotiations cutting across these align-ments. On occasions, France and Germany made common cause in Africa against Britain. Likewise, albeit for her own ends, Germany encouraged, and to some extent was an accomplice of, Russian involvement in the Far East. There were also several attempts, especially in the 1898–1901 period, to start serious negotiations between Germany and Britain because in many respects British and German interests conflicted less seriously than did those of Britain on the one hand, and France and Russia on the other.

As yet another example of the lack of rigidity of the alliances, it has been argued that the Franco-Russian alliance of 1894 was intended not to cement a new European alignment but to restore an old one, in that both states were looking to the past rather than to the future. As A. J. P. Taylor has contended 'each power was still looking over its shoulder. The Russians hoped that the entente would lead Germany to renew the Reinsurance Treaty, the French that it would lead Great Britain to compromise in the Egyptian question.'[19]

Certainly, the alliances did divide Europe into the two core camps that were to fight the war. But it would be too simplistic to accuse them of causing the First World War. The alliances nonetheless provided the working context for the diplomacy of the age:

> the existence of the alliance system and of the less formal *ententes* provided the framework within which the diplomacy of the pre-war years was conducted. It raised expectations about the behaviour of other governments which conditioned the foreign policies and the military plans of the major countries of Europe. And even when the

alliances did not provide the immediate diplomatic support for which
the governments were hoping, this sometimes made the participants
all the more anxious to ensure that the alliance would function more
effectively next time.[20]

Perhaps more important than the original Austro-German alliance
of 1879 was the particular turn that Austro-German relations were to
take in 1906. The German chief of staff, Schlieffen, who had drawn up
a German war plan in the event of a war on two fronts, had thereby
antagonised Austria, first by refusing to coordinate plans with her
and, secondly, because his plan of military operations concentrated on
the west first and only then on the east. That is to say that Schlieffen's
plan was for a quick knock-out blow against France after which
German troops would be transferred to the eastern front. But given
that Austria's collision was likely to be with Russia, this scarcely met
the order of Austrian priorities. Schlieffen's successor, Moltke, set out
in 1906 to repair the damage with Austria and did so by making new
commitments to Austria in order to convince her of Germany's good
faith. By 1909 there is evidence that Moltke was practically encouraging Austria to believe that Germany would back her, even in a war
caused by Austrian provocation. Unfortunately, as various analysts
have pointed out, at the very moment that he was making commitments to Austria that increased the likelihood of war with Russia,
Moltke insisted that the war must be fought in accordance with
Schlieffen's prescription – that is, that it must start with a German
attack on France. In their insistence upon fighting the war in this way,
the military planners ensured that Germany took the initiative in
declaring war on Russia and France and that she invaded Belgium. In
other words, Germany put beyond question the fact that an Austro-
Russian war would be a European war.

Another way of looking at the First World War is to approach it from
the perspective of the long-term interests of Russia and Austria in the
Balkans that were to provide the immediate occasion for the war. To a
certain extent, Europe had preserved the peace by channelling off its
inner tensions into overseas expansion. By the first decade of the
twentieth century, however, Europe began once again to turn in upon
itself. This indicated that the Balkans would be the most likely scene of
conflict.

Austria had seen her options as to possible spheres of influence
steadily foreclosed. The war against Cavour and Louis Napoleon in 1859
had served notice that Italy would no longer be Austria's own preserve
and with the achievement of Italian unification, Austria was largely
excluded from expansion in a south-westerly direction. The same was

to happen in the north. Her defeat by Prussia in 1866 was a signal that Austria would no longer be the preponderant power in Germany. The smaller states of Germany now fell under the sway of Prussia. All that remained was expansion in the direction of the south-east, towards the Balkans, and it was in this direction that Austria was attracted steadily during the late nineteenth and early twentieth centuries.

All might have been well had Russia not made the same decision at the same time. Russian interest in the Eastern question and in securing parts of the disintegrating Ottoman Empire dates back at least to the eighteenth century. However, for the last quarter of the nineteenth century, after being checked in her ambition for a greater Bulgaria by the Congress of Berlin, which ended the Balkan crisis of 1877–8, Russia temporarily shifted the focus of her interest away from this area. The atmosphere for expansion appeared more congenial in Central Asia and in the Far East. However, developments in Europe led Britain and Russia to sign a truce on the Central Asian question in 1907. And, similarly, Russia's humiliating defeat at the hands of Japan, in 1905, foreclosed the Far East as a possible area for Russian expansion at this time. Like Austria, Russia found that her energies were coming increasingly to be concentrated upon the Balkan region. In the end, this was to spell disaster.

The specific question of culpability for the outbreak of the First World War need not detain us here. There is an obvious sense in which Germany's potential strength was disruptive of the European equilibrium but we should be hesitant in proceeding to adduce culpability from this fact alone. It is a perennial feature of international history, and of the structure of conflicts more generally, that the rising power or challenger must seem to be the aggressor state or the disruptive element: such is an inevitable accompaniment of the cyclical rise and fall of states. In consequence, as Germany sought to find her place in an international order in which Britain had hitherto been *primus inter pares*, the impression was created that Germany's *Weltpolitik* was undermining the stability of the system. However, unless the pre-existing order had some special legitimacy associated with it, it is difficult to see how the intrusion of Germany into that structure, by itself renders her culpable.

There may well be a parallel between Germany's challenge to the *Pax Britannica* at the turn of the century and the Soviet challenge, from the 1960s onwards, to the *Pax Americana*. In this latter case, it was the Soviet Union which was the late arrival in terms of global military capacity and in that sense, it must appear that the Soviet attempt to secure her 'place in the sun' is 'destabilising' and 'threatening'. This is,

however, no more than to say that the 'first comer' stands in possession of rights that the aspirant must later challenge and from this
perspective it would seem misleading to confuse a moral situation –
culpability – with a chronological one – change.

Whatever the relationship between the alliances, as the characteristic instrument of the period, and the *outbreak* of the war, there can be
no denying that the alliance structure had a significant impact on its
course. Indeed, if many of the military plans were based on short-war
assumptions, it is perhaps not too much to claim that it was the
alliance system which ensured that a long war of attrition was the most
likely outcome. This in turn created the postwar scene for revolutionary developments in the map of Eastern Europe, as well as for the
emergence of new centres of power, if not for a transformation in the
very nature of state power itself:

> Thus, the alliance system itself virtually guaranteed that the war
> would *not* be swiftly decided, and meant in turn that victory in this
> lengthy duel would go – as in the great coalition wars of the
> eighteenth century – to the side whose combination of both military/
> naval *and* financial/industrial/technological resources was the
> greatest.[21]

It has been the argument of this chapter that international relations
in the 1856–1914 period were – in contrast to the years 1815–54 –
characterised by balance-of-power mechanisms rather than by concert
norms. The real problem lies in trying to explain why this should have
been so. In this context, the immediate dilemma emanates from our
inability to disentangle the alliances as the *source* of the heightened
insecurity of the pre-war generation – and thus as the factor that lent
the period its characteristic mood – from the alliances as a *symptom* of
insecurity and therefore as mere indications of more profound processes of change. Just as we earlier pondered whether the concert
created the peace or simply mirrored it, we are now bemused by the
choice as to whether the balance tactics created the tension, or the
tension demanded the tactics.

Presumably, the relationship is symbiotic, which is a trivial observation, but from it we might make the more important deduction that
moods of international politics, and the characteristic modes of statecraft associated with them, tend to be self-reinforcing, at least in the
short term. Expectations of a concert approach to international problems tend to produce conditions in which a concert can function with
some degree of success: alternatively, expectations of a purely competitive approach tend to ensure that this is the most that the system can
achieve.

One final point needs to be made. If the Concert of Europe seems in hindsight to have fused the twin elements of Great Power tutelage of the international order and of international diplomatic machinery, the period 1856–1914 witnessed once again the bifurcation of these two themes of modern international history. A balance-of-power system is, *de facto*, one in which the major powers have special rights and privileges, and what is interesting about this period, as compared with the earlier part of the century, is that there was little attempt to introduce additional diplomatic norms or conventions over and above the basic rules that a balance system itself prescribes. The hierarchy of power stood out, unsoftened by moderating norms of conduct amongst the Great Powers.

This does not mean that the late nineteenth century was devoid of efforts to ameliorate the practices by means of which states conducted their diplomacy: the attempts to institute some form of arbitration apparatus, which was perhaps the characteristic avenue of exploration of the age, would belie such a statement, as would the international gatherings at The Hague. Nevertheless, these efforts were little more than a faint descant in a diplomatic melody dominated by another mood. While it makes some kind of sense to regard the concert as a fusion of utopian and realist elements, in the latter half of the century the utopian pursuit of peace is a story of its own, largely divorced from the manner in which the hierarchy of states went about its daily task of creating international order.

8 CONCERT WITHOUT BALANCE, 1918–1939

In grossly simplified terms, we might describe the historical periods so far considered in the following way. From 1815 to 1854 there was a stable distribution of power upon which the powers were able to base a successful concert; whereas from 1856 to 1914, while there may well have been periods of equilibrium, the powers were unable to operate a system in which concert principles played any significant part. From this perspective, the period 1918–39 represents a third distinctive form of 'international order' in the sense that its dominant feature was an attempt to operate a highly formalised and institutionalised concert system, namely the League of Nations, but, as there was a funda-mental disequilibrium within the system, the conditions for concert were not present and the actual practice of states bore little resem-blance to the concert principles formally enshrined in the League. In other words, the 1918–39 period may be viewed as having character-istics of both these former ages: like 1815–54 there was a collectivist aspiration and an attempt to introduce new diplomatic norms; like 1856–1914 the powers were thrown back upon their own individual resources and reverted, almost without exception, to traditional balance devices. We might say that as far as the 'heart' was concerned, the inter-war years shared the sentiments of concert diplomacy whilst the 'head' dictated a continuance of late-nineteenth-century balance strategies.

This is possibly to say no more than that the League, as the foremost instrument of the inter-war period, was the beneficiary of a mixed legacy, inheriting both the concert experience of the previous century and also the problem created in the international balance mechanism. As Armstrong has suggested, 'the League probably owed less to the Concert itself than it did to the breakdown of the balance of power which had underpinned the Concert until the emergence of modern Germany'.[1]

The First World War and the settlement that ended it were to have a profound influence on subsequent international relations. Perhaps most obviously, the Versailles treaty defined the structure of international politics in the inter-war period. The war saw the destruction of Europe's three major empires, the Russian, Austro–Hungarian and German. In place of the former Austro–Hungarian Empire, Europe saw the rebirth of several successor states, which greatly complicated the map of the continent. It was in the context of this new territorial distribution that international relations were to be conducted during the next two decades.

However, the consequences of the war were to be more far-reaching than this. In fact, it can be argued that many of the developments that are normally associated with the post–1945 period can more properly be seen to have had their origins in the war of 1914–18 and its immediate aftermath. This point can be made with reference to several aspects of contemporary international relations.

It is often claimed that one of the most salient characteristics of the post-1945 period has been the revolution in military technology. This in turn is said to have resulted in a pronounced decline in the utility of military force. Without minimising the impact of nuclear weapons on current strategic thought and on the political uses of war, there is some validity in the view that, if war can no longer be regarded as an appropriate instrument of political settlement, then the trend towards this point of view was already well established by 1918. The basic argument as it applies to nuclear weapons is that the consequences of nuclear war would far outweigh any possible benefits resulting from the war and that therefore military force is obsolete. Although the scale of magnitude is perhaps different, the First World War led to exactly the same conclusions. Whereas the Bismarckian wars of the nineteenth century had been short and efficient, the 1914–18 war, in terms of its territorial stagnation and its unprecedented loss of life, was to cast serious doubts on the efficacy of military power and on its appropriateness for settling political disputes: that partial erosion of the legitimacy of war which has characterised post-1945 attitudes began in 1918 rather than at Hiroshima.

A second revolution that is generally thought to have been triggered off by the Second World War is the independence movement in the Afro-Asian countries. Again, while as a matter of strict historical detail this is true, there seems to be at least some reason for arguing that several nationalist movements were given a major stimulus by the First World War. The principle of national self-determination was partly adhered to in Eastern Europe and this in itself pointed to the contradictions in denying its applicability outside Europe. To express the point in a wide historical perspective, if the movement for independence in the colonial territories was, in a sense, merely the obverse side of the decline of Europe and of the decline of the imperial Powers, then this decline, although concealed during the inter-war period, certainly dates from the First World War rather than commencing suddenly after the Second. It is true that Britain and France maintained even larger empires after 1918, with new acquisitions in the Middle East, but they were arguably less able to defend them and the security of their positions was more a reflection of the lack of challengers in the 1920s than of their own intrinsic strength.[2]

The First World War was to lead directly to another revolutionary transformation in world politics precipitated by the Russian Revolution of 1917. This suggests another way in which it is possible to argue that the historical creator of the present framework of international relations was the 1914–18 period rather than the aftermath of 1945: both the power-political and the ideological bases of Soviet–American hostility originated in the immediate revolutionary aftermath. The ideological Cold War had its roots in the opposing conceptions of international order put forward by Lenin and by President Wilson: the power-political antagonism between the two states had its origins in direct American military intervention against the Bolsheviks during the civil war within Russia. As Mayer has pointed out, one of the most momentous developments of the war was the simultaneous emergence of Washington and Petrograd as two rival centres of power, both of which momentarily abandoned the old diplomacy.[3] On the Soviet side, the Bolsheviks renounced the former Russian imperial objectives, especially Russian designs on Constantinople, and they published the secret wartime treaties signed with the allies. On the American side, Woodrow Wilson, too, came out against the old diplomacy and advocated its replacement by open treaties openly arrived at. This conflict between the old and the new diplomacy was to have important consequences for future international relations. It postulated two radically different conceptions of foreign-policy formulation. On the one hand, the old diplomacy clung to the idea that foreign policy was best made by professional diplomats behind closed doors and immune from national politics. As against this, the advocates of the new diplomacy argued that such a method had resulted in the 1914–18 war. To remedy this situation, foreign policy should be opened to the influence of public opinion. The argument held that just as increased democratisation of domestic politics had produced important economic and social reforms, so the foreign policies of democratic states could also improve as a result of popular participation and control. In effect, the contention was that unlike the officials of the foreign offices, the public at large would not tolerate aggressive policies. Stimulated by the Russian Revolution on the one side and President Wilson on the other, these ideas increased in influence during 1917–18 and begun to have a powerful effect on the war aims of the allies, culminating in the apparent allied acceptance of Wilson's fourteen points as the basis for a postwar settlement.

The war had thus established a new territorial balance of power, given a boost to anti-colonialist movements outside Europe and wrought changes in attitudes towards war and diplomacy. Most obviously, also, the 1914–18 war gave birth to the League of Nations, which concerns us because, as one historian has expressed it, 'for the first time in history an attempt was made to formalize in law the organization of international order'.[4]

Historically, the lineage of the League may be divided into three periods: first, an evolution from, and a reaction against, international practice in the nineteenth century; secondly, the experiences of the 1914–18 war itself; and thirdly, the particular international configuration that prevailed at the end of the war and provided the environment in which the Versailles treaty was signed and the League was set up.

Intellectually, the origins of the League were manifold. It is possible to trace back a strand of intellectual speculation about the problems of achieving peace almost to the beginning of the European state system itself. Although the various peace projects of the sixteenth, seventeenth and eighteenth centuries were in no sense direct precursors of the League of Nations, they do contain a rich body of philosophical writings that is very much relevant to the problems of maintaining peace between independent states and relevant also to the philosophical basis of any international organisation. It is also possible to distinguish the influence of mid-nineteenth-century liberalism, of the peace movement of the second half of the century, of international socialism, of the various peace societies that sprang up – especially in Britain and the United States – during the war years, and, unmistakably, the emerging Wilsonian ethos of international relations. However, if the intellectual origins of the League were partly the product of evolution, they were also partly the product of a revolution caused by the psychological crisis of the war.

The League was in a very specific sense a reaction to the World War of 1914–18. It must be remembered that with the exception of the few clinical wars of German and Italian unification in the middle of the century, the European powers had enjoyed almost a century of peace.

That is not to say that there were not many crises during the period and perhaps an unprecedented degree of rivalry and conflict between the powers outside of Europe. But at the same time, the 1914–18 war did come as a psychological shock to a generation brought up to think of peace as being the normal state of affairs. Additionally, while the few wars of the nineteenth century had been of short duration, the 1914–18 war, which many had expected to be over by Christmas of 1914, continued until 1918 with casualties at unprecedented levels. It is small wonder that such a war had a powerful and revolutionary effect on statesmen at the time. As has been said

> The Great War . . . by its destructiveness, by its overthrow of all that had been regarded as stable in international politics, compelled men to seek for new and surer terms of organisation. And at the same time, by the associated effort which the war called out for its own purposes, it provided working models for the peace time machinery of the future.[5]

Indeed, when we recall the extent of cooperation in the prosecution of the war, we might accept the verdict that 'the League to come was hardly a step forward. It was a measure of demobilisation in international organisation'.[6] As in 1815, the postwar basis of peace-time diplomacy was to be influenced by wartime precedents of coalition.

If the League was a reaction to the war in general, it was also more specifically a reaction to the international conditions that were believed to have brought it about. Statesmen singled out what they considered to be the main features of international life in the pre-war era and calculated that by eliminating these features peace could be ensured. No one expressed this point of view more vocally than the American President, Woodrow Wilson. His particular target was the morality of the old European diplomacy. If it is true that Americans in general shared a distaste for the methods and practices of European statecraft, Wilson was particularly obsessed with this great evil. It was a sentiment that he was often to repeat:

> It is plain that this war could have come only as it did, suddenly out of secret counsels without warning to the world . . . And the lesson which the shock of being taken by surprise in a matter so deeply vital to all the nations of the world has made poignantly clear is that the peace of the world must henceforth depend upon a new and more wholesome diplomacy.[7]

It was a view that regarded war as the product of the unscrupulous machinations of diplomats, untrammelled by democratic controls.

It is now time to turn to a more detailed analysis of the ideas and practices underlying the League itself. It must be remembered that the League was to be engaged in a whole range of managerial functions – dealing with economic issues, communications, transport, and health. It spawned also the International Labour Organisation. In terms of the subsequent history of decolonisation, a principal function of the League was carried out by its Mandates Commission – the arrangement devised by the League for the supervision of the colonial territories of the defeated powers. However, while these other functions were important, the following observations are confined to the central issue of the League as a peace-keeping institution.

Broadly speaking, the League of Nations may be regarded as a synthesis of three devices that had only partially been realised in the international diplomacy of the nineteenth and early twentieth centuries. These were:

(1) a permanent apparatus for regular conferences;
(2) a system of arbitration directed by a permanent judicial organ;
(3) a system of guarantees

The precise nature of the conference system established by the League is illustrative of the influence of the nineteenth century and of the felt need to improve on that earlier system. Basic features of the League approach were its permanent framework, its regularity of meetings and its approach towards universality. The Bismarckian wars had revealed the speed with which war could be launched in the age of the railway and in consequence the procedure for the summoning of conferences was in need of lubrication if a peace-keeping function was to be performed. Hence the framers of the covenant recognised the need for a secretariat and for fixed procedural rules. Again, while conferences had been a typical means of diplomacy during the nineteenth century, they were sporadic rather than regular; in the words of one historian, 'the medicine of Europe rather than its daily bread'.[8] Thus, the Concert of Europe ceased to function if the national interest of one of the powers demanded that it exercise a free hand: conferences disappeared from the international scene during the wars of Italian and German unification. No conference was summoned in 1914. The shortcomings of such a system the League sought to rectify by regularising the meetings of the Assembly and of the Council.

The institutional structure of the League reflects an uneasy compromise between two conceptions of its membership, a conflict produced by the historical development of the conference system. The nineteenth-century concert was composed essentially of the Great Powers. The reluctance of the powers to share their dominant position in the system was bolstered by wartime experience: if military cooperation during the 1914–18 war proved to be useful experience for future international organisation, it also strengthened the conception of the allies as the directors and executors of the international system, an attitude scarcely concealed at the Versailles conference. However, this elite ethos amongst the powers came into direct conflict with the Wilsonian ideal of self-determination and with any attempt to base the new international system on the moral force of world opinion. Hence the permanent Great Power membership of the Council, originally envisaged as the organ of the victorious powers, was diluted by the inclusion of elected members from amongst the smaller states and the Assembly gained some status as against the Council. The hierarchical concert was thus modified.

Implicit in this ideal of a permanent framework for discussion is the notion of open diplomacy. The preamble to the covenant required 'open, just and honourable' relations between nations, and Article 18 required all treaties to be registered with the League. It is not difficult to see in this an aversion from the alliance diplomacy of the pre-war generation and the high place that secret diplomacy was accorded in the assessments of the causes of tension leading to the war. Also, if Wilson's vision of the League as the tribunal of world opinion was to become operative such openness would be necessary: instigation of the international 'hue and cry' presupposed knowledge of developments in the system that were contrary to the ideals of the League and a threat to international security.

A second major element in the League complex was the apparatus of conciliation described in the convenant. The dual nature of this instrument reflected the two strands of its historical evolution. On the one hand there was to be the process of judicial arbitration by means of the Permanent Court of International Justice. Such a judicial organ had been striven for at The Hague conferences but they merely succeeded in establishing what has been described as a permanent framework for *ad hoc* tribunals.[9]

Disputes not submitted to judicial arbitration were to be presented to the Council, which had to endeavour to effect a settlement of the dispute. In this provision can be distinguished a lineage going back to the congress system and existing in a weaker form in the Concert of Europe whereby the major powers took it upon themselves to preserve the peace of Europe. However, such a blatant form of power politics was considered unacceptable by the exponents of the new diplomacy. The remains of a Great Power directorship of the European order lingered on, however, in the League Council with the qualification, as Inis Claude has expressed it, that if the Council was a new edition of the Concert of Europe, it was at least a significantly revised edition.[10]

The third essential element incorporated in the League of Nations was a system of guarantees. The guarantee was no innovation of the twentieth century: the most notable example of a guarantee in the nineteenth century, the relevance of which was highlighted in 1914, was that accorded by the Powers to Belgian neutrality in 1831. It was also an instrument well known on the other side of the Atlantic, the home of the Monroe doctrine. It can be argued, however, that the guarantee embodied in the covenant was distinctive because of its attempt at universality: its essence was the preservation of the entire *status quo post bellum*. Thus, it has been said that 'the function envisaged for the League was ... to legitimise and stabilise a particular world settlement based upon victory'.[11] In so far as this is true, it is reminiscent of the purposes of the congress system following upon the 1815 Vienna settlement.

The point about this view is that it brings an important perspective to the study of the League of Nations. There is a temptation to regard the League as the almost inevitable outcome of the precedents, organisational precursors and theoretical frameworks of the nine-teenth century. As a corrective to this, it is important to stress the view of the League, implicit in the description of it as the stabiliser of the postwar situation, as the particular response to a specific historical situation. This view emphasises the role of such immediate factors as wartime experience, the prevailing condition of world opinion and the unique energies of the societies and personalities whose ideas helped to shape the covenant. Above all, it should be stressed that the covenant was no sacred document, delivered from on high, like the ten commandments. It was very much a political document and as such was a compromise between the various views of security held by the major powers. Whatever the League owed to earlier ideas about international organisation, it was given its distinctive character by the requirements of national interest as perceived in the specific con-ditions of 1918–19.

How are we to assess the nature of the League, given the attitude with which the powers approached it and the general spirit surround-ing the postwar settlement as a whole? In this context, it is difficult to avoid the conclusion that the League was a veneer underneath which traditional policies were pursued. Such a case can be made against America. Once the rhetoric surrounding the American intervention in the First World War is stripped away, one is left with the harsh reality that America became involved because it would have been contrary to her interests to have had Europe dominated by an expansionist German state. If the American decision to join the war effort did not come until 1917, it is nonetheless significant that it came at a point when Germany was probably closer to victory than at any other stage of the war. If we consider Europe in terms of the traditional balance-of-power system, it looks very much as if America was set to enter the game to take the place of one of the players, Russia, soon to be disabled by domestic turmoil from continuing with her role as a counterweight to Germany. Having thrown her weight into the balance at the crucial moment in order to prevent German predominance, America then reverted immediately to continental isolation. The wish gave birth to the belief that the balance once restored would remain in equilibrium. This failed to take account of the blunt fact that, just as her intervention had restored the European balance in 1918, so her refusal to play a permanent role in Europe was to leave the door open to a further challenge to this balance.

Not only did the United States not join the League but, in some respects, she sponsored agreements outside the context of the League which, by themselves, were perhaps further corrosive of the League's international standing. This was especially the case with the Washington Conference of 1921 which sought to establish a naval and political framework for the Pacific region.[12] Moreover, the unsettled condition of America's domestic political attitudes to the League must call into question the somewhat simplistic notion that, had the United States become a League member, the history of the inter-war period would have turned out otherwise. It is open to reasonable speculation that the balance of political opinion within the United States would have operated against a stronger American foreign policy even within the context of League membership.[13] Non-membership of the League was a symptom, not the cause, of America's uncertainty about her future international role.

France, to sketch out an argument that will be developed in detail below, was obsessed by fears for her own security and saw the League and the Versailles settlement solely in these terms. In a sense French statesmen were more realistic than their Anglo-Saxon counterparts. They realised that the postwar settlement rested on an elaborate fiction. The fiction was that France, after 1919, was the most powerful state in Europe. This was a fiction because the conditions that led to this situation were both artificial and impermanent. They rested on the artificial constraint of Germany through the Versailles provisions. They rested on the fact that these conditions had been imposed on

Germany, not by French power alone but additionally by British and American power. They rested on the temporary exclusion of the Soviet Union from the European scene in the aftermath of the revolution. Probably the French themselves appreciated the artificial nature of the postwar structure better than anyone. That is why they demanded that traditional balance-of-power considerations should be included in the settlement.

Realising that the postwar situation was artificial but realising also that France's security depended on this artificial situation being preserved, France saw the main function of the League of Nations as being the maintenance of the territorial *status quo* established at Versailles. Any form of change could only make this artificial situation less favourable to France. But already there were signs that this fiction could not persist. If France's position depended on being underwritten by Britain and America, then unfortunately these two countries soon made it clear that they would not underwrite the European settlement. America did not ratify the covenant and so did not join the League of Nations.

If the Versailles settlement was in large measure the embodiment of traditional power-objectives on the part of the European states, then this infected also the League of Nations, which came to appear as the instrument for maintaining this settlement. The reason for this was that the League covenant was written into the peace treaties themselves. Even more importantly, the League was an instrument in the hands of the victors and in the hands of those victors most dedicated to security through traditional balance practices. The United States, from which the original idealistic impulse had come, as we have seen, did not become a member of the League. Germany was not to be permitted to join until 1926 when she had demonstrated, through her adherence to the disarmament and reparations clauses of the settlement, that she was fit to be a member of such an international organisation. The Soviet Union and the League viewed each other with mutual distrust and hostility until 1934. In short, the League as an international instrument fell into the hands of France and Britain. Britain, reluctant to undertake enforcement tasks which the existence of the Royal Navy was likely to devolve upon her, was slightly embarrassed by the League and sought to play it down. France, meanwhile, saw it as the only means of preserving the artificial European *status quo* upon which her security depended. If this was the concert, then it was indeed a concert of the most minimal kind.

From what has been said so far, it is clear that the League failed to establish itself as an organisation capable of rising above the individual national interests of the principal member states. It is this fact which forms the basis of E. H. Carr's critique of the League and of the Versailles settlement.[14] The point emerges repeatedly in Carr's discussion of the inter-war period. As he sharply commented of the collective security principles of the League, 'these supposedly absolute and universal principles were not principles at all, but the unconscious reflections of national policy based on a particular interpretation of national interest at a particular time'.[15] In other words, what was described as collective security was little other than the placing of predominant power in the hands of the victor states and thus ensuring that there could be no challenge to the status quo. If we accept this point of view, then it leads to the conclusion that the failure of the League of Nations was not so much the failure of collective security as the failure of those powers entrusted with the monopoly of power in the postwar situation to maintain their temporary preponderance. To quote again from E. H. Carr, who makes a similar point very well, 'it is necessary to dispel the illusion that the policy of these states which are broadly speaking satisfied with the status quo and whose watchword is security is somehow less concerned with power than the policy of the dissatisfied states'.[16] The League did not banish power considerations from international politics only to see them revived in the form of renewed Japanese, Italian and German expansion. Rather, power was basic to the very formation of the League. If a change did occur from the 1920s to the 1930s then it was not a change to power politics; rather it was a change with respect to which states were able successfully to exploit the balance of power – from the status quo to the revisionist states.

It may be appropriate at this stage to draw attention to some of the striking parallels and differences between the settlement of 1815 and that of 1919. Both settlements had been necessitated by the need to repair a European continent severely disrupted by harsh and protracted war. Both witnessed important redrawings of the map of Europe in accordance with political and strategic requirements of security. But while both settlements redrew the map of Europe in accordance with traditional security dictates, at the same time they gave expression to a reaction against the diplomacy that had caused the preceding war. The 1815 settlement gave birth to the congress system whilst the 1919 settlement gave birth to the League of Nations. Each, in its own fashion, was an important experiment in reordering the basic techniques for the management of international relations. While there are these similarities between the two settlements, there is at least one important contrast: that whereas the Vienna settlement was to last, with the exception of the revisions executed in the middle of the century, until 1914, the 1919 settlement did not last two decades. This has led one historian to observe, rather cynically, that in 1815 the framers of the settlement dealt with questions of power and preserved the peace for a century whilst in 1919 statesmen dealt with questions of justice and morality and kept the peace for less than twenty years. This comment is slightly misguided. As we have seen, the 1919 settlement in the final analysis was little more concerned with questions of justice and morality than was that of 1815. In fact, the primary considerations, international security and opposition to internal revolution, were largely the same both in 1815 and 1919.

What, then, explains the apparent success of the Vienna, and the apparent failure of the Versailles, settlement? There are probably several explanations that could be advanced but only one will be mentioned: whereas the 1815 peace left no major power dissatisfied, France having been largely reinstated as a member of the Great Power directorate by 1818, the 1919 settlement was considered to be intolerable by the vanquished Germany and from the very beginning there were appeals for revision of the treaty. How, in turn, this should be explained is another and an extremely difficult question. The following argument is largely an extension of that put forward by Mayer:[17] it hinges on the role of public opinion in the framing of the settlement. Perhaps, in 1815, the professional diplomats had greater freedom to draw up a treaty that was based solely on considerations of balance and security without the intrusion of popular demands for revenge and for the imposition of punitive conditions on the defeated party. It has been said of the Vienna settlement that it was negotiated 'in elegant and ceremonious privacy'.[18] This was not the case in 1919 when a whole host of domestic considerations, not least the need to appease popular political sentiments, impinged on the calculations of the peacemakers. If this appears too simple an explanation, then perhaps we should try to explain why a war-guilt clause was imposed on Germany in 1919 but no such stipulation on France in 1815, and it seems that one reason for this is that such symbolic gestures are designed for the consumption of public opinion. However, the emotional reaction against the war guilt clause was to play a large part in the undermining of the entire Versailles settlement. Perhaps, then, it is not too superficial to explain the relative success of the two settlements in terms of the ages that produced them – the age of aristocratic politics on the one hand and the age of emerging mass politics on the other.

Thus far we have discussed the general atmosphere surrounding the Versailles settlement and the inception of the League. How are we now to analyse the pattern of international order that emerged and developed during the inter-war years? It will be the argument of the remainder of this chapter that the postwar settlement was based on certain false assumptions, already alluded to in passing, and that these assumptions led to a 'schizophrenic' international order in which the policies of the powers were pursued at two quite distinct levels. At the one level, the powers participated in an elaborate myth. At the more profound level, the powers were very consciously aware of the underlying reality of the situation. The most fitting account of the inter-war period is, then, that during the 1920s the myth and the reality managed to coexist with each other whereas in the 1930s the myth was destroyed and only the reality remained.

What were the elements of the myth that permeated the international relations of the 1920s? They were several. First, as we have seen, the central myth was that France could by its own efforts maintain the European system in equilibrium. Ever since 1870, the central factor of European diplomacy had been the fragile balance between Germany and France. The decision of 1918 had reversed that of 1871 in as much as France was this time on the victorious side and regained the territories of Alsace and Lorraine. The desire for revenge that had been such a conspicuous element in France's outlook during the Third Republic from 1870 to 1914, appeared to have been satisfied. But, of course, whereas Prussia had defeated France in 1870 in a direct contest, France had only gained her revenge against Germany as part of a much wider coalition that also included Britain, Russia for a time and subsequently the United States. However, after 1919, the stability of the European balance was to depend on an assumption that France could, by herself, serve as a check and a counterweight to Germany. This was an assumption that, given the increasing discrepancy in industrial power between the two countries and the stagnation in France's population growth, was becoming increasingly unrealistic.

The second myth of the period followed on from the logic of the first: that a self-contained European balance of power still persisted. It had been demonstrated that even the joint efforts of all the European powers combined – Britain, France, Russia and Italy – were barely sufficient to hold Germany in check. In such a situation the traditional balance-of-power mechanism could no longer operate. Consequently, albeit for its own interests, the United States was coopted into the European system and served as an adjunct of the balance system. The defeat of Germany, the revolution in Russia and America's disinclination overtly to commit herself to Europe's long-term political and security arrangements, even while underwriting essential parts of the financial fabric, fostered the image that in 'an artificial way . . . it still seemed a Eurocentric world'.[19]

There was a third myth and that was that the maintenance of a preponderance of power in the hands of the victor powers was tantamount to an effective League of Nations. As long as France was dedicated to the *status quo* that provided her security and as long as France was the predominant military power on the continent – which in view of Germany's forced disarmament she was – no power could challenge the 1919 settlement. This was interpreted as indicating that the League of Nations was operating successfully to avoid war. Clearly, the optimism of the period of the 1920s was unfounded. It was the function of the League to produce peaceful settlement of disputes between states and it was apparent that the most serious disputes would arise with respect to revision of the 1919 treaties. The point is, of course, that there was no military challenge to the treaties in the 1920s because the revisionist powers – those left dissatisfied by the 1919 settlement – did not then have the military capacity to challenge the treaties. The test of the League came in the 1930s when disputes could be, and were, settled by military means. When this occurred the League failed abysmally for the simple reason that, if collective security depended on preponderance of power, those states that supported the League no longer possessed this margin of superiority.

The joint product of all these myths put together was the over-arching myth of the 1920s: the persisting belief that somehow states were living up to the ideals of the covenant and were no longer operating purely in terms of the old immoral power considerations. So powerful was this myth that an elaborate diplomatic framework was established to enshrine it. First, there was the machinery of the League itself. During the later 1920s, it experienced its most successful period as the talking-shop of the diplomatic community. It was fortunate that several of the leading figures of the times developed a regular habit of attending at Geneva and participating in the debates, the period of the so-called 'Geneva Spirit'. But if we were to be cynical we might point to the fact that this same period was to witness the League suffering from severe financial constraints, which perhaps indicated that although all the states saw the value in being members of the club, they were none too willing to pay their subscriptions. Perhaps ultimately the optimism about the League, and its eventual failure, were to be destructively related because the apparent success of the League seemed to belie the need for other tangible efforts to maintain security. The effect was to confuse the democracies with the result, as expressed elsewhere, that

158

'the existence of the League caused cabinets and foreign ministers to wobble between the "old" and the "new" diplomacy, usually securing the benefits of neither . . .'[20]

Apart from the League itself, there was during the 1920s an entire stream of diplomacy that was carried on at the level of mythology. There were the endless disarmament debates of the 1920s and early 1930s. Why should we consign them to the level of mythology? The very fact that the powers considered the time ripe for disarmament talks suggested that the basic problems of international security had been solved: whereas the course that the talks took, in practice, revealed only too clearly the context of extreme insecurity in which these discussions were taking place. The evidence for this is overwhelming. Each power saw the disarmament question in the light of the impact that it would have on its own defensive capacity. Each power came up with definitions of military power that would call for restraint of other parties but leave its own forces intact. In short, each of the powers could come up with the most sophisticated technical reasons for doing itself a good turn. Ultimately, the failure to achieve any progress provided the pretext for Germany's rejection of the limits on its own armed forces, set by Versailles, since she regarded the legitimacy of these restrictions as contingent upon disarmament by the other powers as well.

There were to be numerous other manifestations of diplomacy at the level of mythology during the 1920s. There was the Geneva Protocol of 1924, which was an attempt to strengthen the arbitration procedures of the League. Most conspicuous of all was the Kellogg pact of 1928, which was a solemn declaration by the states to refrain from using war as an instrument of policy. One need only contrast the ease with which all the states signed this document with the slow, grinding lack of progress on disarmament to appreciate where the true concerns of the powers lay. It is part of the conventional mythology that the 1920s were just beginning to show signs of fulfilment of these lofty ideals when circumstances unfortunately intervened to upset the happy course of events. The promise of the 1920s was lost because of the economic crisis of 1929 and the resurgence of militarism in Italy, Japan and Germany: the gradual realisation of the League ideals was suddenly, in 1931, checked by the Japanese takeover of Manchuria. Nothing of course, could be further from the truth. Such a view of the inter-war period can only be sustained by mistaking the mythology of the 1920s for the underlying reality. Moreover, there certainly was a level of reality that, as has been said, managed to coexist with the mythology for some years, but was in stark contrast to all the ideals and all the aspirations of the Geneva spirit and to all the claims of the creators of the League.

The change from the 1920s to the 1930s did not represent a transition from internationalism to conventional power politics. There was a change but that was not in the role of power so much as in the distribution of power. This brings us back to the original point that the inter-war period rested on an elaborate fiction. These various fictions ensured, from 1919, that the mythology of internationalism, peace and harmony would be supplemented by more realistic and practical measures. If the postwar structure rested on a fiction of security that produced the League discussions, disarmament talks, the Geneva Protocol and the Kellogg pact, then the underlying reality was one of insecurity that in turn was to produce a solid stratum of *Realpolitik* throughout both the 1920s and 1930s. While this stratum was concealed by the mythology in the 1920s, in the 1930s it was laid bare as the mythology was stripped away.

It is this underlying level of *Realpolitik* in the inter-war period that must now be considered. It can be done in three contexts:

(1) in the context of French security policy;
(2) in the context of Britain's attitude to France and to Germany;
(3) in the context of the Soviet Union's relations with Germany.

France's search for security was a prominent feature of the Versailles peace talks and of the entire postwar period and the reason why France became so concerned about her security was obvious enough. As we have seen, the settlement was based on an assumption that France could act as a counterweight to Germany, an assumption that was doubted by France herself. But unfortunately, to strengthen France's position against Germany, France was in fact offered not the tangible instruments of security but rather the promise of security that derived from the mythology of the period. France at Versailles sought to achieve certain very specific and very concrete objectives from the settlement. She sought to take the Rhineland away from Germany and so improve France's strategic position on her eastern border. This she was denied. She attempted to give the League of Nations some teeth by having that organisation set up an international military force, but again was unsuccessful. Finally she sought and was offered an Anglo-American guarantee of her eastern border only to see this guarantee lapse when the American Senate refused to ratify the Versailles treaty. Having failed in all these efforts, what did France receive by way of compensation? She received the same guarantee of security that was offered to all the states under this system – the guarantee of collective security as embodied in the League of Nations.

However, it was a collective security that had to depend for its enforcement, not – as the theory required – on an absolute preponderance of power, but on the power of Britain and France.

Faced with this situation, France quickly appreciated the hollowness of her own victory and proceeded to adopt traditional measures. She did this in various ways. First, she called for strict adherence by Germany to the Versailles clauses as one means of preventing a German revival. If the balance between France and Germany at this time was an artificial one, then for France's sake it must be kept artificial. France was, therefore, the great champion of rigid and strict enforcement of the most punitive clauses of the settlement and especially of its reparations clauses. In fact, it was this subject that was to give France the excuse she required in 1923 to invade the Ruhr. If the ostensible purpose of this exercise was to enforce the provisions of the peace treaty, the real reason was French determination to keep Germany down by any means, including display of military force.

There were other signs that under the façade of the League, France had reverted to traditional balance-of-power diplomacy. In 1921 she signed an alliance with Poland and then associated herself with the Little Entente – that grouping of Eastern European states that consisted of Czechoslovakia, Romania and Yugoslavia. An alliance in the east was the time-honoured French device for countering a threat from Germany. This pactomania has been described as a 'forlorn effort to conceal power relationships that they realized were unfavourable to them behind a thick foliage of paper guarantees'.[21] And the culminating example of traditional French tactics was to come in 1935 when France signed a pact with the Soviet Union. Here at last was the revival of the Franco–Russian entente that had been the feature of French foreign policy in the years preceding the First World War. In some ways it was only a shadow of that former alliance, as both signatories to the pact had strong ideological reservations about it. But the strategic situation that gave rise to it was precisely the same as that of 1894. To derive full advantage from it required, however, an eastern Locarno which France was unable to persuade the British to underwrite.[22]

If France, immediately after the Versailles settlement, reverted to traditional *Realpolitik* tactics, she was not alone in this. Britain, too, in her attitude towards France and Germany witnessed a revival of her traditional ambition to serve as the balancer for the European continent. In fact, the re-emergence of this British desire to act as a balancer sprang from the same origins as did the intellectual grounds

161

for appeasement. The emergence of these feelings can be followed in Martin Gilbert's study, *The Roots of Appeasement*, in which he traces the origins of appeasement from the British reaction to the First World War and to the Versailles settlement. There was a powerful section of British opinion that did not share the French inclination to impose a punitive treaty on Germany and thought that the Versailles treaty was overly severe. Appeasement was born then, as Gilbert shows, from a feeling that German demands for revision of the treaty were justified. This feeling increased with the publication by John Maynard Keynes of his *The Economic Consequences of the Peace* in which he argued against the severity of the reparations clauses of the treaty.

In the few years after 1919, Britain and France moved even further apart on the question of the Versailles settlement, France demanding strict adherence to its clauses but Britain, on the other hand, being prepared to allow controlled revision of the treaty. It would be wrong to imagine that the only motive of British policy was a moral reaction against Versailles. In fact, it seems clear that Britain was at this time not at all happy about French predominance in Europe, however artificial it might be, and was guided by her traditional objective of maintaining a balance on the continent. This could only be done by permitting a limited revival of German power. Clearly, on this crucial issue, Britain and France were diametrically opposed. But Britain was able on this occasion to have her way for the simple reason that France could not afford to antagonise her unduly. The great symbol of this British attempt to establish a more natural balance between Germany and France was the Locarno treaty of 1925, described by one historian as being 'fully in the old tradition of partial Great Power guarantees which the League system supposedly rejected'.[23] As a result of its provisions, Britain agreed to guarantee France's eastern frontier, and Germany undertook not to violate this frontier. This was one side of the bargain in which France's demands for security were met. The other side was the execution of the first stage of removal of foreign forces from the Rhineland. Again, the treaty was linked with Germany's admission to the League of Nations, which occurred in 1926. So, to this extent, it met Germany's demands for a revival of her international status. As guarantor of the treaty, it was clear that Britain was the architect of this diplomatic structure. The balance that came out of this bargain was characterised by a limited rebirth of German power and a limited decline in French power; this trend towards equilibrium was controlled and checked by Britain as the holder of the balance.

It is, of course, this view of British policy in the inter-war period that has led some to say that Britain contributed to the outbreak of war by failing to pursue this role of balancer to its logical conclusion. According to this argument, just as Britain had reacted in the 1920s against French preponderance by aiding the revival of Germany, so in the 1930s Britain should have reacted to the changing balance between Germany and France so as to prevent the emerging German preponderance.

Underlying the facade of the League, there was a reversion to typical diplomatic devices on the part of both France and Britain. Another conspicuous example of traditional power-tactics at this period is that provided by German–Soviet relations. It was one of the aims of the League of Nations to prevent the formation of rival international alignments and so a recurrence of the alliance patterns of the pre-1914 generation. In this aim, the League conspicuously failed. No sooner did it exclude the defeated Germany and Soviet Russia from the League as international outcasts, than these two powers came together and signed a treaty at Rapallo in 1922. In fact, as the Rapallo treaty was to demonstrate, German–Soviet relations were to provide the classic example of balance-of-power considerations. This can be seen in the Rapallo treaty itself. For both of the signatories, the treaty offered a way out of the diplomatic isolation in which they had been left as a result of the war and of the revolution. More particularly, Germany needed the Soviet Union in order to overcome the disarmament provisions of the Versailles treaty, as the Soviet Union during the 1920s was to become the main area in which Germany carried out military training and tests on her military equipment. From the Soviet point of view, alliance with Germany was welcomed because the Soviet nightmare was of a united capitalist offensive against the Soviet state. Given this fear, the only tactic available to her was to exploit such divisions as existed within the capitalist camp and, at this particular period, the main division was between the victors on the one hand and Germany on the other.

German–Soviet relations were to pass through several stages in the course of the two decades of the inter-war period and at each stage both powers were guided by their ambivalent attitude towards the western powers. For Germany's part, she had turned to the Soviet Union in 1922 to overcome her international isolation. What brought the partnership to an end was Hitler's rise to power in Germany. By this time, Germany had succeeded in wedging herself in between the West and the Soviet Union and in exploiting her geographical position by playing the one off against the other. How she managed to do so was a result largely of the ambiguous ideological standing of Hitler and of the Nazi movement in Germany. There is in fact a fairly close parallel between the role played by Nazism in German domestic affairs and that on the international scene. It can be argued that in both instances, by a deliberate tactic of confusing accepted political differentiations, Nazism pretended to defend the system as a pretext for in fact overthrowing it. Domestically, it adopted an ambiguous platform on social policy such as to appeal to left and to right, to the workers and to the industrialists. To the masses, Hitler promised a social revolution and at the same time one of Hitler's strongest appeals was as Germany's defender against communism. When Hitler came to power in 1933 both the radicals in his own party and the representatives of the old order in Germany thought that their voice would now be heard. Likewise, on the international scene, Germany made use of her ambiguous posture. She appealed to the Soviet Union as a fellow-outcast – one of the dissatisfied powers of Europe – and at the same time looked towards the west with her capitalist face, claiming to be the western bastion against communism. It is quite clear that many European statesmen, including Churchill, welcomed Hitler's accession to power for precisely the reason that it would check any expansion of communism into Europe.

If all the major European states were playing a fairly traditional power-game under the guise of internationalist rhetoric, the Soviet Union likewise was playing a traditional game under the rhetoric of international revolution. She came to terms with Germany to prevent capitalist encirclement of the Soviet state. But once the German danger revived under Hitler, the Soviet Union reverted to the historical tactic of the alliance with France. Also, having despised the League of Nations in its early years, as a direct consequence of the emergence of Hitler the Soviet Union joined the League and became one of its most loyal members.

There are many questions that can be asked about the inter-war period. Interest in the period can be expressed by asking why the League of Nations failed, why war broke out in Europe once again, or why there was a return to power politics in the 1930s. The question can be phrased in several different ways but basically it is the same question that is being asked. Although the details of the answers may differ, they all have a common origin in the picture of the international situation that has just been described.

The League failed to function in accordance with the ideal for the reason that it was directed towards the satisfaction of narrow national self-interests: by all the victors through the exclusion of Germany; by America, through turning her back on it; more fundamentally, by the antagonistic conceptions of it held by France and by Britain, and by their respective attempts to tailor the guarantee function of the League to these conceptions. There was, then, no return to power in the inter-war years for the simple reason that there had never been a departure from it. What then distinguishes the easy optimism of the 1920s from the tragedy of the 1930s? The answer lies not in a return to power politics but in the restoration of German power to limits more realistically aligned to its potential – in other words in the overthrow of the artificial balance of the 1920s.

The confusion has arisen as a result of the failure to distinguish a return to power from an alteration to the status quo of 1919. The subjugation of Germany was an intrinsic part of that status quo, which represented stability in postwar terms. Britain welcomed change within the system and assumed that change was compatible with the maintenance of stability. The facts of power however were such as to ensure that change would lead to instability, as Germany was potentially a stronger power than France. The problem can be illustrated as follows. The Locarno treaty has been described as an attempt to satisfy both French demands for security and German demands for revival. Given the limited sense in which Locarno permitted a German revival, this object was attained in 1925. However, in the long term, and with the dimensions of Hitler's revival of Germany, the problem was insoluble because French security and German revival were essentially incompatible.

The origins of the Second World War have been variously presented as either 'the culmination of a disintegration of the European order',[24] first manifested in 1914–18, or as a successful European recovery, destroyed by economic and social collapse and the rise of pernicious political forces.[25] If the latter, it still remains to be explained why the European structure was unable to resist the forces unleashed by depression. At base, this can be accounted for only by the unavailability of the coalitions that had been formed earlier against Napoleon or against imperial Germany.[26] Key elements in the traditional equilibrium were no longer present and the status quo was threatened from various quarters. Britain's halting efforts to keep variously Japan, and then Italy, available as potential allies had the unfortunate effect of making all resistance to revisionism half-hearted at best.

So the fundamental fact of the inter-war period was the latent power of Germany. This taught the world an important diplomatic lesson – that if Germany could not be contained by treaty provisions, then she must be contained by more drastic means. It was a lesson which was to lead, ultimately, if not in immediate intention, to the division of Germany after 1945.

In conclusion, the concert that functioned during the inter-war period was a defective one, in terms both of its restrictive membership and its operative norms. Its membership was a reduced one, above all because of the American defection, but also because of the 'exclusivist' tendency within the League's original recruitment drive.[27] Similarly, the conspicuous divergence of opinion between the major powers as to the norms of conduct on which the League was to be based resulted in an insufficient consensus upon which to base a working concert system.

It was pointed out above that the main contribution of the Concert of Europe to the subsequent theory and practice of international order was in its tentative elaboration of a set of ground rules for the diplomatic conduct of the Great Powers: its contribution to international organisation, in the sense of tangible machinery, was negligible.

With the League of Nations, this judgement should arguably be reversed: its distinctive contribution lay in the creation of the infrastructure of international organisation, to the extent of associating the League with a specific geographical location, namely Geneva. It fostered the emergence of international institutions, serviced by a permanent secretariat. When we move on to consider the impact of the League upon the Great Powers' conceptions of international order and how they might best contribute towards it, the period strikes us as sterile. While such a judgement might appear severe, it seems nonetheless appropriate for an era in international relations that told us so much about the need for international cooperation but told us so little about how it was to be achieved. Even more, if the League experiment bequeathed any conspicuous legacies, then it was surely a disenchantment with the notion of concert diplomacy as such: in trying to push the concert idea too far, the League produced a widespread disillusionment with the attempt to transcend basic balance-of-power strategies. Despite the subsequent creation of the United Nations, the inter-war period represented the last occasion to date in which the powers consciously sought to construct an international order that was, at least rhetorically, divorced from the realities of power. The failure of the League persuaded the framers of its successor organisation that international security was best to be attained, not by a rejection of the hierarchical ordering of states, but by due recognition of the need for such hierarchy in any security system.

In consequence, the post-1945 international order reflects the cumulative experience of the preceding century and a half: the conditions for concerted Great Power action do not, for the most part, persist; the costs of wholehearted return to international anarchy are deemed to be too severe; and disillusionment with formalised concerts, unsupported by power, has not yet dissipated after the inter-war debacle. The result, to which we now proceed, is a patchwork order in which elements of the earlier periods are to be rediscovered but in which a return to balance strategies is the single most conspicuous feature.

9 FROM CONCERT TO BALANCE, 1945–1990

There is a pervasive consensus that the post-1945 distribution of power differed in fundamental ways from that which had preceded it. The war severely weakened the traditional powers of Europe and the defeat of Germany was to be succeeded by a temporary, and then enduring, partition of the country. Soviet power had been injected into the heartland of Eastern Europe, at the same time as the United States emerged as the world's foremost economic and technological power.

This postwar order was immediately to be shaped by the twin consequences of the war and of the developing Soviet–American antagonism. Whether that order was the product of aggressive Soviet expansionism, as the traditional Cold War historians would have it, or of a dynamic American capitalism relentlessly pursuing 'Open Door' policies, as the revisionists retorted, or, indeed, whether the Cold War was simply the inevitable structural by-product of the vacuum in postwar Europe, it is certainly the case that more so than in most periods, it was to be the relationship between two dominant states that was to lend the era its characteristic features: to understand the post-1945 order, we need to understand the dynamic superpower relationship.

There is a danger with this period, as with the others, in describing it as if its dominant features persist unchanged throughout several decades. Even a superficial accounting of the change of mood from Cold War to detente and to Second Cold War, or from bipolarity to loose bipolarity or multipolarity, should convince us that this has not been the case. Nevertheless, it is possible to make some generalisations about the nature of international order in the post-Second World War era and about the principal modalities by means of which it has been maintained.

As with the previous chapters, the focus of discussion will be upon the diplomatic procedures and norms of the Great Powers and upon the elements of concert and balance that characterised these. Above all, the conspicuous feature of the post-1945 period has been, not simply a failure to construct a working concert system, but indeed a manifest lack of interest in trying to do so. To this extent, the period under review has much in common with the latter half of the nineteenth century, tempered however by fear of the consequences of war in the nuclear age. Moreover, if this atavism was partially a product of the peculiar conditions of the age, which would have operated against concert diplomacy in any case, it was also symptomatic of a changing intellectual mood. Despite the flurry of discussion and planning about the postwar order that persisted throughout the war years, there is little evidence of confidence that a 'brave new world' could be created. The United Nations was conceived in an age of relative disillusionment with mankind's capacities to shape the future and in this respect the temper of the 1940s was quite different from the early days of the League. Perhaps, in fact, recent League experience was too vivid to allow of such a sense of expectation. At any rate, Martin Wight is no doubt correct when he submits that 'the failure first of the League of Nations, and then of the permanent members of the Security Council to achieve unanimity disabused men of the idea of international order as a work of political construction'.[1]

How, then, should we characterise the main features of order since 1945? First of all, before proceeding to discuss the specific modalities of order, a few general comments on the period are necessary. The first point relates to that just made – namely, a reversion from a 'constructionist' to a *laissez-faire* attitude as far as international order is concerned. To express the same point in a slightly different form, we might say that order in the post-1945 period may well have emerged but it has seldom been consciously pursued. This, in turn, has been viewed as one of the ironies of the present age, in the sense, to quote again from Wight, that 'since 1945 a decline in theoretical concern for international order has paradoxically coincided with a balance of power that has defied pessimists by its durability'.[2] The realists would, of course, contend that this must inevitably be so. Such, at any rate, is the conviction of Henry Kissinger:

> The attainment of peace is not as easy as the desire for it. Not for nothing is history associated with the figure of Nemesis, which defeats man by fulfilling his wishes in a different form or by answering his prayers too completely. Those ages which in retrospect seem most peaceful were least in search of peace. Those whose quest for it seems unending appear least able to achieve tranquility.[3]

Accordingly, Kissinger would see the tragedy of the inter-war period to lie in its over-preoccupation with instituting a novel system of order whereas the postwar world has achieved more by aspiring to less.

A second general observation on the period would be that while it has not been wholly without collectivist policies, these have been articulated in the form of collective defence arrangements rather than as a collective security apparatus. Much more obviously, and more rapidly than in the post-1919 phase, did the accoutrements of collective security give way to the substance of alliance mechanisms. The guarantee of collective security provided by the United Nations was, as we shall see, not only supplemented but supplanted by specific alliance commitments, NATO and the Warsaw pact being the foremost of these.

The third aspect to be considered is central to the continuing theme of this book and this is the nature, and the provenance, of the norms associated with the Great Powers' relations with each other. It was argued previously that the Concert of Europe had two principal facets, one asserting a special position within the international system for the Great Powers and the other mitigating the effects of this by prescribing rules for Great Power conduct. The latter is as central to the concert idea as is the former. This is a point which Hedley Bull, apart from a few saving qualifications, comes close to missing. He sees the Great Powers as contributing to order in two main ways: 'by managing their relations with one another, and by exploiting their preponderance in such a way as to impart a degree of central direction to the affairs of international society as a whole'.[4] Bull then goes on to list the various means by which these two contributions are made and mentions a 'great power concert' under the second category. The whole point is, of course, that a concert, if it is to mean anything, means also 'managing their relations with one another'. Subsequently, however, Bull makes the substantial qualification that these two Great Power roles are closely interconnected and, by doing so, makes his formulation less open to criticism. In his own words:

> The steps the great powers take to manage their relations with one another lead directly to the attempt to provide central direction or management of the affairs of international society as a whole; the steps they take to exploit their preponderance in relation to the rest of international society presuppose some effective management of their relations with one another.[5]

The status of any postwar norms of superpower behaviour is open to question. Indeed, one analyst has expressed his own puzzlement at the very intractability of the Soviet–American relationship:

170

It is not clear whether a security regime regulates superpower relations today. Patterns of behaviour exist ... but the question is whether they are far enough removed from immediate, narrow self-interest to involve a regime. I think the answer is no, but ... lack confidence in this judgment.[6]

There are some obvious reasons why it should have been difficult for a superpower concert to develop. At the very least, there have been a number of medium powers, some formerly Great Powers in their own right, who have resisted such a duopoly. They have done so because they have 'more to lose and sometimes also less to gain' from superpower control than some of the small states within the system.[7] In addition, to an unusual degree, the superpowers have been riven by ideological differences and competing conceptions, not only of a desirable international order, but of the very nature of international order itself. If, in practice, this manifested itself as an American preference for 'universalism', as contrasted with a Soviet preference for 'spheres of influence',[8] then in theory the gulf was even wider as the United States operated within a traditional state-centric prism, whereas the Soviet Union has adhered to a more complex and variegated correlation of forces in which social systems and trans-national classes are paramount.[9] There have been recent indications of convergence[10] and, where this has occurred, Soviet theoreticians have elaborated not only a statist/pluralist view but also a 'Superpower conception of international relations'.[11] As against this, however, there still persists some American reluctance to countenance the Soviet Union as a superpower equal and partner. 'For all its fixation on duopoly', one critic observes, 'American diplomacy has never been willing to offer the Soviets the equal global status they presumably crave'.[12]

Have there been norms of Great Power behaviour in the post-1945 period? Probably the closest that we can come to such a notion is in the form of conventions limiting conflict between the superpowers and we might label these 'rules of crisis management', or simply 'the policy of detente'. Apart from the inherent difficulties with these terms, which will be discussed shortly, there is still the question whether these practices would be sufficient to warrant description as concert diplomacy. At the very least, there is the doubt that a concert can consist of two powers alone, because crisis management and detente, if, and to the extent that, they have been practised, have been norms confined solely to the two superpowers. Thus, Bull is correct to point out that 'it will be necessary, however, to study not only crisis avoidance and control, as it has been practised by the United States

171

and the Soviet Union in the period of their predominance, but also to extend the inquiry to embrace the avoidance and control of crises in a system of several great powers'.[13]

Membership of a concert apart, there is also the issue of its content. If crisis management or detente are seen as behavioural traits of (to use Coral Bell's terminology) an 'adversary partnership', one may legitimately question whether such a partnership can constitute a concert, especially if, as seems to have been the case for much of the postwar period, the 'adversary' element has been more visible than the 'partnership' component. The late Alastair Buchan thought not:

> The development of an awareness of parallel Soviet–American interests during the ten years since the Cuban crisis, in the sense of both tacit and explicit understanding about the rules by which deterrence can be maintained while war may be avoided, has led neither to a super power condominium . . . nor to a significant expansion of the area of political detente . . . The bipolar relationship remains primarily an adversary one.[14]

A fourth issue relates to whether a situation in which the dominant strategic concepts derive from a relationship of nuclear deterrence can appropriately be described as a reversion to balance-of-power practices. The distinctions between 'balance of power' and 'balance of terror' have frequently been reiterated[15] and need not be detailed here. Suffice it to say that the debate centres upon notions of power and equilibrium in the nuclear age, on the increasing subjectivity of estimations of balance, on the decreasing importance of marginal quantities of military power and upon the changing role of alliances or alignments in such a context. It is not the intention of this chapter to argue against these propositions and to maintain that nuclear weaponry has not modified traditional balance-of-power practices. What can be said, however, is that the system of nuclear deterrence is essentially a set of precepts for counterpoising nuclear force against nuclear force in a decentralised milieu and, from that perspective, is much closer to a classical balance system than to any other variant scheme for the management of power between states. The point to be emphasised, then, is that the description of the postwar years as a 'balance' age should not be disallowed on the technicality of the existence of nuclear weaponry.

Fifthly, we must consider the implications for the overall argument of the trend, widely perceived by analysts, towards an increasingly multipolar world structure, a trend beginning in the 1960s but accelerating in the 1970s. To the extent that such a development has taken place, it marks a departure from Wight's outline history in which 'though the field of the balance of power expanded the number of decisive weights has decreased'.[16] If the objection was that balance policies could not be pursued in a bipolar world, then the force of this argument has presumably declined *pari passu* with the 'tightness' of the Soviet–American polarity.

At a very general level, it is an easy enough task to identify the various developments that tended to increase the element of pluralism in international life. These points are familiar and scarcely contentious. There are three facets of the trend worth mentioning:

(1) The first was the tendency towards disintegration within the two Cold War camps. On the Soviet side, the first example of this was the defection of Yugoslavia but of course by far the most important example was the rift between Moscow and Peking. In the course of the 1960s Romania joined the ranks of those eastern states that were gaining a certain amount of autonomy over their own affairs. On the western side, the most conspicuous evidence of friction within the NATO fold were the demonstrative gestures of France but this was no more than the most prominent symptom of a fairly widespread complaint. The 1960s – in the course of which many of the European countries became uneasy about the extent of American foreign investment in the European economies – also witnessed the gradual erosion of faith in America's determination to meet her nuclear guarantees. On the American side, there was growing disillusionment with the sincerity of European efforts to provide a greater contribution to their own defence. These various sources of contention came to a head during the 1960s with France actually withdrawing from NATO's joint military structure in 1966 and in the form of a series of debates about NATO strategy in Europe.

(2) A second reason for the emergence of a more pluralistic international system may well be found in a factor that facilitated the disintegration of the monolithic appearance of the two camps. This was the very fact of the balance that existed between the two camps as the Cold War evolved into the 1950s. There is obviously a sense in which the nuclear stalemate between the two superpowers created greater room for manoeuvre on the part of the lesser members of the opposing alliance systems. China is the example on the one side and France the example on the other. Just as the balance between the two camps created a margin of discretion for the nonaligned states, so that same balance increased the autonomy of some of the states within the rival alliances. Another example of this is in relation to the effect of the Sino-Soviet dispute on Eastern Europe. Here it is possible to see that the existence of conflict between Moscow and Peking strengthened

173

the bargaining hand of certain of the Eastern European states, particularly Yugoslavia and Romania, during the 1960s.

(3) The third factor to be mentioned is the economic recovery of
Europe and of Japan. At least in part, the Cold War between the Soviet
Union and the United States sprang up as a response to the economic
and political collapse of Germany and Japan. If this was the situation
that gave birth to the bipolar order, then clearly by the 1960s this
situation was changing rapidly as Europe and Japan reasserted their
status in world economic terms. It may well be the case, as Calleo
suggests, that this is ultimately more threatening to the Soviet Union
than to the United States. If the resurgence of Japan and Western
Europe has created monetary, trading and alliance difficulties for the
United States, it presents to the Soviet Union the spectre of 'the rise of
those very European neighbours who are historically the principal
threats to Russian security and ambition'.[17]

During the early 1970s, significant changes in the balance of power
seemed to occur, so as to bring to the fore the latent possibilities of a
more genuinely tripolar order. It had been one of the most conspicuous features of American foreign policy in the 1960s that the
existence of the Sino-Soviet dispute made little difference to the
United States' relationship with either China or the Soviet Union.
Neither did China nor the Soviet Union substantially modify their
postures towards the United States solely on account of the friction
that was developing between them. To a large extent all three powers
operated on considerations that took little account of what was
happening on the other two sides of the triangle. As the 1960s came to
an end and the 1970s began, however, the United States found
increasingly that in her dialogue with the Soviet Union, her bargaining
position was deteriorating because of the drain of the Vietnam war in
particular and the shift in the military balance with the Soviet Union
more generally. At the very time when the United States seemed less
willing to meet her global commitments, the Soviet Union was
extending hers – particularly in the Middle East and in the Indian
subcontinent.

The culmination of these various trends was that for the first time
the United States decided to avail herself of the opportunity presented
to her by the Sino-Soviet dispute and to improve her bargaining
position *vis-à-vis* Moscow by initiating a dialogue with Peking. This
was the most basic consideration underlying the Nixon visit to Peking
in 1972 and the admission of China to the United Nations.

Soviet sources provide several clear statements as to how the
Sino-American *rapprochement* was viewed in Moscow. By China's

admission to the United Nations and as a result of the Nixon visit, Peking's status in international terms was greatly increased. Indeed, such an increase in status was the price that Washington had to pay for Peking's agreement to enter into a dialogue that would demonstrate to Moscow that, if the Soviet Union became too ambitious, she would have to face joint opposition from America and China. A few quotes from Russian sources make this point very well. According to one Soviet analyst what the United States was seeking to do was to 'meet half way the Maoists' great power claims and style and to persuade the world public that Washington really regards Peking as a full-fledged global partner'.[18] The reason why she was doing so was that 'the present stage is characterised by a further weakening of the USA's position and prestige in international affairs. In the confrontation with the Soviet Union ... US imperialism now seeks new partners and Washington is trying to find such a partner in China.'[19] By the nature of her overtures to Peking the United States sought to promote the emergence of a tripolar system within which the Soviet Union could be more effectively checked than by the continuance of the purely bipolar arrangement. To quote again from a Soviet commentator, 'the endeavour to stimulate the globalisation of the Chinese factor is closely connected with the adoption of a triangular foreign policy stance ... China is wedging itself into the traditional structure of the present day world and in doing so is transforming this structure by introducing a new additional coefficient of complexity into foreign policy calculations.'[20] This is to say that it would no longer be sufficient to operate on the basis of purely bilateral considerations.

Soviet reactions were as hostile and suspicious as they were also to prove to be premature. By the 1980s, it had become increasingly clear that there were real constraints on an overly close American relationship with China. Under Gorbachev, steps were also to be taken to thaw the long-frozen Sino-Soviet relationship itself. Accordingly, while the emergence of China can be regarded as a significant element in the wider process of diffusion of world power that has continued since the 1960s, a self-conscious tripolarity has failed to sustain itself. If anything, despite their limited military power, Japan and Western Europe have exercised greater influence on the conduct of world affairs than any limited tripolar balance structure.

The sixth general point by way of comment on the post-1945 international order pertains to the very concept of security at the present time. According to some accounts, governments are no longer concerned simply to further the ends of military security but tend to define their security increasingly in economic or 'welfare' terms. It follows from such an interpretation that international relations can no longer be thought to be coextensive with the field of deterrence or strategy and that any concentration on the purely 'military balancing' component of international order is misleading as a general depiction of the age.

The argument is compelling and has had many adherents. It is as a result of this line of reasoning that Herz reaches his conclusion that 'the event which led to the destruction of the balance system was the growing, and now worldwide, inter-connection of economic and other relationships in the industrial age and the ensuing inter-dependence of states'.[21] Keohane and Nye have dubbed this a situation of 'complex interdependence' and more strongly than most argue that 'balance of power theories and national security imagery are also poorly adapted to analysing problems of economic or eco-logical interdependence. Security, in traditional terms, is not likely to be the principal issue facing governments.'[22]

We may accept the general drift of these arguments but it is unclear what their implications are for the present discussion. Even if it is conceded that the distinction between 'high' and 'low' politics is inappropriate under current conditions and that the issues that face present-day governments are distinctively novel, as is the setting of interdependence in which these issues have to be confronted, this need not, however, imply that statecraft itself has been revo-lutionised.

It is now time to move on and consider the specific modalities of order-maintenance in the post-1945 world and, on the basis of that evidence, to try to characterise the main features of the age. The discussion will focus upon the following topics: international economic order; international organisations and the United Nations; nuclear deterrence and arms control; spheres of influence and inter-vention; and crisis management and detente.

INTERNATIONAL ECONOMIC ORDER

In the last three decades, according to the interdependence theorists just mentioned, there has been a pronounced change of emphasis in the nature of the problems that have vexed the world's statesmen. While traditional issues of a politico-strategic nature have not faded from the scene, they have in many instances been tempo-rarily obscured by more pressing demands in the international economic sphere.

What placed economic issues at the head of summit agendas was the confluence of at least three discrete developments. The first was the intrusion into the world's consciousness that all might not be well with mankind's relationship to the environment: as one writer has phrased it, 'by the early 1970s, the macro-ecologists were gathering full voice and, in March of 1972, when the Club of Rome issued the Meadows' Limits of Growth, they reached high C'.[23] The second was the specific element in the 'Doomsday Syndrome', which emphasised the finiteness of certain key resources. And the third development was the tangible experience of the post-October-1973 oil crisis, which was important because it appeared, however erroneously, to validate the general 'attrition of resources' argument.

The elevation of these economic issues to the forefront of international politics was in itself a significant occurrence. However, what was even more interesting was the common property that was shared by each of these problems: the striking feature of these challenges was that they seemed to require a concerted international effort to meet them. What is the rhetoric of international cooperation in the face of this economic challenge? Astonishingly, the purveyors of this rhetoric have not taken the trouble to find their own terminology, but have simply adopted the utopian catch-phrases of the 1920s. Just as President Wilson advocated collective security as a substitute for 'power politics', so the modern idealists have spread the gospel of 'collective economic security'.[24]

More generally, the environmental and ecological concerns of the early 1970s coincided with severe dislocations in the international economy, such as to call into question confidence in the prevailing mechanisms which had operated throughout most of the postwar period. It might be said that international economic issues became politicised to an unprecedented extent during this period as the pursuit of a stable economic order took top priority in national policies.

The analysis of the international economic order brings together in all its complexity the interplay between the politico-strategic and the economic components of order. This is reflected in the widespread assumption that it was political and strategic change which was destabilising the Bretton Woods system insofar as it was undermining the managerial role of the United States within that order and also in the notion that order must extend beyond the confines of the East–West relationship to encompass the economic relationship between the industrialised countries and between North and South.

Arguably, the postwar economic order has been as prominently characterised by hierarchy as the political order and has indeed been

177

interwoven with it. It is claimed, for instance, that such is the uneven development of that order that some five-sixths of all industrial capacity is concentrated in a dozen countries.[25] Likewise, economically speaking, the rich tend to trade and invest amongst themselves. In 1975, some 75 per cent of all multinational corporation investment was placed in developed countries.[26] Such economic stratification is embodied in the financial decision-making institutions of the economic order, such as the IMF and World Bank, in the weighted voting systems of these bodies.

The postwar international economic order had itself been influenced by similar liberal ideas as those behind other international organisations and had equally been influenced by historical experience, particularly that of the 1930s. 'National protectionism and the disintegration of world trade in the 1930s,' Spero writes, 'created a common interest in an open trading order and a realization that states would have to cooperate to achieve and maintain that order'[27] and this provided an impetus to the design of postwar institutions. In addition, the creation of such an order required a concomitance of favourable conditions, including concentration of power in a small number of countries, shared interests, and the presence of a dominant power able to play a leadership role.[28] The last factor, namely the position of the United States, is deemed to be crucial by most analysts.

This newly created order was based on two major pillars, a financial and a trading regime. As regards the former, the IMF and the World Bank complex were the two principal creations. Together, and with subsequent refinements, they oversaw an international financial and exchange rate system which permitted the stable recovery of much of the world in the 1950s. The United States was the apex of this system which, based on fixed exchange rates and gold convertibility, increasingly came to be dollar-based. From its initiation in the late 1940s until 1960, the monetary system was unilaterally managed by the United States as a deliberately contrived American deficit provided an outflow of dollars which, in turn, created the necessary liquidity for economic reconstruction.

This system came under strain in the 1960s as the American deficit became endemic. Management of the order was increasingly multi-lateralised, initially under the Group of Ten, but by the end of the decade the order was coming apart. In 1971, Nixon delivered his shock of taking dollars off the gold standard and instituting a system of flexible exchange rates. Ever since, monetary relations have been characterised by partial measures at imposing order on exchange rates, coupled with market-led disruptions to the system such that two commentators have suggested that 'the 1980s can be seen as a decade of growing, but inadequate, collective management of floating exchange rates'.[29]

The other pillar of the economic order has been the trading regime. Reflecting the widespread assumption that a liberal trading order would be necessary both to avoid a recurrence of the breakdown of the 1930s, as well as to profit American business, the postwar economic architects attempted to institute a stable, and freer, set of trading arrangements. Failing in their efforts to establish a formal international organisation in the shape of the International Trading Organization, they settled for the informal General Agreement on Tariffs and Trade which sought to implement nondiscrimination and a lowering of trading tariffs. It was a measure of its success that between 1950 and 1980, international trade increased from 11.7 per cent of world GNP to 21.2 per cent.[30] The attempt to reduce trade barriers was carried forward in the 1960s and 1970s in the Kennedy and Tokyo rounds of negotiations.

President Nixon's 10 per cent import surcharge in 1971 was a harbinger of the difficulties that were to beset the international trading order through the 1970s and 1980s, reflecting the economic recessions of those years, the disparities in economic achievement between the most successful, such as Japan, and those suffering intensifying balance of trade deficits, such as the United States, and the domestic political pressures for protectionism that built up under the influence of these developments. Threats of trade wars between Japan, Europe and the United States have become part of the trade landscape in the 1980s.

Collectively, these trends demonstrated the declining capacity of the postwar economic order to sustain the demands of the new forces operating in the past twenty years. This was itself a function of political and economic change. As Spero attests of the recovery of Western Europe and Japan, 'the shift toward a more pluralist distribution of economic power led to a renewed sense of political power and to increasing dissatisfaction with American dominance of the international monetary system'.[31] In any event, America's declining economic stature rendered her less capable of sustaining such a dominant role. In her relationship with her erstwhile economic *protégés*, America experienced a 'remarkable reversal of fortunes'.[32] Not only did the erosion of the international economic order betray the shifting political fortunes of the leading states, in turn the economic order was to hold momentous potential consequences for the politico-strategic order as well, so much so that one critic writes apocalyptically

179

that 'America's endemic economic disorder is today a more serious threat to the postwar international liberal order than is any plausible Soviet aggression . . . '[33]

The other aspect of the international economic order to achieve prominence in the 1970s and beyond was that of North–South relations. Arguably, the record of the economic order by this stage was such as to suggest that, not only was there a markedly hierarchical structure, but it was questionable to what extent it could be said that an order existed at all. Healthy growth rates by the less developed countries in the 1950s and 1960s were consumed by population increases and by the 1970s the terms of trade shifted significantly against the disadvantaged exporters. By 1975, the gap in per capita GNP between OECD and less developed countries had increased to $4839 from $2191 in 1950.[34] This has been further aggravated, especially in Africa, by persistent famine in the 1980s. To this extent, the gap between developed and underdeveloped was widening, even after two decades of conscious development strategies. The situation was not, of course, uniformly bleak as the so-called Newly Industrialised Countries (Taiwan, South Korea, Singapore, Hong Kong) returned impressive rates of growth but it was far from clear whether these examples demonstrated the success of orthodox strategies or merely were the exceptions which confirmed the general rule.

The economic difficulties experienced by the poorer countries in the 1970s set the scene for the politicisation of North–South economic issues to an unprecedented level. This was further stimulated by the OPEC action in quadrupling oil prices in 1973–4 which served both to aggravate the position of non-oil-producing underdeveloped countries and to offer an example of successful third world cartelisation which others might emulate. As such, it fostered a collectivist bargaining approach through its chosen instrument of UNCTAD. The succeeding decade witnessed the recycling of oil-producer surpluses, through western financial institutions, into new lending to less developed countries. By the early 1980s, it was clear that many of these were heavily indebted and experiencing difficulty in making repayments. Net capital transfers were taking place from the borrowers to the lenders of $7 billion in 1981, $56 billion in 1983 and $74 billion in 1985.[35] Efforts to renegotiate and reschedule debts were driven not simply by concern for the plight of the debtors but additionally by fears for the future stability of the global financial and banking system in the face of widespread default.

By this stage, prospects for the success of demands for a New International Economic Order seemed increasingly gloomy. The sense of third world bargaining power in the mid-1970s had been translated into specific demands for a new basis for North–South economic relations. These had focussed on various facets of the economic system. In particular, as third world exporter earnings became squeezed between unstable commodity prices and inflated prices for manufactured goods from the industrialised world, the former sought stabilisation measures for commodity prices. Proposals included holding of international stocks and a common fund to sustain prices. They also sought easier access to industrialised markets by reduction of tariffs and elimination of quotas on manufactured goods. As regards their financial situation, they demanded a greater voice in international financial institutions, increased access to international capital markets on favourable terms, and rescheduling of debts to diminish debt burdens. Other proposals were the development of a code of practice for technology transfer by modifying restrictive patent legislation, and a code of conduct for multinational corporations, to avoid the ills of enclave resource development, with minimal benefit to employment and economic development, and of transfer pricing, by means of which corporations could creatively evade contributions to the national exchequer.

It was always unlikely that there would be sufficient unity of political purpose behind these demands to sustain them over the longer term. It was even less likely that the industrialised world would accede to them. What little prospect remained was largely destroyed by the economic recession at the turn of the decade which concentrated western minds on the plight of their own economies to the resultant exclusion of international order concerns.

It is evident from the above that the evolving international economic order has itself included elements of both concert and balance strategies. At times, the system has operated on the basis of purely market mechanisms in which the powerful have held sway. Additionally, however, most of the formal institutions and informal mechanisms of the economic order have been devised and managed by a relatively small coterie of leading industrialised states, exemplifying concert characteristics. It is unlikely that the system can ever gravitate fully to either polar extreme. Some coordination and concerted management is in the interests of all economic participants, even in situations when, as in the 1950s, the central direction of the system is virtually unilateral. On the other hand, important members of the OECD grouping currently adhere to non-interventionist economic philosophies and have fostered the deregulation of much financial activity as the basis of national economic policies. It is difficult to conceive of

181

increasing formalisation of concerted international coordination taking place in a context of declining faith in governmental intervention in economic processes at the national level: market-led philosophies scarcely allow for elaborate international structures of management. This leads some commentators to view the current system as a minimally directed anarchy. Brett thus refers to the 'collapse of authority and order in a system which can no longer be effectively managed by its once dominant power, and is as yet unable to develop a more collective alternative'.[36]

One further comment is necessary on the basis of the international economic order. The economic and institutional patterns described above have largely functioned without the participation of the Soviet bloc. In turn, this leads to two significant conclusions. To the extent that the international economic order has been directed by a concert of powers, it has been by a residual concert, itself as exclusivist and limited as the limited concert of the League of Nations. Secondly, the fact that the Soviet Union, because of its own autarchic policies, has not been actively involved in this order has contributed to a disjunction, in this respect, between the economic and the politico-strategic orders. The Soviet Union, a key element in the military equilibrium, has contributed little to sustain the economic order, either in its industrialised, or in its North–South, dimensions.

INTERNATIONAL ORGANISATIONS AND THE UNITED NATIONS

It is difficult to assess the role and contribution of international organisations in recent international politics and even more so to speculate about their potential role. In part, this reflects the deliberate ambiguity of the United Nations, drawing as it did upon the reformism of the League but also seeking to rectify the League's apparent failure to cope with power. What this ambiguity achieved was to blur 'the distinction so sharply drawn under the League between balance of power and collective security'.[37] Judgements about these organisations consequently tend to vary from the 'power politics in disguise' verdict at one end of the spectrum to the 'incipient world community' at the other, and from seeing international organisations as passive reflections of the state of political play to seeing them as active participants and potential vehicles of change. Keohane and Nye, for instance, believe that international organisations function differently and have a more important role in a world of 'complex interdependence'. As they themselves have argued the case:

182

in a world of multiple issues imperfectly linked, in which coalitions are formed transnationally and transgovernmentally, the potential role of international institutions in political bargaining is greatly increased. In particular, they help set the international agenda, and act as catalysts for coalition formation and as arenas for political initiatives and linkage by weak states[38]

It would, of course, be premature to make any definitive pronouncement upon international organisations and Inis Claude, in discussing the vast quantitative proliferation of these organisations, best reflects the ambivalent, and tentative, nature of our assessment of them:

At the very least, this growth suggests that statesmen are now more willing to emphasize collective rather than merely unilateral approaches to a wide range of issues. At most, it may presage the development of a more effective system for the management of international relations than the world has yet known. In promoting the proliferation of international agencies and the greater scope and variety of their activities, states neither guarantee that result nor provide unequivocal evidence of their dedication to its achievement, but they at least open up the possibility of its achievement.[39]

If we focus exclusively upon the United Nations, we have the same problem with general assessments but also can make some specific, and less equivocal, observations. There is a fairly wide consensus amongst analysts of the UN that there have been, broadly speaking, three distinctive phases in the evolution of the UN's operations. The first of these did not last beyond the original conception of the UN, as the philosophy of the Charter was quickly overtaken by developments in international relations and by the outbreak of the Cold War in particular. The second phase of UN activities is associated with the use of that organisation as an instrument of Western policy: the period was marked by a large Western majority and the use to which this was put was best, if unusually, displayed by the Korean war. The third phase started in the mid-1950s and has, in a sense, lasted ever since; this witnessed the great numerical expansion in UN membership, especially from the Afro-Asian countries, the disappearance of the West's automatic majority, the greater attention devoted to issues of decolonisation and development and the emergence of a new peace-keeping role for the organisation in the shape of small 'policing' ventures rather than the large interventions symbolised by the Korean episode.

The original Charter was, to a large extent, devised on the assumption of a continuance of the Great Power cooperation of the war period. The major role in assuring international order was assigned to

183

the Security Council, which was to be composed of eleven members, six of which would be temporary and five of which would be permanent and of these, clearly the permanent members were pre-eminent – the United States, the Soviet Union, Britain, France and China. If these powers were unanimous on some issue, they could authorise actions binding on the remainder of the UN's membership.

That the Charter placed authority for the future supervision of the international system explicitly in the hands of the Great Powers can scarcely be denied and was amply revealed in the provision that granted the permanent members of the Security Council a veto. This veto was to ensure that the collective security provisions of the Charter could not be applied by one Great Power against another or that the UN could not be used to impose a settlement on a Great Power that dissented from a UN verdict. Inis Claude has developed this point when he argued that:

> the insertion of the veto provision in the decision-making circuit of the Security Council reflected the clear conviction that in cases of sharp conflict among the great powers the Council ought, for safety's sake, to be incapacitated – to be rendered incapable of being used to precipitate a showdown or to mobilise collective action against the recalcitrant power. The philosophy of the veto is that it is better to have the Security Council stalemated than to have that body used by a majority to take action so strongly opposed by a dissident great power that a world war is likely to ensue.[40]

As originally conceived, the UN was based on several principles: first, that overall supervision of security matters should be the firm responsibility of the major powers; secondly, that the UN should not be used against an unwilling Great Power; and thirdly that the UN should have some 'teeth', a development considered necessary in view of the experience of the League of Nations. As part of this effort, the Charter envisaged the creation of a Military Staff Committee, composed of military personnel from the member states of the Security Council.

As noted, the UN embodied in the Charter did not materialise, as it was quickly overtaken by the Cold War. This resulted in a peacekeeping role for the UN quite different from the one originally intended, as a dynamic UN role was very much dependent upon a level of agreement between the superpowers that greatly surpassed that which was possible in the atmosphere of the Cold War. This also had the effect of preventing the fruition of the military clauses of the Charter. Under the circumstances, it is not surprising that the peacekeeping role of the UN should have been tailored and have moved away from a full-scale system of collective security to one in which the UN does little more than provide small-scale emergency 'policing' and 'supervisory' units.

At the level of general assessments of UN performance, we have the same ambivalent attitude with which international organisations as a whole have been regarded. In Goodwin's terminology, it depends very much upon whether one holds to an 'organic' or 'instrumental' view of the organisation, the first seeing it as an 'incipient world community capable of spontaneous growth'[41] and the latter seeing it 'as the instrument of its leading members, to be used as they see fit'.[42] LeRoy Bennett also arrives at an uncertain judgement:

> At the present stage of history, the United Nations system of agencies ... provide a bridge between the old and the new world order. On the one hand, they act as a conservative force against radical change by conforming to the status quo and by further institutionalising the present international framework. On the other hand, they reflect the necessity for orderly, cooperative action in attacking the common problems of humanity.[43]

If we move on to specific aspects of the United Nations, it is, however, possible to be more positive. We can, for instance, clearly perceive how the UN fits into the concept of concert diplomacy developed in this study: it fits not at all well. In fact, if we concentrate on the veto provisions of the Security Council, a case could be mounted for the view that the United Nations is predicated upon an explicit rejection of any notion of concert diplomacy.

How is this so? We have noted that it is a part of the concert idea that the Great Powers, in their relations with each other, should adhere to certain precepts of behaviour – in the European concert, the most important of these being the requirement of formal and common consent to change. This is to say that in concert diplomacy, the powers adhere to some kind of group norm. But the veto provision can be understood only as a statement that, as far as the major powers are concerned, there shall be no such group norm. While the organisational principle for the security of the remainder of international society shall be a collective one, for the Great Powers it is to be strongly individualistic. Moreover, such norms of behaviour as are to apply to international society, such as peaceful settlement of disputes, are not to be enforced upon the Great Powers themselves. It is in this sense, presumably, that Martin Wight made his comment that 'the Great Power veto written into the new international constitution in 1944–5 divorced the notion of the balance of power from the notion of international order'.[44] The balance of power was to be liberated from the artificial constraints of such formal principles as are characteristic of concert diplomacy. There is, therefore, a touch of primitivism, if also of realism, in the *carte blanche* that the major powers were accorded by the terms of the UN Charter.

It followed logically that the balance of power would bypass the UN forum and manifest itself elsewhere. There is, therefore, an important sense in which the Charter's denial of concert diplomacy has made a major impression on the subsequent peacekeeping history of the organisation and this is in the divorce between 'order' and 'power' referred to by Wight and the consequent loss of real power by the UN. As one commentator has pointed out 'in contrast to the intention to draw collective security forces mainly from the great powers, the practice in peacekeeping has been to insulate each situation from major-power involvement, influence or confrontation'.[45] This does not mean that 'power' is no longer exercised or of importance, only that it is exercised outside the UN rather than within it.

In general terms, the inability of the United Nations to extricate itself from the conflicts that have riven Great Power relations, and the consequent incapacity of the Security Council to perform its allotted role as custodian of the international peace, has been a disappointment even to the UN's staunchest supporters. Episodes of Great Power unanimity, and of cooperation, have been all but absent. Some have drawn comfort from the unprecedented unanimity which the Security Council displayed in 1987 in calling for a cease-fire in the Gulf war between Iran and Iraq and in the ensuing initiatives taken by the Secretary-General in bringing this into effect. Whether this represents the beginning of a new phase of harmonious superpower action through the UN, or whether it will remain as an isolated episode brought about by an unusual coincidence of interests, remains to be seen.

NUCLEAR DETERRENCE AND ARMS CONTROL

As the nuclear balance of terror is a pervasive component of the post-1945 international order, some comments must be made upon it. To the extent that the postwar order is a hierarchical one in which the Great Powers enjoy privileges commensurate with their status, this has been reinforced by the unequal distribution of nuclear force throughout international society.

Nuclear weaponry has intruded itself into international political processes in various ways, modifying our conceptions of war and our ideas about the political uses of violence. One of the most famous treatises on the nature of war was that produced by the Prussian soldier and philosopher von Clausewitz in the aftermath of the Napoleonic wars. His book *On War* is probably best remembered because it contains the well-known dictum that war is the continuation of politics by other means. This was in fact the basic thesis of the work. What Clausewitz did was to describe the essence of war and he did so in terms that emphasised the political ends that war was intended to achieve. In writing his book, Clausewitz discussed his subject as if war was, in fact, subject to political constraints but what he should perhaps have been saying is that war ought to be subject to such constraints. Thus he writes in one place that 'the political object, as the original motive of the war, will be the standard for determining both the aim of the military force and also the amount of effort to be made'. This is a statement that wars do not follow their own military logic but are subject to political supervision and that it is political decisions that will determine the course and the extent of the war.

Clausewitz was able to write about war as if this was its fundamental nature because he generalised from the actual experience of the eighteenth century. What Clausewitz believed to be inherent in the very nature of war was little more than a historical accident produced by a set of fortuitous circumstances. During the eighteenth century wars were fought for limited purposes and one of the main reasons why this was so was the limited resources and the limited technology at the disposal of rival monarchs. In other words, war was a strictly political exercise not because of its inherent nature but because the constraints of the monarch's purse ensured that force would be employed only within the limits of the political ambitions and the financial resources of king or emperor.

In fact, at the very moment that Clausewitz wrote his treatise, the historical conditions that underlay this view had already begun to change dramatically. The main source of this transformation was the French Revolution and the consequent emergence of nationalism as one of the main political forces in Europe. By placing war in the service of the nation–state, nationalism was to provide a political end of overriding legitimacy. The point is this – while political control of war was a relatively simple matter in days of limited political objectives, it was to be seriously impaired by the development of the political ideas of nationalism that justified almost any action that was in the interest of the nation state. The contradiction between limited means and nationalist ends was not at first apparent and was successfully concealed by the practitioners of *Realpolitik* – the Bismarcks

187

and Cavours – who managed to combine the conception of clinical warfare with the pursuit of a national – albeit still limited – interest.

The contradiction could not, however, be concealed forever. With the turn of the century, it was difficult to pretend that an expansive political end defined in nationalistic terms could be attained in harmony with rigorous political control over the military means: if the survival of the nation–state is the ultimate political end, then there is no logical reason for limiting any military means that will achieve this objective. In other words, once the decision to defend the state is taken, by the logic of the situation control of operations must then be handed over to the military, who will determine the course of the war in accordance with purely military considerations – the only important issue being that of victory. The central concern of the strategist was to discover how the forces at his disposal might best be employed in order to accomplish the end of destroying the enemy's army. It remained only for technology to realise the full potential of 'total' war that was already latent in the political changes of the preceding century.

As a general statement, it can be argued that the net impact of nuclear weapons was to produce a striking decrease in the utility of military power in terms of its actual use. Their very destructiveness appeared to sever the rational connection between the use of military means and the achievement of political ends. It might be said that technological advance was already making military operations dispro-portionate to the goals for which they were intended and that nuclear weapons only pushed this development to its logical conclusion. In any case, whether as a result of evolution or of the nuclear evolution, the relationship between war and politics needed to be viewed from a new perspective.

This change has occurred in two directions: there has been a militarisation of political thinking and, simultaneously, a politicisation of military thinking.

First, we will analyse the militarisation of political thinking. The most obvious outcome of the development of nuclear weapons, and of the view that these weapons were too dangerous to be employed, has been a shift in emphasis from the use of military power in war to the use of military power short of war. In other words, there has been a change of emphasis from the use of war to the threat of war. Deterrence is a continual process and as its basic instrument is a military one, it is possible to argue that this has led to the militarisation of international political processes because, ultimately, the threat of nuclear war underlies any conflict between the superpowers.

Another way of saying the same thing is to argue that nuclear weapons have blurred the distinction between peace and war in that they have given the threat of force an increased visibility even in times of 'peace.' Given the interest of the superpowers in avoiding a 'hot' war between themselves, this has led to a situation in which latent threats to use force are pitted against each other far short of actual hostilities. If this blurring of the distinction between war and peace has led to the militarisation of political practice, it has also had the opposite, and possibly more welcome, consequence of fostering the establishment of greater political restraints over war itself.

How has this come about? At this point it is necessary to introduce an important distinction – that between diplomacy and force. Diplomacy is a form of bargaining through negotiation: force is an attempt to impose one's will and is thus the very reverse of bargaining. Traditionally wars have been contests of force – the negotiations have broken down and both sides have attempted to impose their will on the other by means of pure force. But a nuclear confrontation is not like a conventional war. It is a process of bargaining. It is, as Schelling has pointed out, not an attempt to overcome the opponent's strength by brute force but rather to structure his motives by the threat of the infliction of pain.[46] What a state seeks from its military forces is not the power to overcome physically but the bargaining power that comes from its capacity to inflict this pain.

It is because of the inherent power of destruction of nuclear weapons that there has been a need to integrate more closely the threat of war with political objectives. If in a conventional war it is at the point of surrender that political considerations usually take over from purely military ones, and if, as we have seen, nuclear confrontation resembles this point of greatest potential violence, then obviously it is necessary that the political factor should enter the proceedings long before war has actually broken out. Unlike in a conventional war, it is no longer possible to await the outcome of a contest of military forces before initiating a process of bargaining. Rather, bargaining must run through the entire pre-war period when nuclear weapons are involved.

It is because the use of force, in a nuclear context, has come to be directed against the minds of men rather than in a physical sense that the political element in force is now so conspicuous. The sole purpose of military force is not physical coercion but an attempt to affect the intentions of the opponent through putting psychological pressures upon him. Thus even in the case of the bombs that were dropped on Japan in 1945, it can be argued that their real targets were not

Hiroshima or Nagasaki but the politicians in Tokyo. As a general rule then, in the writings of most contemporary strategists, it can be seen that there has been a shift in emphasis from the military use of force to its psychological use. Or as one analysis has expressed it 'the principal deficiency of the thesis of military obsolescence lies less in its depreciation of the *utility* of war than in its failure to appreciate the subtle and varied role of military power short of war'.[47]

It is at this stage that it becomes apparent that nuclear deterrence is based on a striking paradox. What has been suggested so far is that because of the disproportion between the destructive power of nuclear weapons and any conceivable political end, the actual use of nuclear weapons in a war situation is hard to visualise. At the same time the latent threat to use these weapons has come to play a greater role in international affairs. It is this distinction that some strategists refer to when they say that the *utility* of nuclear weapons should not be confused with their *usability*. While this is a distinction, it also is something of a paradox: as deterrence rests on the posing of mutually credible threats, how can a credible threat be posed on the basis of weapons the use of which is incredible? Or to put it another way, the more successful deterrence is in practice, the more suspect it becomes in theory. This fundamental paradox in nuclear deterrence has been seized on by numerous writers. One study has argued that 'if the utility of war is greatly diminished or nullified, it is difficult to imagine threats of war indefinitely performing all the functions of war itself . . . In the long run a threat of senseless violence never carried out may lose its credibility.'[48] Similarly, it has been hypothesised that 'if the use of force has lost its utility, and has in fact become obsolescent the threat of force may be expected to share a similar fate'.[49] This, in turn, leads to a further paradox: to ensure the prevention of war, the threat of it must be increased. Even worse perhaps, is the apparent contradiction that in order that nuclear weapons will never have to be used, we must have more of them and they must be technically superior.

In order to minimise some of these paradoxes, and in order to create a stable nuclear relationship between themselves, the superpowers have sought to create certain foundations of credible deterrence over the years. With the signing of the ABM Treaty in 1972, the United States and the Soviet Union seemed to subscribe to the notion that mutual vulnerability was an essential condition of stable deterrence, with neither side able to defend itself and thus escape the threat of retaliatory punishment. However, under pressure of the Reagan presidency's Strategic Defence Initiative, this element of the nuclear posture has been called into question as the Americans have espoused, what the Soviet leadership had always seemed to have a greater interest in practising, namely a defensive rather than simply an offensive doctrine of deterrence.

Secondly, they have sought to stabilise deterrence by assuring the survivability of their retaliatory strategic nuclear forces. The invulnerability of second-strike forces has come to be recognised as the touchstone of credible deterrence, particularly in its association with seemingly undetectable submarine-launched missiles. However, the quest for invulnerability has also been pursued in land-based systems, by hardening of silos, concealment of systems and by mobility. The difficulties the United States has experienced in finding a convincing, and cost-effective, basing mode for its MX missile serves as a guide to the high priority attached to securing the survival of strategic forces. Unfortunately, at the present moment the superpowers are aware that some ranking of priorities, and possible trade-offs, may be required. What is beneficial in terms of ensuring survival of forces, such as mobility and concealment, is detrimental in terms of arms control, as these systems are that much more difficult to verify.

Thirdly, the incredibility of potential nuclear use, and its consequent undermining of deterrent strategies, has been tackled by a number of attempted politico-technical solutions. The deployment by NATO of a number of Intermediate Nuclear Forces in Europe, beginning in 1983, was such an effort to enhance the deterrent threat by increasing the credibility of nuclear response. The rationale underlying this deployment decision was that since these American-owned systems could reach Soviet soil, there would be no possibility of superpower territory remaining sanctuary and, to this extent, the defence of Western Europe would be more effectively 'coupled' to the American strategic deterrent. As part of a strategy of flexible response, a seemingly incredible threat would be strengthened by being tied to a series of incrementally escalatory military responses.

Fourthly, in order to address the same problem, the credibility of using nuclear weapons has been addressed by seeking to hold out a promise of limiting the amount of resulting damage. To this extent, the various strategies declared by the United States, such as the no-cities doctrine of the Macnamara era, and the countervailing and prevailing doctrines of the Carter and Reagan periods, have all been devised with essentially the same objective, namely to restore credibility to the use of these weapons by targeting postures which might hold out some prospect of limiting the resulting damage in a nuclear war.[50] Such strategies have, perhaps, become marginally more plausible given advances in the accuracy of missile systems but serious questions still remain about the plausibility of the technical and political command and control systems allowing for such limited outcomes.[51]

With these few general remarks on the impact of nuclear weaponry, it remains only to summarise their significance in the context of Great Power tutelage of the international system. Two points are worthy of mention. First, as already mentioned, possession of nuclear weaponry has emphasised the hierarchical dimension of international society, creating a new category of 'have' and 'have not' states. To that extent, by marking off a well-defined nuclear peer-group from the rest of society, it might be considered that nuclear weaponry has created a precondition of a successful concert system since such a system depends upon the existence of an elite grouping of powers with a shared interest in managing the system and with the capacity to do so. In practice, however, beyond a staunch attempt to check the further proliferation of nuclear weapons, the nuclear powers have been too riven by disagreements in other areas to be able to give the system 'concerted' direction. Indeed, it has been suggested that the seeming stability of the nuclear relationship, however real or illusory it might be, could have actually stymied further efforts to develop a more formalised concert or security system.[52]

Secondly, nuclear weapons might have assisted the emergence of a concert system by inculcating within the Great Powers an ideological consensus, in the shape of a shared body of ideas about nuclear diplomacy and a shared set of concepts about nuclear deterrence. In fact, such an ideological convergence is by no means assured and is not, in any case, irreversible: it is a continuous process that must be constantly worked at. It is from this perspective that some analysts see the major significance of arms-control dialogues, such as SALT – not that they will eventuate in any substantial reduction in weaponry but that they might assist the states involved to think about nuclear issues in a mutually intelligible fashion.

To what extent, then, might arms control be said to have contributed towards a superpower concert? An assessment can be offered by considering the objectives of arms control, its record of achievement and the obstacles to its further advancement.

Attitudes towards arms control, and its objectives, cover the spectrum. Freedman has usefully distinguished between the 'reformers' who support arms control 'only if it produces major changes in the international system' and thus regard arms control as both a measure of fundamental change and as an instrument for bringing it into being. Alternatively, there are the 'managers' who more modestly seek, not to change the fundamental realities of the nuclear age but 'to ensure that the antagonism does not get out of hand'.[53] Measuring the success of arms control, or assessing its effect upon superpower relations, depends upon what the purpose of arms control is deemed to be.

It might be argued that, unlike classical disarmament which saw reduction in armaments as its only ostensible function, arms control has a prior interest in stabilising deterrence. Not only may this be achieved without actual reduction in numbers of weapons, but it can plausibly be argued that smaller nuclear arsenals might be more, rather than less, dangerous. According to this view, it is the nature of the cuts, and the characteristics of the remaining forces, that are more important than absolute numbers in themselves. If the residual forces after an arms accord are both highly accurate and vulnerable, it could then be contended that crisis instability has been heightened and such an agreement therefore undesirable.

Beyond this, the objectives of arms control may be deemed to lie outside the intrinsic strategic relationship itself. In these terms, arms control might be sought to reduce the economic cost of arms competition and to control expensive areas of technological rivalry. Additionally, some might think that the political results of arms control are more important than their strategic dividends: what is crucial is the *process* of arms control, rather than the substance of specific agreements, because it is a vital element in sustaining a healthy political dialogue between the superpowers.

The record of arms control to date reflects a mixture of strategic, political and economic motives. If anything, the Reagan administration, at least in its early years, took the view that arms control must be justified in its own strategic terms and that militarily undesirable deals should be avoided, whatever contribution they might make to political atmospherics.

Of the SALT agreements of 1972 and 1979, little remained into the 1980s. The ABM Treaty of SALT I remained in force but was under increasing strain as a result of renewed interest in strategic defence and because of reinterpretations of the treaty by the US administration. The SALT II agreement, although unratified, was broadly adhered to until the mid-1980s when its sub-limits were symbolically transgressed. Further negotiations were temporarily broken off in the wake of the INF deployment of 1983. Talks were resumed by the mid-1980s and culminated in the INF agreement of December 1987. This accord was significant as representing the first arms agreement to remove an entire class of missiles from current arsenals, namely land-based systems with ranges between 500–5500 kilometres.

193

There are substantial obstacles to further agreements. Old difficulties of what to count (what is a strategic system?) are now compounded by a proliferation of weapon systems, especially cruise missiles, which are difficult to count and verify. Fundamentally, the superpowers still remain far from resolving the problems associated with the asymmetrical structures of their respective arsenals, the United States retaining a preponderance of its warheads on submarines while the Soviet Union persists with a strategic force which is largely land-based. Arms control has thus far not reduced the gap between the superpowers in this respect.

Hopes nonetheless remain alive for a further treaty limiting strategic systems and it is widely mooted that 50 per cent reductions are envisaged. However, it is recognised that major impediments remain to be overcome and it is not at all clear that by the end of the second decade of arms control the superpowers had achieved much doctrinal congruence. As contrasted with the considerable consensus of the early 1970s that stable deterrence required an abandonment of strategic defences and an emphasis on large-scale retaliatory attacks, the realm of arms control at present betrays the complexities and uncertainties that have entered deterrence calculations over the previous two decades: there is uncertainty about what constitutes stable strategic targeting and whether single or multiple warhead systems are preferable; there is some disaffection with offensive deterrence and a revival of defensive deterrence concepts; there is disagreement about the virtues of mobility and concealment. In sum, current negotiations for a strategic forces reduction agreement are taking place in the absence of any clear and shared overall doctrine of deterrence. To this extent, the contribution of arms control to a deterrence philosophy shared between the superpowers has been considerably less than was anticipated in the early 1970s.

In summary, it might not be an unfair judgement on the record of arms control to suggest that it has served mainly as a barometer of the superpower relationship rather than as an independent factor capable of moderating that relationship if it is otherwise recalcitrant.

SPHERES OF INFLUENCE AND INTERVENTION

Analyses of the role played by the superpowers in the post-1945 order can be superficially divided into two polar interpretations. According to what might be termed the 'imperial model', it is the superpowers themselves that represent the greatest threat to international order. They are expansive and use their power to dominate regional neighbours as well as distant clients. They compete globally for influence, are rivals in the world's grey areas, fight wars by proxy and stimulate regional conflicts to maintain or further their own influence. Spheres of influence are a salient example of such infamous behaviour. Alternatively, an 'international order' view would emphasise the positive role played by the superpowers as the custodians of the international order. In its terms, the superpowers exercise restraint over clients, seek to defuse preexisting regional tensions and introduce elements of stability by the exercise of their hegemonial roles within demarcated spheres of influence.

In this section, we will consider the role of spheres of influence in the maintenance of post-1945 international order. However, before doing so, a brief examination of the concept of imperialism is needed in the belief that the two ideas are closely related: indeed, spheres of influence may be seen as a specific manifestation of the more general phenomenon of imperialism. Additionally, both concepts are open to the same difficulties of definition and interpretation.

The main problem with the idea of imperialism is as follows. If we look at the second half of the nineteenth century and especially the period 1880–1900, thought by many to represent the zenith of imperialistic activity, we find that its most striking feature was the annexation and partition of overseas territories by the European powers. Britain acquired Burma, France seized Indo-China and various islands in the Pacific. Germany too acquired territories in the Pacific. The United States annexed, amongst other places, Hawaii and the Philippines. Shortly after the turn of the century, Japan was to annexe Korea. Russia during the 1850s and 1860s had engulfed much of Central Asia and had extended her effective reach to the Pacific by the end of the century. The most dramatic partition was to occur in Africa. In 1875 only 10 per cent was controlled by the European powers whereas by 1900 90 per cent of Africa had been divided up amongst them. All in all, during the last quarter of the century about one-fifth of the globe fell into the possession of the European powers.

By contrast, if we look at the post-1945 period, we find that one of the salient features of the age is the break-up of the former colonial empires. The British withdrew from India and from South-East Asia. The Dutch were expelled from Indonesia, the French from Indo-China. The United States granted independence to the Philippines and in the course of the 1950s and 1960s most of Africa attained independent statehood.

The paradox is this. The term imperialism is said to characterise the latter period just as it did the former. We hear as much of imperialism today as in the late nineteenth century. Clearly this suggests some major definitional problems. If imperialism is to be taken as referring to a specific phenomenon that occurs in international relations, then it follows from the contrast drawn above that the manifestations of this phenomenon are not the same for every historical period. But then, we may legitimately ask, if the face of imperialism can change so dramatically over such a short span of time, are we not begging the question by assuming that, beneath these various masks, there is an underlying reality, a persisting set of characteristics that gives meaning, identity and continuity to a concept of imperialism? And if there is not, are we not in fact talking about discrete historical phenomena rather than about one concept?

One way out of this problem is to view imperialism in the most general of terms as a recurrent relationship of control but allowing that the precise means by which this control is attained varies from historical period to period. How does this pertain to a discussion of spheres of influence? According to this conception of imperialism as a relationship of control, spheres of influence would be one technique for its exercise. Moreover, spheres of influence themselves have changed in precisely the same way as imperialism in general and can be used as an illustration of the point that, although the imperialist urge to control is fairly constant, the specific manifestations of it vary from one historical period to another.

In other words, changes in the nature of spheres of influence have reflected the more general changes that have taken place in the nature of imperialistic control over the past century or so. As one analyst of spheres of influence has written:

> the formal agreements of the late 19th and early 20th centuries often preceded any actual influence and were intended to prevent or limit conflict which might occur between European powers as they expanded into Africa and Asia. In this respect, they are unlike contemporary spheres of influence. To the extent that contemporary spheres of influence have limited conflict, this has been an effect and not a cause of them.[54]

There was, then, a type of spheres-of-influence agreement that was appropriate to the annexationist phase of imperialism and now there is a new form of sphere of influence appropriate to the non-annexationist phase.

How would we define such a sphere? One writer has discerned three integral parts of the concept of a sphere of influence in post-1945 world politics and, although his formulation leaves some questions unanswered, they are worth reproducing at this stage. The three are: a declared interest of a power to achieve such a dominating status; recognition of this claim by other important members of the world community; and acquiescence of the local regimes or their resignation to a condition of dependency.[55]

The questions raised by the notion of spheres of influence all relate directly to issues of hierarchy. As our historical survey of the evolution of the international system has shown, there has been a perennial tendency to ascribe special rights to the Great Powers in accordance with their power status. The point about this is that some writers would argue that a hierarchical arrangement of states and an inegalitarian distribution of privileges within that hierarchy constitutes a valuable contribution to international order. As Hedley Bull has put it:

> Because states are grossly unequal in power, certain international issues are as a consequence settled, the demands of certain states (weak ones) can in practice be left out of account, the demands of certain other states (strong ones) recognised to be the only ones relevant to the issue in hand ... The inequality of states in terms of power has the effect, in other words, of simplifying the pattern of international relations.[56]

Put crudely, this means that hierarchy enhances international order by avoiding recourse to war every time a dispute occurs: since we know in advance that a big power will defeat a small one, we can proceed directly to a solution of the dispute by simply letting the big power have its way.

Those analysts who see virtue in spheres of influence base their case on much the same kind of reasoning. They see spheres of influence as a positive contribution to international order in the sense that they serve to limit conflict between the superpowers and they do so by demarcating areas considered vital to the respective superpowers and by stabilising each power's enjoyment of rights within its respective sphere. For instance, the Soviet Union could invade Hungary and Czechoslovakia in 1956 and 1968 without any fear of reprisal from the West. Had these two states not fallen unequivocally within the Soviet sphere of influence, there might well have been a danger of serious conflict between the superpowers. But the existence of this sphere of influence and its recognition by the West effectively removed this area as a possible source of conflict between the rival superpowers.

This argument that spheres of influence contribute to international order by limiting the areas of competition between the major powers can be illustrated negatively by the case of the Cuban crisis in 1962. Essentially, the significance of the Cuban crisis was that it represented a Soviet attempt to change the boundaries of the American sphere of influence or, at least, amounted to a Soviet refusal to recognise the traditional contours of the American sphere. As a consequence, the world was pushed towards the brink of nuclear war. Spheres of influence, therefore, are thought to prevent confrontations of the Cuban kind – as long as both sides' spheres are mutually recognised.

There are several difficulties in coming to terms with spheres of influence and in assessing their place in the post-1945 international system. In the first instance, as was noted in a quotation above, their contribution to conflict-prevention is incidental to their primary role, which we have said is as an expression of the imperialist urge to control. Any assessment of spheres would be derelict if it did not take this into account.

Additionally, there is the problem of discerning in what sense spheres of influence are based upon conscious agreements or formally accepted rules of the game. To the extent that they are, they may well be regarded as a form, albeit limited, of group norm of the kind that has underlain Great Power concert diplomacy of the past. Here, however, the basis of agreement appears too tenuous to support a working concert system: Bull is undoubtedly correct when he states that 'Soviet–American spheres-of-influence understandings have so far been negative in content rather than positive.'[57] It was also argued in relation to the Concert of Europe that one of its operative rules was the requirement of 'formal consent'. Likewise, the attempt to build a post-1918 concert was based on the formal rules of the covenant. In this sense, because spheres of influence are informal, there is difficulty in knowing their status in the eyes of the superpowers. Kaufman points out this problem when he notes that 'it is hard to establish that a mutual agreement does exist reciprocally legitimising the rule of the rival superpowers in their respective spheres of influence', but he lamely begs the question when he concludes that 'it seems most probable that an understanding does exist to a certain degree'.[58]

Lastly, while spheres of influence may contribute to order by reducing the areas of rivalry between the superpowers, it surely has to be insisted that they undermine other constituents of international order? In any recounting of the principles upon which order has traditionally been based, sovereignty and non-intervention in domestic affairs would figure prominently and yet these are the principles that have most obviously been subordinated to the order sustained by spheres of influence.

This provides a tangible illustration of the conflict between 'realist' and 'charter' conceptions of international order. As one writer has expressed his indignation, 'we can no more identify the conventions of super-power domination with a morally satisfactory international order than we can identify the most iniquitous command of a Hobbesian sovereign with justice'.[59] At the same time, such practices as spheres seem ingrained in the very fabric of international relations. They may well enhance a superpower-preferred international order, but they are immune to utopian expressions of outrage. In the words of their foremost analyst, 'the history of spheres of influence suggests that radical reform is a pious and elusive hope'.[60]

Of the various tacit expectations about superpower behaviour concerning spheres of influence, that which seems to be on firmest ground is the expectation of military non-intervention within each other's sphere because such reciprocity introduces 'a reasonably stable pattern of mutual expectations in the crucial areas of superpower coexistence'.[61] This leads to the more general topic of intervention in international relations and its relationship to patterns of order.

Intervention falls precisely at the interstices of the various conceptions of order depicted in this volume. It is a principal instrument of both the 'imperial' and the 'international order' perspectives upon superpower behaviour. It is the single issue around which the realist and the Charter conceptions of order most flagrantly diverge, the former accepting it as a contribution to order and the latter as the most palpable evidence of violation of international norms. The topic also opens the wider issue of international versus world order since many of the notions of intervention and non-intervention have been crafted around statist conceptions which do little to accommodate the behaviour of states in a world in which human rights occupy a more significant legal and rhetorical position.

The subject is also diffuse, so much so that 'interventionary activity of one kind or another is so widespread that it is sometimes said to be endemic or "structural" in nature'.[62] Thus far, intervention has been considered only in cases of overt military intervention in spheres of influence, such as that sanctioned by the Brezhnev Doctrine. However, intervention can take many forms, ranging from the covert to the direct, and from political and economic to the overtly military.

In the post-1945 period, a number of variant forms of forceful intervention may be distinguished and it is around such typologies that the normative debate concerning which types of intervention may be justified has been conducted. Walzer, for instance, believes that some interventions in support of secessions, in support of counterinterventions in a civil war, and humanitarian interventions may be both justified and obligatory.[63] For present purposes, three broad

199

types of intervention – in civil wars, in external wars, and humanitarian – will be delineated.

The first has represented the typical form of superpower intervention during the period. Faced with a regime threatened by internal or external forces of resistance, the superpowers have intervened or counterintervened to support their preferred candidates for power. The level of support has again ranged from the outright military, through encouragement of proxy intervention and to covert and material assistance. The Soviet intervention in Afghanistan and the American role in Vietnam might be thought to correspond to the first; the Soviet sponsorship of Cuban participation in support of the MPLA in the Angolan civil war to the second; and American subventions variously to UNITA forces in Angola and the Contras in Nicaragua to the third. Indeed, during the 1980s the Reagan administration came close to elevating such a policy to that of a doctrine by systematically encouraging 'freedom fighters' against communist regimes in Angola, Nicaragua, Afghanistan and Kampuchea.

The second category is epitomised in superpower support of clients involved in regional conflict situations and while thus representing intervention in third-party disputes, does not represent intervention in domestic affairs to the same extent. Superpower involvement in the Middle East wars of 1967 and 1973, largely through the medium of arms supplies, polarised superpower stances in relation to the Indo-Pakistani war of 1971, and superpower embroilment in the war in the Horn of Africa in 1977–8 are all typical of this situation.

Thirdly, it is widely suggested that there is a separate category of humanitarian intervention. This is purportedly brought about in situations where governments perpetrate gross violations of human rights against their own populations. In cases where this occurs, it has been suggested that there may be justification for outside intervention, and some might say an onus upon the wider international community to take action. It is a moot point whether such action should be taken collectively by the international community, acting through its agencies, or unilaterally by individual states. Widely cited instances in recent experience where major violations of human rights have taken place include the treatment of its eastern half by the Pakistani authorities prior to the secession of Bangladesh in 1971, the genocide conducted by the Pol Pot regime in Kampuchea in the 1970s and Idi Amin's reign of terror in Uganda. In each of these cases, there was to be intervention by outside parties in the shape of India, Vietnam and Tanzania. The case has been made that these were justified humanitarian interventions to remove intolerably oppressive regimes although, in fact, this has seldom been presented in international forums as the actual reason for such interventions.[64] Not surprisingly, state authorities are reluctant to allow this particular genie to escape the bottle.

It is apparent from this, as well as from earlier discussion of intervention that it finds a place both in conservative international, and in radical world, conceptions of order. With a Metternich, intervention in the domestic affairs of other states to suppress revolutionary movements – because of their potential to disrupt the international order – is justified. From the other end, radical human right interventionists clamour for international overthrow of disreputable regimes, such as that in South Africa, on the grounds of a violated universal human rights order to which the non-interventionary ground-rules of the international system must be subordinate. Despite the immense gulfs between their political philosophies and political prescriptions, both conservatives and radicals nonetheless make similar appeals to the need for intervention.

A case can be made that, just as with annexationist forms of imperialism, the temper of the contemporary international system is set against the cruder and more overt forms of military intervention.[65] Nonetheless, the practice of intervention in its various forms is all but universal. It gives rise also to other facets of superpower behaviour. It is the risk that competitive interventions in support of clients, either in internal or external wars, will lead unwittingly to higher levels of superpower confrontation than is thought safe or desirable that has contributed to the quest for crisis management regimes. And it is the endeavour to restrain interventions in the grey areas of the third world that stimulated the quest for detente in the 1970s, at least in the American understanding of it. The norms associated with these two superpower practices can be explored in turn.

CRISIS MANAGEMENT AND DETENTE

Can the conventions of crisis management or the rules of detente provide a sufficiently coherent framework for concert diplomacy in the post-1945 era, even if only a limited concert of two superpowers? There is little reason to think so. In fact, as with some of the previous regulatory systems considered in this book, there is a suggestion that such rules of superpower relations as have been observed have been a product of the post-1945 order rather than the cause of it – a reflection of the specific balance of power rather than of conscious adherence to formalised precepts.

That this is so is amply revealed in the central ambiguity within the very concept of crisis management. On the one hand, the term has been used to denote the art of winning diplomatic victory: a crisis is 'managed' if the opponent is made to back down. On the other, crisis management has been used to refer to a set of practices whereby the superpowers 'ride' a crisis and consciously seek to avoid the outbreak of war between them. On the basis of this distinction, there is reason for believing that, in their responses to crises, the respective superpowers have acted more often on the basis of a calculation of unilateral advantage than out of a concern for shared managerial interest.

We might characterise the main difference between these two conceptions of crisis management as that between conflict-utilisation and conflict-avoidance. The distinction is amply summarised by P. Williams. He says of the former conception that:

> crises are not regarded as pathological or distasteful but rather as an opportunity for aggrandisement. It is the opposing state and not the crisis itself that is the enemy. Far from being a partnership, there is fierce competition or rivalry in which every attempt is made to manipulate or influence the adversary's behaviour in desired directions.

Of the latter, he observes that:

> implicit in this view is the notion of a crisis as a pathological occurrence to be ended or defused as quickly as possible. The aim is to control the situation and dampen down the conflict ... The crisis itself is the real enemy and the participants are actually partners in the task of eliminating the dangers of war and restoring things to normal.[66]

The vast majority of post-1945 crises have been managed in the former, rather than the latter, sense and have, therefore, been exercises in the balance of power rather than displays of a superpower concert. Even in such cases where management of the latter kind seems to have occurred, there can be no assurance that the powers have been moved in their behaviour by acceptance of 'rules' and 'conventions' or, whether the tactical demands of specific events have not produced a fortuitous convergence of interests.

The 'conventions' that have developed for the conduct of crises seem to fall into two broad categories, the former a hardware or technical, and the latter a political or diplomatic, set of guidelines for handling of crises. Examples of the former would be means of communication, such as the post-Cuba hot-line (since upgraded) and various systems of secure command and control. Examples of the latter would be a delimitation of objectives, controlled escalation (choosing a naval quarantine rather than an air strike on Cuba in 1962), leaving the opponent a dignified means of backing down, and tacit forms of communication or signalling. The optimists would tend to argue that the technical environment has improved and that, through learning, statesmen are now better equipped to handle crises than previously. The pessimists would emphasise that an increasingly complex technical hardware, and greater reliance upon it, has heightened the dangers of accident or malfunction. Indeed, some would lament that the faith placed in technology is corrosive of political judgement. 'Good crisis management cannot be fabricated from communication nodes' chastises Lebow, and suggests that 'in a complete reversal of Clausewitzian logic, technology, divorced from politics, has come to dominate strategy'.[67]

The question as to whether the superpowers consciously adhere to crisis conventions is the crucial one and has been by no means resolved in favour of the theorists of crisis management. A useful example is provided in Coral Bell's seminal work.[68] In her discussion of the Quemoy crisis of 1958, she refers to American 'creative use of ambiguity' in its diplomatic signalling, whereby President Eisenhower and Secretary of State Dulles emitted two very different forms of signal. However, the reader is somewhat perplexed to be told that this 'diplomatic success' had been gained 'largely by a *conscious or unconscious* use of ambiguity'.[69] If the ambiguity was conscious, all is well and we can perhaps speak of crisis management (although for this to be regarded as a 'group norm', it would also be necessary for the receivers of the ambiguous signals to appreciate their significance). If, however, the ambiguity was not conscious or intended, what we have instead is a typical piece of bureaucratic bungling with one voice of government saying one thing and another voice saying something else – diplomatic mismanagement rather than crisis management. The point about this example is that it is extremely difficult to tell whether the participants in a crisis are actually operating in accordance with a code of crisis etiquette or whether the academic analyst is merely reading such a code into behaviour that is random and undisciplined.

There is a further problem. By which criteria should we measure whether, and how successfully, crisis management has taken place? Do we assess it in terms of the interests of one of the superpowers, in terms of a common superpower interest in avoiding conflict or can we relate it to some wider notion of the interests of international society? For instance, the superpowers may manage a third-party crisis, such as that in the Middle East, so as to minimise hostilities but without necessarily settling the underlying issue. Can we speak of 'management' in such a context? If crisis management is designed to avoid conflict rather than settle issues, should we necessarily assume that what is convenient for the superpowers is also in the best interests of the other members of international society? In any event, how much confidence ought to be placed in the ability of the superpowers to control the behaviour of their clients, a question prompted particularly by the Middle East crisis of 1973?

One final comment on crisis management is worth making. In some of the literature, there is the not-unreasonable suggestion that, given the existence of nuclear weapons and the enormity of nuclear violence, crisis management can be regarded as a kind of functional substitute for actual war. In this case, as war can no longer be regarded as politically rational, but as the system still requires some mechanism for reaching political decisions, the management of the crisis and the diplomatic manoeuvring that accompanies it is the new means of resolving conflicts. If we push this interpretation to its ultimate conclusion, the powers involved in a crisis are in a quasi-war situation and playing for big stakes and it is scarcely conceivable that the 'game' would be played out according to neat and tidy gentlemen's rules. In other words, if the provenance of crisis conventions is a limited one, we should not have expected it to be otherwise.

There is some overlap between the notions of crisis management and detente, both having been seen as patterns in post-1945 superpower relations, with the major distinction being that detente has been a diplomatic technique for overall superpower relations rather than simply a code that is activated when crisis occurs. C. Bell's conception of detente is as 'a diplomatic strategy for a triangular power balance',[70] and she sees it as having been the dominant mode of managing the central balance since 1969.

There are various views of detente. It has been defined as a 'process of easing of tension between states whose interests are so radically divergent that reconciliation is inherentlly limited'.[71] Others have sought to distinguish between detente as a 'policy instrument' (process) and as a 'policy objective' (substance or goal).[72]

Beyond this, detente might either be seen as simply a phase in an ongoing superpower relationship or, alternatively, as a substantially new departure to implement concert principles in their relationship.

The former view tends to see the post-1945 Soviet–American relationship as a succession of phases, some characterised by tension, others by relative relaxation. The periods 1947–53, 1958–62, 1967–8, and 1977–83 might all be offered as belonging to the former category:

1954–7, 1963–6, 1969–75 and the late 1980s as periods of the latter. In these terms, there was nothing distinctive about the detente of the early 1970s; it was simply one phase in a cycle of such phases.

As against this, detente may be viewed as a qualitative innovation. Stevenson thinks it distinctive for its positive element in that the 'Moscow detente sought to establish a framework for competition and a basis for cooperation'.[73] We can discern substantial reasons for this. The Soviet Union sought strategic equality, sought relief from the economic pressure of arms competition and economic benefit from expanded trading and technological contact with the West, as well as the sanctification of the post-1945 division of Europe. For the United States, a new relationship with the Soviet Union would allow for a recovery from the debacle of Vietnam, permit the incorporation of China into the power balance and enable a diversion of attention away from East–West military issues to the now looming West–West economic issues.

The substance of detente can then be seen as representing a set of principles both for managing the superpower relationship and for imparting some direction to the international order as a whole. It is best embodied in attempts to manage the strategic nuclear balance, to create a 'legitimate' international order by enmeshing the Soviet Union in a web of mutual interests, by efforts to develop a crisis-prevention regime, and by concerted actions to manage third-party crises, such as that of 1973 in the Middle East.

How then should we locate the strategy of detente within our spectrum ranging from balance to concert policies? Does detente signify a substantial modification of balance strategies as the Concert of Europe did, if only partially, and as the League attempted to do, but without success? Coral Bell's comments are instructive. Given the adversary context in which detente arose, and as in the case of crisis management, Bell is insistent that 'it does not in any way imply an end to the contest for diplomatic influence, only a mode of making the contest less dangerous'.[74] She adds, and here we should recall the Concert of Europe, that 'detente should certainly not be mistaken for peace. Peace is an objective, detente is a diplomatic mode or strategy by which that objective (or others) may be sought.'[75] Both of these statements, while not in themselves descriptive of detente as a superpower concert, are at least fully compatible with such an interpretation. However, Bell subsequently makes it clear that she does not regard detente as a set of concert principles for the superpowers: 'Obviously a balance of power underlay the nineteenth-century concert of powers, or it would not have proved viable, just as a balance of power is now necessary as the foundation of the detente, which is not a concert of powers.'[76] The phraseology implies that such a concert may nonetheless be in the process of emergence although no indication is given as to how it will materialise. Indeed, in view of Bell's approving citation of Castlereagh's opinion that in a concert system the powers feel a common duty as well as a common interest, one is left wondering what the source of this common duty will be perceived to be by the powers involved.

With hindsight, we can now see that the detente of the 1970s faltered and gave way to a further tense period, often described as a Second Cold War.[77] The failure of the detente is most commonly attributed to mutual misunderstandings about the principles of detente, the United States mistakenly believing that it would induce moderation in Soviet behaviour in the third world, and the Soviet Union disappointed in the 'equality' allowed by the United States. It is worth also pointing out that detente, and the more hostile relationship which succeeded it, have both been attributed to superpower attempts to stabilise their control of world affairs. It was perhaps unsurprising that, in the face of the more pluralistic world balance of the late 1960s, the superpowers should have reached some accommodation in order to control an increasingly volatile and diffuse international system. Similarly, the heightened tension between the superpowers in the late 1970s has been attributed to the superpower desire to bring recalcitrant allies to heel by emphasising their dependence for security upon their superpower protectors.

Is it then, appropriate to characterise the post-1945 order as a reversion to balance policies in which a concert system hás not simply failed but has not even been aspired to? It must be conceded that the posing of the issue in these terms creates a genuine problem of interpretation and it may well be impossible to arrive at an assessment acceptable to all schools of thought.

On the one hand, we can be confident in our conclusion, which has been the thesis of this chapter, that the behaviour of the major powers, in their relations with each other, has not been sufficiently regulated by formally accepted rules for us to be able to speak of a functioning post-1945 concert system. The reasons for such a conclusion have been cogently stated by Bull elsewhere but bear repetition at this point:

> There has been no attempt to formalise a Soviet–American concert. There is no regular attempt to concert, in the sense of the holding of regular discussions concerned to define common and unique objectives, to map out a common strategy for attaining them and for distributing the burdens of such a strategy . . . Nor has there been

enunciated any theory or ideology of world order, such as underlay the Holy Alliance or the later European concert, that would give direction and purpose to a Soviet–American concert.[78]

On the other hand, if not as a concert, how are we to characterise the Great Power tutelage of the post-1945 order? The problem from this perspective is that many reasonable analysts have given weighty reasons why a description of postwar international relations in balance terminology would not be appropriate. Morse, for one, has roundly declaimed that 'the world simply does not conform to the patterns established in the Westphalian framework'[79] and that 'the balance of power has ceased to be useful as a description of the international system'.[80]

We can be sympathetic to this line of reasoning but reject its ultimate conclusion. Of course international life is now vastly more complex than previously, with a host of new state actors, as well as many non-state ones, with a change of emphasis to new, and in many cases non-military, issues and with a greater degree of 'linkage' or 'interdependence' within the whole. This much must be readily conceded. Nonetheless, when we consider the ways in which international security has been maintained, and the ways in which the Great Powers have related to each other, it is difficult to deny totally the validity of the balance concept. The conclusion that suggests itself, unsatisfactory as it might appear, is that until the balance system becomes something else, it remains a balance system even if altered in form. As no one can adequately define what has taken the place of the previous system, and as we can be sure that it is not diplomacy by concert, then the description of the post-1945 world as an age of balance is, perhaps, the least misleading of the alternatives.

CONCLUSION

This book has been concerned with both ideas and practices in relation to international order and its potential for reform. As such, it has explored continuity and change both in the ideology of international order and in its historical practice. It remains only to summarise the assessment of change, both as regards ideas about international relations and the actual conduct of international affairs. Finally, the conclusion will comment upon the mutual interaction between ideas and practices. That images of international order and historical patterns of international order affect each other is uncontroversial but trite: meanwhile, the precise nature of this inter-relationship resists adequate analysis.

IDEOLOGY

It has been noted in the course of this study that optimism and pessimism, whether in relation to the need for international reform or the possibility of its attainment, have been persistent attitudes of mind. At the same time, one or other of these moods has tended to become dominant during various phases of history: we tend to associate some periods with a prevailing mood of optimism or pessimism and these moods fluctuate, if not in cyclical fashion, then at least at fairly regular intervals.

It is, of course, possible to discern why some intellectual moods do arise. Most obviously, fears and hopes about the nature of international order are generated by events in the real world of international relations, be it in the form of current experience, or recent memories, or imminent expectations. Dramatic events, such as wars, exercise the most profound influence but can, as we have seen, inspire hope even as they fill us with fear and despair. If the mood of the 1920s was one of confidence, then this was surely a product of the League experiment and the appearance, even if superficial, of a new international order having been inaugurated, just as the despondency of the 1930s was associated with the highly visible failure of the League experiment and the seeming reversion to naked power politics: intellectually, a predominantly utopian temperament was superseded by a predominantly realist one. Similarly, it could be argued that, as far as the climate of international politics was concerned, nuclear weaponry cast a more gloomy shadow over the 1950s than over the 1960s if for no other reason than the growing to maturity of a generation that, in the cliché, has learned to live with the bomb. The student of the 1970s who opened Inis Claude's impressive *Power and International Relations*, written at the height of the Cold War, could not fail to detect a slightly alien mood in the stark and sombre opening passages to the effect that 'mankind stands in grave danger of irreparable self-mutilation or substantial self-destruction' and that 'the march of military technology is so rapid that it is no longer premature to contemplate the danger of the annihilation of the human race'.[1] The possibility of such an occurrence had not lessened in the interval but the seeming durability of the 'nuclear peace' had fostered its own acceptance. By the late 1970s and early 1980s, attitudes towards nuclear weapons had regained their former tone of despair and anxiety and writings on the subject were once more apocalyptic. This reflected the deterioration in superpower relations of that period and the associated disquiet about nuclear strategies prompted by decisions to deploy new theatre nuclear weapons, by the seeming failure of arms control, by the emergence of new 'war-fighting' nuclear strategies and by careless talk of limited nuclear wars in Europe.

At the same time, moods of optimism and pessimism appear also to have their sources in a type of theoretical speculation that may itself be divorced from the current practice of international politics. The realist reorientation within the academic discipline of international relations, which established itself during the 1940s, was as much a reaction to the theoretical inadequacies of the previous generation of writers as it was to the specific international events of the 1930s. We could also insist that there was no very obvious diversity in historical experience to account for the differing temperaments of Rousseau and Kant. In other words, the very moods of those who think seriously about the nature and patterns of international order appear to derive from a mixture of practical and theoretical concerns.

Whether optimistic or pessimistic, theories of international order are also a complex combination of assumptions about continuity and about change. It might be thought that the dichotomies are simple and that it is the pessimists who stress continuity whereas the optimists emphasise change. The situation is not quite so straightforward.

Whence derives the perception of continuity in international relations? There is a simple answer to this question which appears to satisfy but on reflection gives rise to a series of consequent questions. It has been provided, amongst others, by P. Savigear and its initial premise is that international politics are no more than the untidy fringes of domestic politics and, as such, are not susceptible to the same progressive developments as have occurred within states. Savigear explains why the philosophy of international relations has remained static while political philosophy generally has been dynamic:

> The state has changed – the precise form of that change may be in dispute, some would say from dynastic to absolutist and to democratic for example – and the philosophy of the state has changed with it. Thought about International Relations, and indeed International Relations themselves, have not so changed . . . There is not the same sense of moving forward through the history of thought that characterizes the traditional presentation of political theory because in a way there was a progression in the changing nature of the relationship between ruler and ruled . . . The conception of the state was thus eroded from within by the theorists of the internal ordering of the state, but this did not happen for those writers who drew their arguments about International Relations from political philosophy.[2]

Put simply, international politics is about the relationships between states, regardless of the nature of the states themselves, and changes in patterns of domestic order do not, in turn, lead to new patterns of international order.

As a characterisation of the theory of international relations this, as will be argued below, is a half-truth. Before pursuing this issue, however, it is worth asking why there should be this disjunction in thought between internal order and international order. Why, in the course of the past two centuries, have all domestic political systems been faced with, and acceded to, demands for major restructuring while the international polity has remained obdurate to pressures for change? Could the tentative answer be that people have expected much less from the international system? This, in turn, is explicable in terms of the inability of people to discern readily how the international system benefits them or harms them: their demands are directed at, and their wants are assumed to be satisfied by, domestic polities. The affects of the international system upon individual lives are, as a generalisation, but dimly perceived beyond the names of dead soldiers on countless local cenotaphs.

It is worth observing that, if the theorists of 'complex inter-dependence' are correct, then this situation may be changing and the international polity may become the focal point of increasing demands. As people come to recognise the impotence of individual governments, primarily but not exclusively in economic terms, they will more consciously direct attention to the nature of international order and seek satisfaction in that quarter. The appeals for a new international economic order may illustrate this trend to the extent that they are based on a recognition of the fact that individual third world governments cannot deliver 'development' without some adjustment of the world's economic system.

As mentioned above, the theory of inter-state relationships appears to have been static, in spite of the many changes that have taken place within the state itself. The implication of this is that there is no such thing as a 'progressive' theory of international relations. Are we to accept this as a valid characterisation of theoretical speculation in the field of international relations?

In one sense, there is some truth in this proposition. In terms of 'progressive' international theories, we have already confronted such a doctrine in the shape of the Kantian model of international change. However, we would surely have to concede that, although optimistic in its ultimate prognosis about the future international order and although firmly grounded on a theory of progress, the Kantian model remains a fearsome and distressing one? The view has been expressed that 'history does not move forward without catastrophe'.[3] This, like the Kantian, is a theory of progress but the manner of its attainment casts its own depressing shadow.

Were the Kantian vision the only progressive theory of international relations, there might well be grounds for saying that no genuine theory of international progress exists. However, the simple propo-sition that change is impossible because international relations are derivative of state practice leaves out of account the theory of the state itself, much of which emphasises its dynamic nature. International relations may be practised in a constant framework of inter-state relations but the states themselves are changing, yielding a new substance to their contacts. Competing perspectives on the state – contractual, organic, liberal, marxist, repressive, administrative and interventionist – reflect differences of theoretical interpretation, but also the heterogeneity of the world's many states as well as the historical evolution of the state in recent centuries. Only by creating 'black boxes' can we equate the rudimentary security-fiscal state of the seventeenth century with the socio-economic provider of the twentieth. To the extent that the boxes have changed, what occurs in the interstices of their relationships will have changed substantially as a consequence. Continuity thus comes from the structure of the international system but change from the transformation of the individual units. Paradoxically, theories of international order have suffered both from too much concentration on the state and from too little elaboration of its evolving nature.

There are a number of bodies of progressive theory which deserve consideration in this context: functionalism, liberal–democratic 'internationalism' and the general Marxist–Leninist tradition all contain within them theories of international progress. A brief comment may be made on each.

Functionalism may be viewed as one of the major peace theories of the twentieth century, although many of its intellectual components stretch back at least into the eighteenth century. Its classic formulation is to be found in Mitrany's *A Working Peace System*. The body of ideas associated with functionalism was, like the internationalist idealism of Woodrow Wilson, a reformist ideology – a prescription for improving the world and especially for eliminating violence at the international level. Unlike Wilsonian idealism, however, advocates of functionalism were suspicious about efforts to attain peace by the mere construction of international organisations such as the League. In fact, the functionalist creed represented an alternative to the more traditional efforts at ensuring peace in that it explicitly disavowed such facile constitutional–institutional solutions to the problems of international order.

The central concept of functionalism is that of basic human needs and its contention is that human loyalties will be directed toward the source of the fulfilment of these needs. While the state has traditionally been viewed in this role of 'provider', there are now important areas of human needs that, far from being furthered by the state, are positively thwarted by the existence of separate national jurisdictions. As these needs come to be fulfilled outside the state, so will loyalties come to be redirected towards new supra-national organisations. Unlike constitutional solutions to international order, functionalism does not advocate a direct challenge to the national sovereignty of the state: rather it expects that eventually, in the face of extending functional cooperation across national boundaries, these boundaries will become of decreasing political relevance. As with Marxism, functionalism presents an essentially materialist view of historical development and argues that, as a consequence of changes in the ways in which needs are satisfied, there will be corresponding changes in the international political superstructure. To some extent, as with traditional Marxism, the state will simply wither away. In this sense, functionalism constitutes an important instance of a theory of international progress.

A second such 'progressive' school is that represented by liberal–democratic internationalism, a set of beliefs that was most clearly influential in the early years of the present century. Its intellectual force derived from its adoption of many liberal–democratic beliefs and assumptions of the nineteenth century and from its attempt to apply them in a different context – as having an applicability to international, and not simply to internal, politics.

The central pillar of this doctrine was to be the beneficial role of 'public opinion'. Broadly speaking, there were two reasons why the liberal internationalists wished to foster a greater role for public opinion in international affairs. The first of these was the increasingly 'democratic' nature of warfare itelf: the experience of the First World War and its widespread slaughter, its far greater impact upon civilian populations and the tentative beginnings of air power – all of these technological aspects of warfare had the common effect of ensuring that war would make itself felt within much wider sections of society than had hitherto been the case. Moreover, since warfare was likely to be universal in its effects, the democratic 'progressives' believed it only right that the public at large should be more intimately involved in the processes of international politics in order to try to prevent wars. In other words, while war was the sport of princes, it may have been permissible to leave diplomacy to the princes' close advisers but now that war was impinging more directly upon each and every life, the public at large was entitled to be consulted.

The second reason why the liberal internationalists emphasised the role of public opinion was a reflection of their faith in the inherent good sense of that opinion and of their faith that public opinion would act as a restraint upon the belligerent policies pursued by autocratic states. In this sense, we are back with Kant's proposition that a 'republican constitution' would be the best guarantee of peace. The belief rests upon two assumptions: that only in a democratic system will governmental representatives be accountable to, and controlled by, the people: and that because of the inherent moral good sense of the people, they will not permit their governments to pursue unscrupulous or warlike policies. Woodrow Wilson was a foremost champion of this position:

> No nation is admitted to the League of Nations that cannot show that it has institutions which we call free ... Nobody is admitted except

213

> the self-governing nations, because it was the instinctive judgement of every man who sat around that board that only a nation whose government was its servant and not its master could be trusted to preserve the peace of the world.[4]

Even more succinctly, he contended that:

> a steadfast concert for peace can never be maintained except by a partnership of democratic nations. No autocratic government could be trusted to keep faith with it or observe its covenants.

Liberal internationalism was, therefore, another example of a progressive doctrine. It held to the position that the international order would be improved as a concomitant of the internal processes of democratisation that were occurring within states. Democratically-constituted states would yield a peaceful and harmonious international order, without need for any further adjustment to international political structures.

Thirdly, and lastly, Marxism–Leninism may be said to embody a theory of international progress. It has often been observed that orthodox Marxism lacks any explicit theory of international relations whatsoever. This is not the place to enter into such a debate. Suffice it for present purposes to note that Marxist theory in general, because of its exposition of a series of sequential historical stages, is inherently 'progressive'. Each stage, for Marx, in some important sense represents an improvement upon the stage that preceded it. Moreover, progressive development is ensured by the dialectics of history. Finally, of course, the process culminates in the achievement of a communist society. As far as international relations are concerned, the relevance of the Marxist–Leninist tradition may be confined to the following observation. In as much as international competition and the outbreak of wars are to be explained in terms of the contradictions of the capitalist system, then the resolution of these conflicts in the attainment of communist society will also resolve international conflict. If not explicit in Marxist theory, it is at least implicit, that the achievement of communist society would lead to major international restructuring, if for no other reason than the withering-away of the class-based state.

There are, of course, differences in the nature of the 'progress' postulated in these theories, and we might, with Paul Taylor, distinguish between 'episodic' and 'evolutionary' progress. In Taylor's analysis, the League of Nations was to constitute 'episodic' progress:

> The fourteen points were very much in the tradition of the Lockean social contract; there was to be a single stage transition from a period of disgrace in which diplomacy was private and evil in its effects to a

period of grace in which diplomacy would be open, democratic, and just. Progress in international society was thought to have a beginning and an end: it had to begin in present deficiencies and would finish on a kind of eternal plateau populated with contented and benign states.[5]

Such conceptions have tended to be superseded by 'evolutionary' notions:

> That approach to the problems of world order called Functionalism is also more evolutionary than episodic; it stresses the ongoing and adaptive processes of international integration rather than a particular condition of integration.[6]

The three doctrines briefly discussed may, nonetheless, be taken as examples of 'progressive' international theories. However, in support of Savigear's observation that theories of international relations have not developed in the same way as have theories of the state itself, it might be objected legitimately that none of these three doctrines constitutes a theory of *autonomous* international progress. They are all derivative in as much as the progress that is prescribed for the international order is, in each case, parasitic upon internal domestic changes in the nature of the state. Once again, it may be argued that just as international relations emerged as a side-effect of the modern nation–state, so our theories of international progress are equally 'dependent' and we might see any restructuring of the international order to be contingent upon changes in the state units themselves.

Certainly, in each of the three bodies of theory we have considered, changes to the international order can be seen to be derivative from changes to the internal order within states, whether it be by the democratisation of the state or its gradual withering from within. This leads us to the important issue of the relationship between international order and internal domestic order and we might observe that, even if international order is something more than the sum of domestic orders, it remains true that the two cannot be divorced from each other. In other words, it is impossible to visualise any form of satisfactory international order, however one might want to define it, that is not itself constructed upon satisfactory domestic orders.

This expresses the point rather abstractly and it may clarify matters to provide an example. We have already referred to the prominent position of economic demands by third world countries in present debates about the nature of a desirable international order. The point is simply that such demands for overall restructuring of the economic order would be pointless on their own if they were not taken in conjunction with measures to effect economic redistribution within individual third world countries. This is not to take sides in the debate as to where the true causes of world poverty are to be located but, less ambitiously, to emphasise the uncontentious fact that the two dimensions of the problem, external and internal, are inter-related.[7] In short, a more equitable international order would not by itself suffice to ensure the improvement of the economic lot of the poorest sections of the world's population.[8]

Such an analysis is identical with that found within the school of Wilsonian internationalism discussed above. Its fundamental premise is that a stable international political order can only be achieved in unison with the creation of the domestic democratic orders necessary to sustain it. This again draws attention to the tensions between international and world order within differing ideological frameworks. If it is true that some international orders are derivative from domestic orders, likewise is it so that world orders can both be sustained, and violated, by the interplay between international and domestic orders. At the level of individual security, there is little succour for the citizen when the state turns predator: the Kampuchean atrocities demonstrate the extent to which world order can be subverted when the international order is permissive of domestic butchery. Arguably, in this case the structure of international order was too strong to make possible the saving of human lives. At the other extreme, the recent fate of Lebanon reveals the threat to individual security from a domestic political order too weak to keep the intrusions of the international system at bay. Individual human rights, visualised in a world order framework, are thus threatened equally by pernicious domestic and international orders but neither are they sustainable without such orders.

The static quality of much of the ideology of international order, coupled with its traditional incapacity to come to terms with the individual human beings who inhabit the hierarchy of states, are both ultimately explicable by their statist preoccupations. The notion of the timeless interplay of states both militates against international progress and prevents the inception of a serious philosophical dialogue about the individual's place in an international society. Donelan's plea is surely an apt summation of this state of affairs:

> if the starting-point of the study of international relations is a world of separate states, a political theorist is right not to be interested in the subject. There is nothing for him to say. International relations is concerned with a mere space between states . . . If, on the other hand, we must not start with this assumption of separate states, there is all

216

the international theory in the world to be done. For there is now a primordial community of mankind; separate states are but an arrangement of it.[9]

PRACTICE

There are a number of difficulties in ascertaining the degree of continuity and change, historically, in the practice of international order. Not the least of these is the problem of distinguishing between superficial and fundamental change. A number of examples serve to illustrate this point.

Firstly, there is the danger that a changing distribution of power will be mistaken for fundamental change in the nature and role of power in inter-state relations. The seemingly endless 'rise and fall' of the powers reinforces the perception of dynamic movement. However, shifts in the balance of power do not amount to a change in the nature of the regulatory instruments of international order. As argued above, it was one of the weaknesses of the 1920s that superficial changes of the former kind were mistaken for evidence of fundamental change of the latter.

Secondly, the geographical expansion of the international system gives rise to the question whether this has simply extended the stage on which the traditional game is played or whether the greater economic diversity and cultural heterogeneity of the post-1960 international order does not amount to a major watershed. If there is presently a 'revolt against the West', is a pattern of international order originally derived from the west sustainable in these circumstances?

Thirdly, there is difficulty in distinguishing short-term cycles from long-term restructuring. Regarded within the short-term perspective of individual periods, the 1920s and the 1970s fostered the belief in long-term change whereas, with wider hindsight, both are better understood as repetitive cycles rather than as harbingers of secular change. If there is substance to the interpretations of 'long cycles' in world politics, a movement within a cycle from periodic global wars to periods of general peace, before declining legitimacy leads to a new challenge, may be misunderstood to represent the breaking out from a cycle into a new order.[10]

What does the historical record demonstrate? One theme running through the past century-and-a-half of international experience is that of conflict between the interests of the small powers and the interests of the greater powers. As such, it penetrates to the core of the hierarchical nature of the international order. This was an issue that

217

was first raised explicitly in connection with the congress system in as much as that system appeared to be a flagrant example of the Great Powers running the international show with scant respect for the interests of the small states. In their settlements, the Great Powers casually determined the fate of the lesser states on no principle other than their own convenience. It was to be likewise with the alliance systems at the end of the century. It was the Great Powers that were involved in the alliances and it was the smaller states, and also the colonial territories, that were employed as mere objects for changing or restoring the balance between these great powers.

The dispute between the smaller and the greater powers was to be opened again in relation to the drafting of both the Covenant of the League and the Charter of the United Nations. The former gave the major role to the Great Powers but made substantial concessions to the other states both in the Assembly of the League and in the Council. By way of contrast, the United Nations Charter, much more forcefully than the Covenant, asserted the special role of the Great Powers in international affairs.

There is something paradoxical about this. It is a fairly conventional view that in some sense the effort to establish international organisations represents the expression of the aspiration towards an improved international order. If this is so, and if there has been any progress from the days of the Concert of Europe to the establishment of the United Nations, then it would be reasonable to suppose that the UN represents the ethical ideals of international relations as they have developed over the past couple of centuries. At the same time, it is frequently stated that one of the most ethically abhorrent aspects of international relations has been this perpetual dominance of the Great Powers over the lesser members of the international system. Certainly this was one of Woodrow Wilson's major complaints about the traditional system of power politics. But if the UN represents the progress of ideas about a more equitable international society, then on this precise question of the relationship between, and the relative powers of, the great and small states, there would seem to have been no progress whatsoever. In fact, the UN in its original conception represented a quite definite return to the days of the congress system and refused to make even those concessions to small-power opinion that had been made in the League Covenant.

What, then, are we to make of this apparent paradox? There are at least two views that we might take of it – the 'whig' and the 'tory' interpretations respectively.

According to the whig account, the lack of progress on the issue of constructing a more egalitarian international order can be explained by the deceit and cunning of the Great Powers themselves. Butterfield noted of the whig interpretation that through its 'system of immediate reference to the present-day, historical personages can easily and irresistibly be classed into the men who furthered progress and the men who tried to hinder it'.[11] That is to say that history is populated by heroes and villains. At the international level it is the Great Powers themselves who are the villains: there has been no diminution of the hierarchical aspects of international order because the Great Powers did not desire any and because they had the means to prevent any 'progressive' developments on this issue.

There is another view that could be regarded as the tory interpretation. According to this, the drafters of the Charter had a clearer perception of the realities of international order than did Wilson and his contemporaries. They realised that international order would be made more, not less, stable by emphasising hierarchical arrangements and not by attempting to eliminate them. No ethical sentiment or egalitarian impulse can change the fact that some states are inherently more powerful than others and that these Great Powers, if thwarted in their vital interests, can do much more damage to international order than can dissatisfied small states. It was in this connection that some have argued that the doctrine of formal equality, at the international level, represents 'a spurious application of a nominally democratic principle to the unsuitable environment of international relations'. Vincent continues:

> Thus, in regard to the United Nations, it might be argued that the doctrine of one-state-one-vote that follows from the principle of equality gets in the way of the efficient working of the organization. It does so by preventing the writ of the powerful, on whose support the survival of the organization depends, from running and by allowing resolutions to be carried by coalitions of small states of whose acceptance in the international community at large there is little prospect.[12]

In short, the attempt to give institutional expression to a basic equality among states is, in any case, misconceived and we should not bemoan the lack of 'progress' in that direction.

Anyone who studies the recent development of the international political system cannot fail to be struck by another evident paradox. If we concede, as we surely must, that the performance of the international order has been deficient in many respects, and if we also conclude that there has been little change in the nature of that order, is there not something puzzling in the manner in which this inefficient polity has tenaciously maintained its basic characteristics? The extent of this puzzle depends, of course, on how deficient one assumes the system to have been but even Oran Young's relative equanimity does not conceal this puzzle from him. He is led to observe that 'the international polity constitutes a curious case in which a rather poor performance record along other dimensions is coupled with an impressive exhibit of durability'.[13] Arguably, the international political system has experienced less change in its central structures and its operating norms than any other political system that has functioned during the period since 1815.

One last point remains to be made. The principal theme of the book has been the various ways in which states have sought to manage the relations between them and these can mostly be reduced to a wavering between balance-of-power operations and a more highly organised concert system. The consensus about the present international order seems to be that if the system is not yet operating as a multipolar balance, then this is at least the general trend of development. Whatever its precise configuration, there can be little doubt that its basic operative principles derive from the balance-of-power model. As George Liska has written in the foreword to a book, comparing it with a study he had written some twenty years previously: 'Whereas the early effort dealt with international organization of collective security and stressed the smaller powers, the present one emphasises great states involved in the balances of land- and sea-based power in the raw.'[14]

Throughout the period under review, the irreducible minimum that the states have had between them by way of a regulatory mechanism has been the balance of power. If the present system is no more than a balance one, then it would appear that the search over the past one-and-a-half centuries for a more highly developed form of international order has, at least temporarily, come to a halt. Instead, the states appear to see virtue in the resurrection of the old balance system: they seem little disposed towards the elaboration of concert diplomacy. What is important, and in a sense striking, is that statesmen are openly declaring that, in the present circumstances, the best means of maintaining international order is on the basis of the primitive model of the balance of power. For those who seek for progress, this is a dismal note on which to conclude. As Alastair Buchan has lamented, 'it would be a sorry world and one that risked alienating not only the lesser powers but our own younger generation as well if they were asked to believe that a balance of power is the highest political achievement of which the new great powers are capable'.[15]

PRAXIS

Theory and practice of international order come together in various ways. Not least of the difficulties in assessing the extent of change is that the real world of international relations must be interpreted through an ideological prism. The danger with this is that change may be recognised only in so far as it is compatible with initial theoretical assumptions. The realist dismissal of the inter-war period as 'power politics in disguise', apt as it is with hindsight, tells us more about the theoretical assumptions of this set of ideas than about the nature of the historical situation: it was not simply that fundamental change had not taken place but rather that it could not have occurred, in principle, because a realist perception makes no allowance for such change.

Nonetheless, in some accounts, it is the intervention of ideas, as part of a learning process, that can contribute to change even within a relatively constant structure of international conflict. This is the semi-optimistic prognosis of Modelski, derived from his theory of long cycles which, rather than supporting a purely realist vision of recurrence and repetition, allows for adaptation:

> the experience of the long cycle has been richer than that. While clearly repetitive in its pattern the process has also been associated with undeniable ... variations in system performance. For it is precisely such changes in performance levels that are brought about through learning.[16]

There is a further difficulty in attempting to relate practices to ideas in the history of international order. In this historical survey, a recurring theme of analytic interest has been the effects, in terms of peace or stability, of the application of specific 'norms' of inter-state behaviour. At the most general level, it has been asked implicitly in the foregoing discussion whether concert or balance practices tend to be the more beneficial in their contribution to international order and it should already be clear that no satisfactory answer can be given to this question.

The problem that we started out with, which has not been resolved, is whether various kinds of international norms are creative of specific conditions of peace and stability or whether, conversely, it is the prior existence of conditions of stability that facilitates the adoption of cooperative norms. Did the norms of concert diplomacy create the peace of 1815–54 or was the concert parasitic upon the peace? Likewise, did the League produce the peace of the 1920s or did the peace of the 1920s create the illusion of an effective League system? Is its impotence revealed by its inability to cope with the real problems that arose in the 1930s? Is the post-1945 peace attributable to the rules of nuclear deterrence and the conventions of crisis management or have these norms been adopted because other factors rendered them acceptable?

If ideas about international order are not themselves 'independent variables', and if the effects of specific attempts to apply norms of international order are themselves so uncertain, then it is surely fair to conclude that the inter-relationship between ideas and practices is a complex one in which it is impossible to analyse how images of desirable international orders come to be, or fail to be, turned into reality. The proposition of one writer who contends that ideas and practices may be mutually reinforcing – in a progressive direction – is, accordingly, over-simple. His argument is as follows:

> The view that there is indeed progress is thus capable of generating a circle of mutually supporting arguments in the ideology of the society of international relations theorists: there is an order in international society which can be understood; if we understand we are better able to control and direct; the ability to control and direct allows us to cause improvements, which, in time, confirm our improving and understanding of international society.[17]

Were we all optimists, this might well be so. However, the circle of pessimistic thought is equally self-perpetuating and the real world reflects the tensions of the two competing claims. Ideas for reform of the international order have largely been countered by ideologies resistant to change. In practice, this has yielded a hierarchy of states many of the features of which have persisted since 1815.

NOTES

Introduction

1 F. Meinecke, *Machiavellism*, English translation (Routledge and Kegan Paul, 1957).

2 C. Holbraad, *Middle Powers in International Politics* (Macmillan, 1984), p. 19.

3 K. Waltz, *Theory of International Politics* (Addison-Wesley, 1979), pp. 114–16.

4 For a discussion of 'Regulative Forces' see R. Rosecrance, *International Relations: Peace or War?* (McGraw Hill, 1973), ch. 5.

5 F. H. Hinsley, 'The Rise and Fall of the Modern International System', *Review of International Studies* (January 1982), p. 4.

6 A. James. 'Law and Order in International Society', in James (ed.), *The Bases of International Order* (Oxford University Press, 1973), pp. 61–3.

7 H. Butterfield, *The Whig Interpretation of History* (Bell Edition, 1950), p. v.

8 *Ibid.*, p. 12.

9 C. van Doren, *The Idea of Progress* (Praeger, 1967), p. 3.

10 *Ibid.*, pp. 373–4.

11 F. H. Hinsley, *Power and the Pursuit of Peace* (Cambridge University Press, 1963), p. 13.

12 S. G. Goodspeed, *The Nature and Function of International Organisation* (Oxford University Press, 2nd edn, 1967), p. 670.

13 H. Kohn, *World Order in Historical Perspective* (Harvard, 1942), p. 270.

14 *Ibid.*, p. 279.

15 D. C. O'Brien, 'Modernisation, Order and the Erosion of a Democratic Ideal', *Journal of Development Studies*, 8, no. 4 (1972), p. 353.

16 Quoted in W. Camp, *The Glittering Prizes* (MacGibbon and Kee, 1960), p. 216.

17 G. Schwarzenberger, *Power Politics* (Stevens and Son, 3rd edn, 1964), part 2.

18 H. Bull, *The Anarchical Society: A Study of Order in World Politics* (Macmillan, 1977), p. 239.

19 I. L. Claude, *Swords into Plowshares: The Problems and Progress of International Organisation* (University of London, 1965), p. 14.

20 R. D. McKinlay and R. Little, *Global Problems and World Order* (Pinter, 1986).

21 M. Banks (ed.), *Conflict in World Society: A New Perspective on International Relations* (Wheatsheaf, 1984), p. 15.

22 S. Hoffmann, 'Rousseau on War and Peace', *American Political Science Review*, (June 1963), p. 333.

1 Order and international relations

1 See the general introduction in R. Falk and S. Mendlovitz, *Regional Politics and World Order* (Freeman and Co., 1973), p. 6.
2 Bull, *The Anarchical Society*, p. 94.
3 Stanley Hoffmann, 'An American Social Science: International Relations', *Daedalus* (Summer 1977), p. 57.
4 A. Bozeman, *Politics and Culture in International History* (Princeton, 1960).
5 Oran Young, 'On the Performance of the International Polity', *British Journal of International Studies*, 4 (1978), p. 191.
6 Richard Falk, 'The World Order Models Project and its Critics: A Reply', *International Organization* (Spring 1978), p. 542.
7 Bozeman, *Politics and Culture*, p. 520.
8 J. Weltman, 'On the Obsolescence of War: An Essay in Policy and Theory', *International Studies Quarterly* (December 1974), p. 405.
9 F. A. M. Alting von Geusau, *European Perspectives on World Order* (Sijthoff, 1975), p. 301.
10 M. Mandelbaum, 'International Stability and Nuclear Order: the first Nuclear Regime', in D. Gompert, M. Mandelbaum, R. L. Garwin and J. H. Barton, *Nuclear Weapons and World Politics* (McGraw-Hill, 1977).
11 There is an extensive body of literature on this question. For recent contributions, see e.g. G. Snyder and P. Diesing, *Conflict Among Nations* (Princeton, 1977), ch. 6; also C. Ostrom and J. Aldrich, 'The Relationship between Size and Stability in the Major Power International System', *American Journal of Political Science* (November 1978).
12 E. Luard, *Types of International Society* (Free Press, 1976), p. 303.
13 Young, 'Performance', p. 197.
14 A. Rapoport in his introduction to Clausewitz, *On War* (Penguin edn, 1968).
15 H. Bull, 'Society and Anarchy in International Relations', in H. Butterfield and M. Wight (eds.), *Diplomatic Investigations* (Allen and Unwin, 1966), p. 35.
16 G. Modelski, 'World Order-Keeping' in G. Goodwin and A. Linklater (eds.), *New Dimensions of World Politics* (Croom Helm, 1975), p. 54.

2 International and world order

1 K. J. Holsti, *The Dividing Discipline: Hegemony and Diversity in International Theory* (Allen and Unwin, 1987), p. 2.
2 R. Little, 'Structuralism and Neo-Realism', in M. Light and A. J. R. Groom (eds.), *International Relations: A Handbook of Current Theory* (Pinter, 1985), p. 76.
3 For a succinct summary, see e.g. M. Banks, 'The Inter-Paradigm Debate' in *ibid.*
4 R. Pettman, *State and Class: A Sociology of International Affairs* (Croom Helm, 1979), p. 65.

5 R. B. J. Walker (ed.), *Culture, Ideology, and World Order* (Westview Press, 1984), p. 190.

6 K. Waltz, 'Theory of International Relations', in F. Greenstein and N. Polsby (eds.), *International Politics*, Handbook of Political Science, vol. 8 (Addison-Wesley, 1975), pp. 39–40.

7 R. Keohane and J. Nye, *Power and Interdependence* (Little, Brown and Co., 1977), p. 21.

8 A. L. Burns, *Of Powers and Their Politics* (Prentice Hall, 1968), p. 266.

9 A. James, *Sovereign Statehood: The Basis of International Society* (Allen and Unwin, 1986).

10 Bull, *Anarchical Society*, p. 207.

11 See e.g. *North–South: A Programme for Survival* (Brandt Commission) (Pan, 1980).

12 S. D. Krasner, *Structural Conflict: The Third World Against Global Liberalism* (University of California Press, 1985), p. 83.

13 T. Nardin, *Law, Morality and the Relations of States* (Princeton University Press, 1983), pp. 43–4.

14 A. Giddens, *The Nation–State and Violence* (Polity Press, 1985), p. 255.

15 M. Frost, *Towards a Normative Theory of International Relations* (Cambridge University Press, 1986), p. 11.

16 E.g. C. Beitz, *Political Theory and International Relations* (Princeton University Press, 1979); C. Beitz et al. (eds.), *International Ethics* (Princeton University Press, 1985); S. Hoffmann, *Duties Beyond Borders* (Syracuse University Press, 1981); and A. Linklater, *Men and Citizens in the Theory of International Relations* (Macmillan, 1982). There is also an extensive literature on the ethics of war.

17 Beitz, *Political Theory*, p. 65.

18 Nardin, *Law, Morality*, p. 46.

19 See I. Clark, *Waging War: A Philosophical Introduction* (Clarendon Press, 1988). Important contributions have been M. Walzer, *Just and Unjust Wars* (Basic Books, 1977), B. Paskins and M. Dockrill, *The Ethics of War* (Duckworth, 1979) and J. T. Johnson, *Can Modern War be Just?* (Yale University Press, 1984).

20 M. Banks (ed.), *Conflict in World Society*, p. 7.

21 Beitz, *Political Theory*, p. 121.

22 R. J. Vincent, *Human Rights and International Relations* (Cambridge University Press, 1986), p. 125.

23 See e.g. H. Shue, *Basic Rights* (Princeton University Press, 1980), Beitz et al. (eds.), *International Ethics*, section V.

24 Beitz, *Political Theory*.

25 *Ibid.*, p. 151.

26 *Ibid.*, p. 128.

27 *Ibid.*, pp. 182–3.

28 W. T. R. Fox, 'E. H. Carr and political realism: vision and revision', *Review of International Studies* (January 1985), p. 12.

3 Kant and the tradition of optimism

1 M. Banks, 'The Inter-Paradigm Debate', in M. Light and A. J. R. Groom (eds.), *International Relations*, pp. 14–15.

2 Judith Shklar, *After Utopia. – the decline of political faith* (Princeton University Press, 1957), p. vii.

3 Paul Seabury, 'Practical International Futures', in A. Somit (ed.), *Political Science and the Study of the Future* (Dryden Press, 1974), pp. 286–7.

4 Hinsley, *Power and Pursuit of Peace*, p. 3.

5 This classification is used by L. R. Beres and H. R. Targ (eds.), *Planning Alternative World Futures* (Praeger, 1975), pp. xiv–xv.

6 R. W. Cox, 'On Thinking about Future World Order', *World Politics*, 28, no. 2 (January 1976). Cox specifies three paradigmatic approaches to future world order: the natural-rational; the positivist-evolutionary; the historicist-dialectical.

7 *Ibid.*, pp. 177–8.

8 J. Camilleri, *Civilization in Crisis: Human Prospects in a Changing World* (Cambridge University Press, 1976), p. 183.

9 Hedley Bull, 'The Theory of International Politics 1919–69', in B. Porter (ed.), *The Aberystwyth Papers* (Oxford University Press, 1972), p. 34.

10 Karl Mannheim, *Ideology and Utopia* (Routledge, 1960), p. 179.

11 A. Linklater, *Men and Citizens*, p. 302.

12 This point is discussed in E. H. Carr, *The Twenty Years' Crisis* (Macmillan, 1939), parts 1 and 2.

13 M. Frost, *Towards a Normative Theory*, p. 55.

14 G. Evans, 'Some Problems with a History of Thought in International Relations', *International Relations*, 4, no. 6 (November 1974), p. 720.

15 J. Bentham, *Plan for an Universal and Perpetual Peace* (Grotius Society, 1927), p. 43.

16 Lord Robert Cecil, *The Way of Peace* (Kennikat, 1968, original edn, 1928), p. 138.

17 See Carr, *Twenty Years' Crisis*, ch. 4.

18 A. E. Zimmern, 'The Future of Civilization', in R. Bourne (ed.), *Towards an Enduring Peace* (American Association for International Conciliation, 1916), p. 226.

19 See e.g. Hinsley, *Power and Pursuit of Peace*, ch. 4; K. Waltz, 'Kant, Liberalism and War', *American Political Science Review*, 56 (June 1962).

20 M. G. Forsyth, H. M. A. Keens-Soper and P. Savigear (eds.), *The Theory of International Relations* (Allen and Unwin, 1970), p. 211. All quotations from Kant are taken from the selections of his writings reproduced in this book.

21 *Ibid.*, p. 220.

22 *Ibid.*, p. 183.

23 *Ibid.*, p. 213.

24 W. B. Gallie, *Philosophers of Peace and War* (Cambridge University Press, 1978), p. 20.

25 *Ibid.*, p. 24.

26 Forsyth *et al.*, *Theory of International Relations*, p. 198.

27 *Ibid.*, p. 194.

28 *Ibid.*, pp. 194–5.
29 *Ibid.*, p. 185.
30 *Ibid.*, pp. 183–5.
31 Gallie, *Philosophers*, p. 29.
32 *Ibid.*, p. 32.
33 Cited in S. Rosen and W. Jones, *The Logic of International Relations* (Winthrop, 2nd edn, 1977), p. 429.
34 L. R. Beres, 'Behavioural Paths to a new World Order', in Beres and Targ, *Alternative World Futures*, p. 273.
35 R. Falk draws attention to the same three reformist reactions in *This Endangered Planet* (Vintage, 1971), pp. 283–4.
36 Quoted in K. Thompson, *Political Realism and the Crisis of World Politics* (Princeton University Press, 1960), p. 28.
37 Carr, *Twenty Years' Crisis*, p. 8.
38 E. Harris, *Annihilation and Utopia* (Allen and Unwin, 1966).
39 R. M. Hutchins, 'The Constitutional Foundations for World Order', in H. Morgenthau and K. Thompson (eds.), *Principles and Problems of International Politics* (Knopf, 1950), p. 143. (Emphasis added.)
40 Richard Falk, 'Reforming World Order: Zones of Consciousness and Domains of Action', in Beres and Targ, *Alternative World Futures*, p. 198.
41 Karl Jaspers, *The Future of Mankind*, English translation (University of Chicago Press, 1958), p. 14.
42 *Ibid.*, p. 327.
43 R. Niebuhr, 'The Myth of World Government', *The Nation* (16 March 1949), reproduced in Morgenthau and Thompson, *International Politics*, p. 137.
44 For an example of a less than optimistic appraisal, see A. J. Miller, 'Doomsday Politics: Prospects for International Co-operation', *International Journal*, 28, no. 1 (1972), pp. 122–33.
45 W. Wagar, *Building the City of Man* (Freeman and Co., 1971), p. 29.
46 Camilleri, *Civilization in Crisis*, p. 185.
47 G. Hirschfield, Preface in W. Wagar (ed.), *History and the Idea of Mankind* (University of New Mexico Press, 1971), p. vii.
48 Falk, *Endangered Planet*, p. 101.
49 Falk, 'Reforming World Order', in Beres and Targ, *Alternative World Futures*, p. 198.
50 Quoted in J. A. R. Marriott, *Commonwealth or Anarchy? A Survey of Projects of Peace* (Columbia University Press, 1939), p. 76.
51 Hinsley, *Power and Pursuit of Peace*, p. 1.
52 Quoted in Forsyth *et al.*, *Theory of International Relations*, p. 183.
53 Bull, *Anarchical Society*, p. 262.
54 L. P. Shields and M. C. Ott, 'The Environmental Crisis: International and Supranational Approaches', *International Relations*, 4, no. 6 (November 1974), pp. 645–6.
55 *Ibid.*, p. 647.
56 George Kennan, 'To Prevent a World Wasteland: A Proposal', *Foreign Affairs*, no. 3 (April 1970), p. 413.
57 A. Rapoport, *Conflict in Man-Made Environment* (Penguin, 1974), p. 162.
58 Mannheim, *Ideology and Utopia*, pp. 190–205.

59 *Ibid.*, p. 201.
60 Jaspers, *The Future of Mankind*, p. 324.

4 Rousseau and the tradition of despair

1 B. Porter, 'Patterns of Thought and Practice: Martin Wight's International Theory', in M. Donelan (ed.), *The Reason of States* (Allen and Unwin, 1978), p. 71.
2 Evans, 'Some Problems with a History of Thought', p. 720.
3 Waltz, 'International Relations', in Greenstein and Polsby, *International Politics*, p. 35.
4 F. Parkinson, *The Philosophy of International Relations*, Sage Library of Social Research, 52 (Sage Publications, 1977), p. 158.
5 Hedley Bull, 'The Theory of International Politics 1919–1969', in Porter (ed.), *Aberystwyth Papers*, p. 36.
6 Quoted in Thompson, *Political Realism*, p. 31.
7 John Herz, *The Nation–State and the Crisis of World Politics* (D. McKay, 1976), p. 74.
8 *Ibid.*, pp. 72–3.
9 E. L. Morse, *Modernization and the Transformation of International Relations* (Free Press, 1976), p. 37.
10 F. Ajami, 'The Global Logic of the Neoconservatives', *World Politics* (April 1978), p. 463.
11 R. Niebuhr, *The Structure of Nations and Empires* (Scribner's, 1959), pp. 292–3.
12 Carr, *Twenty Years' Crisis*, pp. 87–8.
13 Niebuhr, 'The Myth of World Government', p. 289.
14 R. W. Fox, 'Reinhold Niebuhr and the Emergence of the Liberal Realist Faith, 1930–1945', *The Review of Politics*, 38, no. 2 (April 1976), p. 247.
15 Thompson, *Political Realism*, p. 160.
16 R. Jervis, 'Co-operation under the Security Dilemma', *World Politics* (January 1978), p. 167.
17 Meinecke, *Machiavellism*, p. 15.
18 Forsyth *et al.*, *The Theory of International Relations*, p. 167. All quotations from Rousseau are taken from the selection of his writings reproduced in this book.
19 *Ibid.*, p. 132.
20 Cornelia Navari, 'Knowledge, the State and the State of Nature', in Donelan (ed.), *Reason of States*, p. 119.
21 Forsyth *et al.*, *The Theory of International Relations*, p. 132.
22 *Ibid.*, p. 156.
23 *Ibid.*
24 *Ibid.*, p. 150.
25 *Ibid.*
26 Hoffmann, 'Rousseau on War and Peace', p. 321.
27 Quoted in K. Waltz, *Man, the State and War* (Columbia, 1954), p. 181.
28 Forsyth *et al.*, *The Theory of International Relations*, p. 170.
29 *Ibid.*, p. 175.

30 *Ibid.*, p. 147.

31 *Ibid.*, p. 131.

32 *Ibid.*

33 Hoffmann, 'Rousseau on War and Peace', p. 317.

34 H. Kissinger, *Years of Upheaval* (Weidenfeld and Nicolson, 1982), p. 50.

35 H. Bull, 'Kissinger: The Primacy of Geopolitics', *International Affairs* (Summer 1980), p. 486.

36 H. J. Morgenthau, *Politics Amongst Nations* (5th edn, Knopf, 1973), p. 4.

37 *Ibid.*, p. 6.

38 Niebuhr, *Nations and Empires*, p. 292.

39 Kissinger, *A World Restored* (Grosset and Dunlop, 1964), p. 317.

40 Quoted in R. Falk, 'What's Wrong with Henry Kissinger's Foreign Policy?', *Alternatives* (March 1975), p. 88.

41 Kissinger, *A World Restored*, p. 2.

42 K. Thompson, 'Moral Reasoning in American Thought on War and Peace', *Review of Politics* (July 1977), p. 389.

43 A. R. Coll, *The Wisdom of Statecraft: Sir Herbert Butterfield and the Philosophy of International Politics* (Duke University Press,1985), p. 152.

44 Kissinger, *A World Restored*, p. 173.

45 Kissinger, *Nuclear Weapons and Foreign Policy* (Harper, 1957), p. 202.

46 The same could be said for Hobbes: 'There is no sense in Hobbes of the glorification of war, nor of relish for the game of power politics as an end in itself, nor of willingness to abdicate judgments in favour of the doctrine that anything in the international anarchy is permissible.' H. Bull, 'Hobbes and the International Anarchy', *Social Research* (Winter 1981), p. 729.

47 Thompson, 'Moral Reasoning', p. 388.

48 Niebuhr, *Nations and Empires*, pp. 289–90.

49 Carr, *Twenty Years' Crisis*, p. 93.

50 G. Evans, 'E. H. Carr and International Relations', *British Journal of International Studies*, 1 (1975), p. 89.

51 Thompson, 'Moral Reasoning', p. 392.

52 *Ibid.*, p. 393.

53 Morgenthau, *Politics Amongst Nations*, p. 10.

54 See K. Thompson, 'Idealism and Realism: Beyond the Great Debate', *British Journal of International Studies*, no. 3 (1977).

55 Waltz, *Theory of International Politics*.

56 See R. O. Keohane (ed.), *Neorealism and its Critics* (Columbia University Press, 1986).

57 R. Little, 'Structuralism and Neo-Realism' in Light and Groom (eds.), *International Relations*.

58 R. O. Keohane, 'Theory of World Politics: Structural Realism and Beyond', in Keohane (ed.), *Neorealism*, p. 159.

59 J. Nye, 'Neorealism and Neoliberalism', *World Politics* (January 1988), p. 245.

60 R. O. Keohane, *After Hegemony: Cooperation and Discord in the World Political Economy* (Princeton University Press, 1984), p. 67.

61 *Ibid.*, p. 245.

62 S. D. Krasner, *Structural Conflict*, p. viii.

63 Nye, 'Neorealism', p. 236.
64 R. W. Cox in R. B. J. Walker (ed.), *Culture, Ideology, and World Order*, p. 266.
65 Meinecke, *Machiavellism*, pp. 15–16.
66 Kissinger, *A World Restored*, p. 316.
67 Kissinger, *American Foreign Policy* (Norton, 1969), p. 46.
68 Thompson, *Political Realism*, ch. 4.
69 Quoted by Thompson in 'Moral Reasoning', p. 390.
70 Morgenthau, *Politics Amongst Nations*, p. 5.
71 Thompson, *Political Realism*, p. 3.
72 A. L. Burns, *Of Powers and their Politics*, p. 3.
73 J. W. Burton, *World Society* (Cambridge University Press, 1972), p. 90.
74 L. Mumford, *The Story of Utopias* (Viking edn, 1962), pp. 8–9.

5 Order and change in the international system, 1815–1990

1 P. W. Schroeder, 'The 19th-Century International System: Changes in the Structure', *World Politics* (October 1986), p. 12.
2 H. Bull, 'The Emergence of a Universal International Society', in H. Bull and A. Watson (eds.), *The Expansion of International Society* (Clarendon Press, 1984), p. 123.
3 G. Barraclough, *An Introduction to Contemporary History* (Penguin, 1964), p. 108.
4 See R. F. Holland, *European Decolonization 1918–1981* (Macmillan, 1985).
5 P. M. H. Bell, *The Origins of the Second World War in Europe* (Longman, 1986).
6 A. Iriye, *The Origins of the Second World War in Asia and the Pacific* (Longman, 1987).
7 R. B. J. Walker (ed.), *Culture, Ideology, and World Order* (Westview Press, 1984), p. 183.
8 Krasner, *Structural Conflict*, p. 75.
9 P. Kennedy, *The Rise and Fall of the Great Powers* (Unwin Hyman, 1988), p. 143.
10 I. Wallerstein, *The Modern World-System* (Academic Press, 1974).
11 A. G. Frank, *Capitalism and Underdevelopment in Latin America* (Monthly Review, 1967).
12 P. O'Brien, 'Europe in the World Economy', in Bull and Watson (eds.), *Expansion*, pp. 50–1.
13 *Ibid.*, p. 50.
14 A. S. Milward and S. B. Saul, *The Development of the Economies of Continental Europe 1850–1914* (Allen and Unwin, 1977), p. 469.
15 Cited in *ibid.*, p. 480.
16 *Ibid.*, pp. 484–5.
17 J. Foreman-Peck, *A History of the World Economy: International Economic Relations since 1850* (Wheatsheaf, 1983), p. 182.
18 *Ibid.*, p. 127.
19 M. S. Anderson, *War and Society in Europe of the Old Regime* (Fontana, 1988), p. 204.

20 J. R. Hale, *War and Society in Renaissance Europe* (Fontana, 1985), p. 45.

21 W. H. McNeill, *The Pursuit of Power* (Blackwell, 1983).

22 H. Strachan, *European Armies and the Conduct of War* (Unwin Hyman, 1983), p. 40.

23 See M. van Creveld, *Supplying War* (Cambridge University Press, 1977).

24 On remaining, and new, problems, see Strachan, *European Armies*, pp. 121–4.

25 See P. Paret (ed.), *Makers of Modern Strategy* (Princeton University Press, 1986).

26 Strachan, *European Armies*, p. 128.

27 M. Gowing, *Britain and Atomic Energy* (Macmillan, 1964).

28 F. H. Hinsley, 'The Rise and Fall of the Modern International System', *Review of International Studies* (January, 1982), p. 8.

29 M. Howard, 'The Military Factor in European Expansion', in Bull and Watson (eds.), *Expansion*, p. 41.

30 Schroeder, 'The 19th-Century International System', p. 11.

31 *Ibid.*, pp. 10–11.

32 J. G. Ruggie 'Continuity and Transformation in the World Polity: Toward a Neorealist Synthesis', *World Politics*, January 1983, p. 268.

33 See V. G. Kiernan, *European Empires from Conquest to Collapse 1815–1960* (Fontana, 1982).

34 L. Freedman, *Atlas of Global Strategy* (Macmillan, 1985), p. 51.

35 R. Gilpin, *War and Change in World Politics* (Cambridge University Press, 1981), p. 144.

36 D. Calleo, *Beyond American Hegemony: The Future of the Western Alliance* (Wheatsheaf, 1987), p. 131.

37 Gilpin, *War and Change*, p. 156.

38 R. Gilpin, 'The Politics of Transnational Economic Relations', in Keohane and Nye (eds.), *Transnational Relations and World Politics* (Harvard University Press, 1971), especially pp. 55–7.

39 R. Keohane, *After Hegemony: Cooperation and Discord in the World Political Economy* (Princeton University Press, 1984), p. 37.

40 Kennedy, *Rise and Fall*, p. 515.

41 Calleo, *Beyond American Hegemony*, p. 9.

42 Keohane, *After Hegemony*, p. 49.

43 Kennedy, *Rise and Fall*, p. 533.

44 Gilpin, *War and Change*, p. 210.

45 For a recent argument stressing continuities in diplomacy, see S. Sofer 'Old and New Diplomacy: a Debate Revisited', *Review of International Studies* (July 1988), pp. 195–211.

46 G. Mattingly, *Renaissance Diplomacy* (Houghton Mifflin, 1955).

47 D. McKay and H. M. Scott, *The Rise of the Great Powers, 1648–1815* (Longman, 1983), pp. 201–2.

48 M. Wight, *Power Politics* (Penguin, 1979), p. 115.

49 R. Albrecht-Carrié, *A Diplomatic History of Europe since the Congress of Vienna* (Methuen, 1958), p. 8. See also, A. Watson, *Diplomacy: The Dialogue Between States* (Methuen, 1982), p. 109.

50 F. R. Bridge and R. Bullen, *The Great Powers and the European States System 1815–1914* (Longman, 1980), p. 19.
51 Hinsley, *Power and Pursuit of Peace*, pp. 261–2.
52 See extracts of evidence from the 1861 Report from the Select Committee on the Diplomatic Service in D. P. Heatley, *Diplomacy and the Study of International Relations* (Clarendon Press, 1919), pp. 251–3.
53 Wight, *Power Politics*, p. 120.
54 *Ibid.*, p. 117.
55 Watson, *Diplomacy*, p. 159.
56 *Ibid.*, p. 18.
57 *Ibid.*, p. 95.
58 Sofer, 'Old and new diplomacy', p. 202.

6 From balance to concert, 1815–1854

1 F. R. Bridge and R. Bullen, *The Great Powers*, p. 20.
2 P. W. Schroeder, 'The 19th-Century International System: Changes in the Structure', *World Politics* (October, 1986), p. 1.
3 See in particular C. Bell, *The Conventions of Crisis – A Study in Diplomatic Management* (Oxford University Press, 1971).
4 I. C. Nichols, *The European Pentarchy and the Congress of Verona, 1822* (Nijhoff, 1971), p. 326.
5 F. Northedge and M. Grieve, *A Hundred Years of International Relations* (Duckworth, 1971), p. 200.
6 *Ibid.*, pp. 278–9.
7 R. B. Elrod, 'The Concert of Europe: A Fresh Look at an International System', *World Politics* (January 1976), p. 167.
8 R. Albrecht-Carrié, *The Concert of Europe 1815–1914* (Harper, 1968), p. 5.
9 Elrod, 'Concert of Europe', p. 163.
10 P. W. Schroeder, *Austria, Great Britain and the Crimean War: The Destruction of the European Concert* (Cornell University Press, 1972), p. 409.
11 W. N. Medlicott, *Bismarck, Gladstone and the Concert of Europe* (Athlone Press, 1956), p. 18.
12 C. Holbraad, 'Condominium and Concert', in Holbraad (ed.), *Super Powers and World Order* (Australian National University, 1971), p. 13. See also C. Holbraad, *The Concert of Europe* (Longman, 1970).
13 Inis Claude, *Swords into Plowshares* (University of London Press, 1965).
14 *Ibid.*, p. 24.
15 The whole point about Bell's 'Conventions of Crisis' is that they circumvent, or are a substitute for, the organisational machinery of the United Nations.
16 Schroeder, *Austria, Britain, Crimean War*, p. 404 (emphasis added).
17 Elrod, 'Concert of Europe', p. 161.
18 C. Bartlett, 'Britain and the European Balance, 1815–48', in A. Sked (ed.), *Europe's Balance of Power* (Macmillan, 1979), pp. 162–3.
19 Kennedy, *The Rise and Fall*, p. 163.
20 M. Wright (ed.), *The Theory and Practice of the Balance of Power* (Dent, 1975), pp. xiv–xv.

21 *Ibid.*, p. xviii.
22 E. V. Gulick, *Europe's Classical Balance of Power* (Norton edn, 1967).
23 *Ibid.*, p. 159.
24 *Ibid.*, pp. 305–6.
25 Schroeder, 'The 19th-Century International System', p. 17.
26 Hinsley, *Power and Pursuit of Peace*, p. 225.
27 R. Bridge, 'Allied Diplomacy in Peacetime', in Sked (ed.), *Europe's Balance*, p. 53.
28 Bridge and Bullen, *The Great Powers*, p. 4.
29 Medlicott, *Bismarck, Gladstone, Concert of Europe*, p. 18.
30 F. S. Northedge, *The International Political System* (Faber and Faber, 1976), p. 84.
31 Elrod, 'Concert of Europe', p. 160.
32 Nardin, *Law, Morality*, p. 96.
33 R. Langhorne, *The Collapse of the Concert of Europe: International Politics 1890–1914* (Macmillan, 1981), p. 4.
34 G. Goodwin, 'International Institutions and International Order', in James (ed.), *International Order*, p. 163.
35 R. Jervis, 'Security Regimes', in S. D. Krasner (ed.), *International Regimes* (Cornell University Press, 1983), p. 184.
36 Hinsley, *Power and Pursuit of Peace*, p. 226.
37 Holbraad, 'Condominium and Concert', p. 15.
38 Elrod, 'Concert of Europe', pp. 172–3.
39 Schroeder, *Austria, Britain, Crimean War*, p. 407.
40 Albrecht-Carrié, *Concert of Europe*, pp. 15–16 (emphases added).
41 Medlicott, *Bismarck, Gladstone, Concert of Europe*, p. 18.
42 Albrecht-Carrié, *Concert of Europe*, p. 17.
43 *Ibid.*, p. 19.

7 Balance without concert, 1856–1914

1 Bridge and Bullen, *The Great Powers*, p. 111.
2 Some analysts, for instance, argue that there was a major change during the 1870s alone. See B. Healy and A. Stein, 'The Balance of Power in International History', *Journal of Conflict Resolution* (September 1973).
3 J. Joll, *Europe Since 1870* (Weidenfeld and Nicolson, 1973), ch. 1.
4 Bridge and Bullen, *The Great Powers*, p. 125.
5 Hinsley, *Power and Pursuit of Peace*, p. 249.
6 *Ibid.*, p. 254.
7 M. S. Anderson *The Ascendancy of Europe* (Longman, 1972), pp. 54–5.
8 A. J. P. Taylor, *The Struggle for Mastery in Europe* (Oxford University Press, 1954), p. 82.
9 Langhorne, *The Collapse*, p. 70.
10 See e.g. Bridge and Bullen, *The Great Powers*, p. 133.
11 G. Barraclough, *An Introduction to Contemporary History* (Penguin, 1964), pp. 98–9.
12 F. Fischer, *Germany's Aims in the First World War* (Norton, 1967).
13 Langhorne, *The Collapse*, p. 22.

14 Northedge and Grieve, *International Relations*, p. 81.
15 Langhorne, *The Collapse*, p. 74.
16 G. Martel, *The Origins of the First World War* (Longman, 1987), pp. 5–7.
17 I. Geiss, 'Origins of the First World War', in H. W. Koch (ed.), *The Origins of the First World War* (Macmillan, 2nd edn, 1984), p. 65.
18 Joll, *Origins of the First World War*, p. 167.
19 Taylor, *Struggle for Mastery*, p. 336.
20 Joll, *The Origins*, p. 55.
21 Kennedy, *Rise and Fall*, p. 256.

8 Concert without balance, 1918–1939

1 D. Armstrong, *The Rise of the International Organization* (Macmillan, 1982), p. 6.
2 R. J. Overy, *The Origins of the Second World War* (Longman, 1987), p. 7.
3 A. J. Mayer, *Political Origins of the New Diplomacy* (Yale University Press, 1959).
4 R. Albrecht-Carrié, *The Unity of Europe* (Secker and Warburg, 1966), p. 199.
5 A. Zimmern, *The League of Nations and the Rule of Law* (Macmillan, 1936), p. 137.
6 Schwarzenberger, *Power Politics*, p. 273.
7 From an extract in A. Lijphart (ed.), *World Politics* (Allyn and Bacon, 2nd edn, 1971), p. 290.
8 Zimmern, *League of Nations*, p. 78.
9 *Ibid.*, p. 110.
10 Claude, *Swords Into Plowshares*, p. 38.
11 *Ibid.*, p. 44.
12 G. Ross, *The Great Powers and the Decline of the European States System* (Longman, 1983), p. 113.
13 F. S. Northedge, *The League of Nations* (Leicester University Press, 1986), p. 286.
14 Carr, *Twenty Years' Crisis*.
15 *Ibid.*, p. 87.
16 *Ibid.*
17 A. J. Mayer, *Politics and Diplomacy of Peacemaking* (Weidenfeld and Nicolson, 1968).
18 Quoted in *ibid.*, p. 12.
19 P. Kennedy, *The Rise and Fall*, p. 277.
20 *Ibid.*, p. 290.
21 A. W. Deporte, *Europe between the Superpowers* (Yale University Press, 1979), p. 28.
22 Bridge and Bullen, *The Great Powers*, p. 86.
23 Northedge, *The League*, p. 97.
24 P. M. H. Bell, *The Origins*, p. 14.
25 *Ibid.*, p. 38.
26 Kennedy, *The Rise and Fall*, pp. 317–18.

27 The tension between 'universalist' and 'exclusivist' conceptions of the League's membership is described in G. Schwarzenberger, *The League of Nations and World Order* (Constable, 1936).

9 From concert to balance, 1945–1990

1 M. Wight, 'The Balance of Power and International Order', in James, *International Order*, p. 113.
2 *Ibid.*, p. 112.
3 *A World Restored*, p. 1.
4 Bull, *Anarchical Society*, p. 207.
5 *Ibid.*
6 R. Jervis, 'Security Regimes', in S. D. Krasner (ed.), *International Regimes* (Cornell University Press, 1983), p. 187.
7 Holbraad, *Middle Powers*, p. 139.
8 A. Schlesinger, 'Origins of the Cold War', *Foreign Affairs* (October, 1967).
9 See M. Light, *The Soviet Theory of International Relations* (Wheatsheaf, 1988); A. Lynch, *The Soviet Study of International Relations* (Cambridge University Press, 1987).
10 Lynch, *The Soviet Study*, p. 67.
11 *Ibid.*, p. 105.
12 Calleo, *Beyond American Hegemony*, p. 17.
13 Bull, *Anarchical Society*, p. 212.
14 A. Buchan, *Power and Equilibrium in the 1970s* (Praeger, 1973), p. 16.
15 See e.g. A. Burns, 'From Balance to Deterrence', *World Politics*, 9 (1957); G. Snyder, 'The Balance of Power and the Balance of Terror', in Lijphart, *World Politics*: J. H. Herz, 'Balance Systems and Balance Politics in a Nuclear and Bipolar Age', in P. Toma and A. Gyorgy (eds.), *Basic Issues in International Relations* (Allyn and Bacon, 1967).
16 M. Wight, 'The Balance of Power', in Butterfield and Wight, *Diplomatic Investigations*, p. 167.
17 Calleo, *Beyond American Hegemony*, pp. 122–3.
18 V. P. Lukin, 'American–Chinese Relations: Concept and Reality', *USA – Economics, Politics, Ideology*, no. 2 (February 1973).
19 Moscow Radio, 1 August 1971.
20 Lukin, 'American–Chinese Relations'.
21 Herz, *Nation–State*, p. 59.
22 Keohane and Nye, *Power and Interdependence*, p. 8.
23 J. Lewis, 'Oil, Other Scarcities and the Poor Countries', *World Politics* (October 1974), p. 69.
24 E.g. J. Nye, 'Collective Economic Security', *International Affairs* (October 1974).
25 E. A. Brett, *The World Economy since the War: The Politics of Uneven Development* (Macmillan, 1985), p. 88.
26 *Ibid.*, p. 87.
27 J. E. Spero, *The Politics of International Economic Relations* (Allen and Unwin, 2nd edn 1981), p. 75.
28 *Ibid.*, p. 23.

29 S. Gill and D. Law, *The Global Political Economy* (Wheatsheaf, 1988), p. 181.
30 *Ibid.*, p. 145.
31 Spero, *The Politics*, p. 49.
32 R. Gilpin, *War and Change in World Politics* (Cambridge University Press, 1981), p. 173.
33 Calleo, *Beyond American Hegemony*, p. 126.
34 Brett, *The World Economy*, p. 187.
35 Gill and Law, *The Global Political Economy*, p. 183.
36 Brett, *The World Economy*, p. 131.
37 Banks (ed.), *Conflict in World Society; A New Perspective on International Relations* (Wheatsheaf, 1984), p. 9.
38 Keohane and Nye, *Power and Interdependence*, p. 35.
39 Claude, 'The Growth of International Institutions', in Porter, *Aberystwyth Papers*, p. 286.
40 Inis Claude, *Power and International Relations* (Random House, 1962), p. 160.
41 Goodwin, 'International Institutions', in James, *International Order*, p. 160.
42 *Ibid.*, p. 183.
43 A. LeRoy Bennett, *International Organizations* (Prentice-Hall, 1977), p. 389.
44 Wight, 'Balance of Power', in James, *International Order*, p. 111.
45 LeRoy Bennett, *International Organizations*, p. 132.
46 T. C. Schelling, *Arms and Influence* (Yale, 1966), p. 3.
47 R. Osgood and R. Tucker, *Force, Order and Justice* (Johns Hopkins, 1967), p. 26.
48 *Ibid.*, p. 15.
49 *Ibid.*, p. 225.
50 See e.g. L. Freedman, *The Evolution of Nuclear Strategy* (Macmillan, 1981); I. Clark, *Limited Nuclear War* (Martin Robertson, 1982); D. Ball and J. Richelson (eds.), *Strategic Nuclear Targeting* (Cornell University Press, 1986).
51 D. Ball, *Can Nuclear War be Controlled?* (IISS, Adelphi Paper No. 169, 1981); P. Bracken, *The Command and Control of Nuclear Forces* (Yale University Press, 1983).
52 Jervis, 'Security Regimes', in S. Krasner (ed.) *International Regimes* (Cornell University Press, 1983), p. 194.
53 L. Freedman, *Arms Control: Management or Reform?* (Routledge and Kegan Paul, 1986), pp. 2–3.
54 P. Keal, 'Spheres of Influence and International Order' (Ph.D. thesis, Department of International Relations, Australian National University). For a full discussion, see Keal, *Unspoken Rules and Superpower Dominance* (Macmillan, 1983).
55 E. Kaufman, *The Superpowers and their Spheres of Influence* (Croom Helm, 1976), p. 10.
56 Bull, *Anarchical Society*, p. 206.
57 *Ibid.*, p. 224.
58 Kaufman, *The Superpowers*, p. 23.
59 M. Cohen 'Moral Skepticism', in C. Beitz *et al.* (eds.), *International Ethics* (Princeton University Press, 1985), p. 47.
60 Keal, *Unspoken Rules*, p. 212.

61 I. I. Dore, *International Law and the Superpowers* (Rutgers University Press, 1984), p. 52.
62 H. Bull (ed.), *Intervention in World Politics* (Clarendon Press, 1984), p. 5.
63 M. Walzer, *Just and Unjust Wars* (Basic Books, 1977), pp. 86–108.
64 See M. Akehurst, 'Humanitarian Intervention', in Bull, *Intervention*, p. 97.
65 Bull, *Intervention*, p. 148.
66 P. Williams, *Crisis Management* (Martin Robertson, 1976), p. 28.
67 R. N. Lebow, *Nuclear Crisis Management: A Dangerous Illusion* (Cornell University Press, 1987), pp. 18, 59.
68 Bell, *Conventions of Crisis*.
69 *Ibid.*, p. 75.
70 Bell, *The Diplomacy of Detente* (St Martin's Press, 1977), p. vii.
71 R. W. Stevenson, *The Rise and Fall of Detente* (Macmillan, 1985), p. 11.
72 B. White, 'The Concept of Detente', *Review of International Studies* (July 1981), pp. 168–9.
73 Stevenson, *The Rise and Fall*, p. 145.
74 Bell, *Diplomacy*, p. 5.
75 *Ibid.*
76 *Ibid.*, p. 25.
77 F. Halliday, *The Making of the Second Cold War* (Penguin, 1982).
78 Bull, *Anarchical Society*, pp. 226–7.
79 Morse, *Modernization*, p. 44.
80 *Ibid.*, p. 45.

Conclusion

1 Claude, *Power*, pp. 3–4.
2 P. Savigear, 'European Political Philosophy and International Relations', in T. Taylor (ed.), *Approaches and Theory in International Relations* (Longman, 1978), p. 35. The same point has been made by M. Wight, see his 'Why is there no International Theory?', in Butterfield and Wight, *Diplomatic Investigations*.
3 Quoted in S. Pollard, *The Idea of Progress* (Penguin, 1971), p. 167.
4 H. Foley (ed.), *Woodrow Wilson's Case for the League of Nations* (Kennikat, 1967), p. 64.
5 P. G. Taylor, 'International Relations Theory, the Idea of Progress and the Role of the International Civil Servant', *Political Studies*, 3 (1972), p. 267.
6 *Ibid.*
7 See e.g. R. Rothstein, *The Weak in the World of the Strong* (Columbia, 1977).
8 For one discussion of this relationship, see J. Galtung, 'The New Economic Order in World Politics' in A. W. Singham (ed.), *The Nonaligned Movement in World Politics* (Lawrence Hill, 1977).
9 M. Donelan, 'The Political Theorists and International Theory' in Donelan (ed.), *Reason of States*, p. 90.
10 On 'long cycles', see G. Modelski, *Long Cycles in World Politics* (Macmillan, 1987).
11 Butterfield, *Whig Interpretation*, p. 11.

12 R. J. Vincent, 'Western Conceptions of a Universal Moral Order', *British Journal of International Studies*, 4 (April 1978), p. 37.

13 O. Young, 'On the Performance of the International Polity', *British Journal of International Studies*, 4 (1978), p. 199.

14 G. Liska, *Quest for Equilibrium* (Johns Hopkins, 1977), p. ix.

15 A. Buchan, *Power and Equilibrium in the 1970s* (Praeger, 1973), p. 111.

16 Modelski, *Long Cycles*, p. 126.

17 Taylor, 'International Relations Theory', p. 268.

BIBLIOGRAPHY

Ajami, F., 'The Global Logic of the Neoconservatives', *World Politics*, April 1978.

Albrecht-Carrié, R., *A Diplomatic History of Europe since the Congress of Vienna* (Methuen: London, 1958).

The Unity of Europe (Secker and Warburg: London, 1966).

The Concert of Europe 1815–1914 (Harper: New York, 1968).

Allison, G., *Essence of Decision: Explaining the Cuban Missile Crisis* (Little Brown: Boston, 1971).

Alting von Geusau, F. A. M., *European Perspectives on World Order* (Sijthoff; Leyden, 1975).

Anderson, M. S., *The Ascendancy of Europe* (Longman: London, 1972).

War and Society in Europe of the Old Regime, 1618–1789 (Fontana: London, 1988).

Armstrong, J. D., *The Rise of the International Organization* (Macmillan: London, 1982).

Aron, R., *Peace and War* (Weidenfeld and Nicolson: London, 1966).

Ball, D., *Can Nuclear War be Controlled?* (IISS, Adelphi Paper No. 169: London, 1981).

Ball, D. and Richelson, J. (eds.), *Strategic Nuclear Targeting* (Cornell University Press: Ithaca, 1986).

Banks, M. (ed.), *Conflict in World Society: A New Perspective on International Relations* (Wheatsheaf Books: Brighton, 1984).

Barraclough, G., *An Introduction to Contemporary History* (Penguin: Harmondsworth, 1964).

Bartlett, C. J., *The Global Conflict: The International Rivalry of the Great Powers, 1880–1970* (Longman: London, 1984).

Beitz, C., *Political Theory and International Relations* (Princeton University Press: Princeton, 1979).

Beitz, C. *et al.* (eds.), *International Ethics* (Princeton University Press: Princeton, 1985).

Bell, C., *The Conventions of Crisis: A Study of Diplomatic Management* (Oxford University Press: London, 1971).

The Diplomacy of Detente (St Martin's Press: New York, 1977).

Bell, P. M. H., *The Origins of the Second World War in Europe* (Longman: London, 1986).

Bentham, J., *Plan for an Universal and Perpetual Peace* (Grotius Society: London, 1927).

Beres, L. R. and Targ, H. R. (eds.), *Planning Alternative World Futures* (Praeger: New York, 1975).

Best, G., *War and Society in Revolutionary Europe, 1770–1870* (Fontana: London, 1982).

Bond, B., *War and Society in Europe, 1870–1970* (Fontana: London, 1984).

Bourne, R. (ed.), *Towards an Enduring Peace* (American Association for International Conciliation: New York, 1916).

Bozeman, A., *Politics and Culture in International History* (Princeton University Press: Princeton, 1960).

Bracken, P., *The Command and Control of Nuclear Forces* (Yale University Press: New Haven, 1983).

Brandt Commission, *North–South: A Programme for Survival* (Pan: London, 1980).

Brett, E. A., *The World Economy since the War; The Politics of Uneven Development* (Macmillan: London, 1985).

Brewer, A., *Marxist Theories of Imperialism: A Critical Survey* (Routledge and Kegan Paul: London, 1980).

Bridge, F. R. and Bullen, R., *The Great Powers and the European States System, 1815–1914* (Longman: London, 1980).

Buchan, A., *Power and Equilibrium in the 1970s* (Praeger: New York, 1973).

Bull, H., *The Anarchical Society: A Study of Order in World Politics* (Macmillan: London, 1977).

  'Kissinger: The Primacy of Geopolitics', *International Affairs*, Summer 1980.

  'Hobbes and the International Anarchy', *Social Research*, Winter 1981.

  (ed.). *Intervention in World Politics* (Clarendon Press; Oxford, 1984).

Bull, H. and Watson, A. (eds.), *The Expansion of International Society* (Oxford University Press: Oxford, 1984).

Burns, A. L., *Of Powers and their Politics* (Prentice-Hall: Englewood Cliffs, 1968).

  'From Balance to Deterrence', *World Politics*, 1957.

Burton, J. W., *World Society* (Cambridge University Press: Cambridge, 1972).

Butterfield, H., *The Whig Interpretation of History* (Bell: London, 1950).

Butterfield, H. and Wight, M. (eds.), *Diplomatic Investigations* (Allen and Unwin: London, 1966).

Buzan, B. and Barry Jones, R. J., *Change and the Study of International Relations: The Evaded Dimension* (Pinter: London, 1981).

Calleo, D. P., *Beyond American Hegemony: The Future of the Western Alliance* (Wheatsheaf: Brighton 1987).

Camilleri, J., *Civilization in Crisis: Human Prospects in a Changing World* (Cambridge University Press: Cambridge, 1976).

Carr, E. H., *The Twenty Years' Crisis* (Macmillan: London, 1939, Harper, 1964).

Cecil, Lord Robert, *The Way of Peace* (Kennikat: Port Washington, 1968).

Clark, I., *Limited Nuclear War: Political Theory and War Conventions* (Martin Robertson: Oxford, 1982).

  Waging War: A Philosophical Introduction (Clarendon Press: Oxford, 1988).

Claude, I., *Power and International Relations* (Random House: New York, 1962).

Swords into Plowshares: The Problems and Prospects of International Organization (University of London Press: London, 1965).

Coll, A. R., *The Wisdom of Statecraft: Sir Herbert Butterfield and the Philosophy of International Politics* (Duke University Press; Durham, 1985).

Cox, R. W., 'On Thinking about Future World Order', *World Politics*, January 1976.

'Ideologies and the NIEO', *International Organization*, No. 2, 1979.

Creveld, M. van, *Supplying War: Logistics from Wallenstein to Patton* (Cambridge University Press: Cambridge, 1977).

Dehio, L., *The Precarious Balance: The Politics of Power in Europe, 1494–1945* (Chatto and Windus: London 1963).

Deporte, A. W., *Europe Between the Superpowers* (Yale University Press: New Haven, 1979).

Donelan, M. (ed.), *The Reason of States* (Allen and Unwin: London, 1978).

Dore, I. I., *International Law and the Superpowers* (Rutgers University Press: New Brunswick, 1984).

Doren, C. van, *The Idea of Progress* (Praeger: New York, 1967).

Elrod, R. B., 'The Concert of Europe: A Fresh Look at an International System', *World Politics*, January 1976.

Evans, G., 'Some Problems with a History of Thought in International Relations', *International Relations*, November 1974.

'E. H. Carr and International Relations', *British Journal of International Studies*, No. 1, 1975.

Falk, R., *This Endangered Planet* (Vintage Books: New York, 1971).

'What's Wrong with Henry Kissinger's Foreign Policy?', *Alternatives*, March 1975.

'The World Order Models Project and its Critics; A Reply', *International Organization*, Spring 1978.

and Mendlovitz, S. (eds.), *Regional Politics and World Order* (Freeman and Company: San Francisco, 1973).

Farer, T., 'The Greening of the Globe: A Preliminary Appraisal of the World Order Models Project', *International Organization*, Winter 1977.

Fischer, F., *Germany's Aims in the First World War* (Norton: New York, 1967).

Foley, H. (ed.), *Woodrow Wilson's Case for the League of Nations* (Kennikat: New York, 1967).

Foreman-Peck, J., *A History of the World Economy: International Economic Relations since 1850* (Wheatsheaf: Brighton, 1983).

Forsyth, M. G., *et al.* (eds.), *The Theory of International Relations* (Allen and Unwin: London, 1970).

Fox, R. W., 'Reinhold Niebuhr and the Emergence of the Liberal Realist Faith, 1930–1945', *The Review of Politics*, April 1976.

Fox, W. T. R., 'E. H. Carr and Political Realism: Vision and Revision', *Review of International Studies*, January 1985.

Frank, A. G., *Capitalism and Underdevelopment in Latin America* (Monthly Review: New York, 1967).

Freedman, L., *The Evolution of Nuclear Strategy* (Macmillan: London, 1981).

Atlas of Global Strategy (Macmillan: London, 1985).

Arms Control: Management or Reform? (Routledge and Kegan Paul: London, 1986).

Frost, M., *Towards a Normative Theory of International Relations* (Cambridge University Press: Cambridge, 1986).

Gaddis, J. L., *The United States and the Origins of the Cold War 1941–1947* (Columbia University Press: New York, 1972).

Gallie, W. B., *Philosophers of Peace and War* (Cambridge University Press: Cambridge, 1978).

George, A. and Craig, G., *Force and Statecraft: Diplomatic Problems of our Time* (Oxford University Press: New York, 1983).

Giddens, A., *The Nation–State and Violence* (Polity Press: Cambridge, 1985).

Gill, S. and Law, D., *The Global Political Economy* (Wheatsheaf: London, 1988).

Gilpin, R., *War and Change in World Politics* (Cambridge University Press: New York, 1981).

Gompert, D. *et al.*, *Nuclear Weapons and World Politics* (McGraw-Hill: New York, 1977).

Goodspeed, S. G., *The Nature and Function of International Organisation* (Oxford University Press: London, 2nd edn, 1967).

Goodwin, G. and Linklater, A. (eds.), *New Dimensions of World Politics* (Croom Helm: London, 1975).

Gowing, M., *Britain and Atomic Energy, 1939–1945* (Macmillan: London, 1964).

Greenstein, F. and Polsby, N. (eds.), *International Politics, Handbook of Political Science*, vol. 8 (Addison-Wesley: Reading, 1975).

Grosser, A., *The Western Alliance* (Macmillan: London, 1980).

Gulick, E. V., *Europe's Classical Balance of Power* (Norton: New York, 1967).

Hale, J. R., *War and Society in Renaissance Europe* (Fontana: London, 1985).

Halle, L. J., *The Cold War as History* (Chatto and Windus: London, 1967).

Halliday, F., *The Making of the Second Cold War* (Penguin: London, 1982).

Handel, M. (ed.), *Clausewitz and Modern Strategy* (Frank Cass: London, 1986).

Harris, E., *Annihilation and Utopia* (Allen and Unwin: London, 1966).

Healy, B. and Stein, A., 'The Balance of Power in International History', *Journal of Conflict Resolution*, September 1973.

Heatley, D. P., *Diplomacy and the Study of International Relations* (Clarendon Press: Oxford, 1919).

Herz, J., *The Nation–State and the Crisis of World Politics* (D. McKay: New York, 1976).

Hinsley, F. H., *Power and the Pursuit of Peace* (Cambridge University Press: Cambridge, 1963).

'The Rise and Fall of the Modern International System', *Review of International Studies*, January 1982.

Hoffmann, S., *Duties Beyond Borders* (Syracuse University Press: Syracuse, 1981).

'Rousseau on War and Peace', *American Political Science Review*, June 1963.

'An American Social Science: International Relations', *Daedalus*, Summer 1977.

Holbraad, C., *The Concert of Europe* (Longman: London, 1970).

Middle Powers in International Politics (Macmillan: London, 1984).

(ed.), *Super Powers and World Order* (Australian National University Press: Canberra, 1971).

Holland, R. F., *European Decolonization, 1918–1981* (Macmillan: London, 1985).

Holsti, K. J., *The Dividing Discipline: Hegemony and Diversity in International Theory* (Allen and Unwin: Boston, 1987)

Howard, M., *War in European History* (Oxford University Press: Oxford, 1976). *War and the Liberal Conscience* (Temple Smith: London, 1978). *Clausewitz* (Oxford University Press: Oxford, 1983).

Iriye, A., *The Origins of the Second World War in Asia and the Pacific* (Longman: London, 1987).

James, A., *Sovereign Statehood: The Basis of International Society* (Allen and Unwin: London, 1986).

(ed.), *The Bases of International Order* (Oxford University Press: London, 1973).

Jaspers, K., *The Future of Mankind* (University of Chicago Press: Chicago, 1958).

Jervis, R., 'Co-operation under the Security Dilemma', *World Politics*, January 1978.

Johnson, J. T., *Can Modern War Be Just?* (Yale University Press: New Haven, 1984).

Joll, J., *Europe since 1870* (Weidenfeld and Nicolson: London, 1973). *The Origins of the First World War* (Longman: London, 1984).

Kaufman, E., *The Superpowers and their Spheres of Influence* (Croom Helm: London, 1976).

Keal, P., *Unspoken Rules and Superpower Dominance* (Macmillan: London, 1983).

Kennan, G., 'To Prevent a World Wasteland: a Proposal', *Foreign Affairs*, April 1970.

Kennedy, P., *The Rise and Fall of the Great Powers: Economic Change and Military Conflict from 1500 to 2000* (Unwin Hyman: London, 1988).

Keohane, R. O., *After Hegemony: Cooperation and Discord in the World Political Economy* (Princeton University Press: Princeton, 1984).

(ed.), *Neorealism and its Critics* (Columbia University Press: New York, 1986).

Keohane, R. O. and Nye, J., *Power and Interdependence* (Little, Brown and Company: Boston, 1977).

Keohane, R. O. and Nye, I. (eds.), *Transnational Relations and World Politics* (Harvard University Press: Cambridge, 1971).

Keylor, W. R., *The Twentieth-Century World: An International History* (Oxford University Press: New York, 1984).

Kiernan, V. G., *European Empires from Conquest to Collapse, 1815–1960* (Fontana: London, 1982).

Kissinger, H., *Nuclear Weapons and Foreign Policy* (Harper: New York, 1957). *A World Restored* (Grosset and Dunlop: New York, 1964). *American Foreign Policy* (Norton: New York, 1969). *Years of Upheaval* (Weidenfeld and Nicolson: London, 1982).

Koch, H. W. (ed.), *The Origins of the First World War* (Macmillan: London, 2nd edn, 1984).

Kohn, H., *World Order in Historical Perspective* (Harvard University Press: Cambridge, 1942).

Krasner, S. D. (ed.), *International Regimes* (Cornell University Press: Ithaca, 1983).

Structural Conflict: The Third World Against Global Liberalism (University of California Press: Berkeley, 1985).

Langhorne, R., *The Collapse of the Concert of Europe: International Politics 1890–1914* (Macmillan: London, 1981).

Lasswell, H. D., 'The Promise of the World Order Modelling Movement', *World Politics*, April 1977.

Lebow, R. N., *Nuclear Crisis Management: A Dangerous Illusion* (Cornell University Press: Ithaca, 1987).

Leroy Bennett, A., *International Organizations* (Prentice-Hall: Englewood Cliffs, 1977).

Lewis, J., 'Oil, Other Scarcities and the Poor Countries', *World Politics*, October 1974.

Light, M., *The Soviet Theory of International Relations* (Wheatsheaf Books: Brighton, 1988).

Light, M. and Groom, A. J. R. (eds.), *International Relations: A Handbook of Current Theory* (Pinter: London, 1985).

Lijphart, A. (ed.), *World Politics* (Allyn and Bacon: Boston, 2nd edn, 1971).

Linklater, A., *Men and Citizens in the Theory of International Relations* (Macmillan: London, 1982).

'Realism, Marxism and Critical International Theory', *Review of International Studies*, October 1986.

Liska, G., *Quest for Equilibrium* (Johns Hopkins University Press: Baltimore, 1977).

Luard, E., *Types of International Society* (Free Press: New York, 1976).

A History of the United Nations (Macmillan: London, 1982).

Lukin, V. P., 'American–Chinese Relations: Concept and Reality', *USA – Economics, Politics, Ideology*, February 1973.

Lynch, A., *The Soviet Study of International Relations* (Cambridge University Press: Cambridge, 1987).

McKay, D. and Scott, H. M., *The Rise of the Great Powers, 1648–1815* (Longman: London, 1983).

McKinlay, R. D. and Little, R., *Global Problems and World Order* (Pinter: London, 1986).

McNeill, W. H., *The Pursuit of Power* (Blackwell: Oxford, 1983).

Mandelbaum, M., *The Nuclear Revolution* (Cambridge University Press: Cambridge, 1981).

Mannheim, K., *Ideology and Utopia* (Routledge: London, 1960).

Manning, C. A. W., *The Nature of International Society* (Macmillan: London, reissued, 1975).

Marriott, J. A. R., *Commonwealth or Anarchy? A Survey of Projects of Peace* (Columbia University Press: New York, 1939).

Martel, G. (ed.), *The Origins of the Second World War Reconsidered* (Allen and Unwin: London, 1986).

The Origins of the First World War (Longman: London, 1987).

Mattingly, G., *Renaissance Diplomacy* (Houghton Mifflin: Boston, 1955).

Mayer, A. J., *Political Origins of the New Diplomacy* (Yale University Press: New Haven, 1959).

Politics and Diplomacy of Peacemaking (Weidenfeld and Nicolson: London, 1968).

244

Medlicott, W. N., *Bismarck, Gladstone and the Concert of Europe* (Athlone Press: London, 1956).

Meinecke, F., *Machiavellism* (Routledge and Kegan Paul: London, 1957).

Mendlovitz, S. (ed.), *On the Creation of a Just World Order* (Free Press: New York, 1975).

Miller, A. J., 'Doomsday Politics: Prospects for International Co-operation', *International Journal*, no. 1, 1972.

Milward, A. S. and Saul, S. B., *The Development of the Economies of Continental Europe, 1850–1914* (Allen and Unwin: London, 1977).

Modelski, G., *Long Cycles in World Politics* (Macmillan: London, 1987).

Morgenthau, H. J., *Politics Amongst Nations* (Knopf: New York, 5th edn, 1973).

Morgenthau, H. J. and Thompson, K. (eds.), *Principles and Problems of International Politics* (Knopf: New York, 1950).

Morse, E. L., *Modernization and the Transformation of International Relations* (Free Press: New York, 1976).

Mumford, L., *The Story of Utopias* (Viking: New York, 1962).

Nardin, T., *Law, Morality and the Relations of States* (Princeton University Press: Princeton, 1983).

Nicholas, H. G., *The United Nations as a Political Institution* (Oxford University Press: London, 4th edn, 1971).

Nichols, I. C., *The European Pentarchy and the Congress of Verona, 1822* (Nijhoff: The Hague, 1971).

Niebuhr, R., *The Structure of Nations and Empires* (Scribner's: New York, 1959).

Northedge, F. S., *The International Political System* (Faber and Faber: London, 1976).

The League of Nations (Leicester University Press: Leicester, 1986).

and Grieve, M., *A Hundred Years of International Relations* (Duckworth: London, 1971).

Nye, J. S., 'Collective Economic Security', *International Affairs*, October 1974.

'Neorealism and Neoliberalism', *World Politics*, January 1988.

O'Brien, D. C., 'Modernisation, Order and the Erosion of a Democratic Ideal', *Journal of Development Studies*, no. 4, 1972.

Osgood, R. and Tucker, R., *Force, Order and Justice* (Johns Hopkins University Press: Baltimore, 1967).

Ostrom, C. and Aldrich, J., 'The Relationship between Size and Stability in the Major Power International System', *American Journal of Political Science*, November 1978.

Overy, R. J., *The Origins of the Second World War* (Longman: London, 1987).

Paret, P. (ed.), *Makers of Modern Strategy: From Machiavelli to the Nuclear Age* (Princeton University Press: Princeton, 1986).

Parkinson, F., *The Philosophy of International Relations* (Sage: Beverly Hills, 1977).

Paskins, B. and Dockrill, M., *The Ethics of War* (Duckworth: London, 1979).

Pettman, R., *State and Class: A Sociology of International Affairs* (Croom Helm: London, 1979).

Pollard, S., *The Idea of Progress* (Penguin: Harmondsworth, 1971).

Porter, B. (ed.), *The Aberystwyth Papers* (Oxford University Press: London, 1972).

Rapoport, A., *Strategy and Conscience* (Harper and Row: New York, 1964).
  Conflict in Man-Made Environment (Penguin: Harmondsworth, 1974).
  (ed.), *On War*, by C. von Clausewitz (Penguin: Harmondsworth, 1968).
Rosecrance, R., *International Relations: Peace or War?* (McGraw Hill: New York, 1973).
Rosen, S. and Jones, W., *The Logic of International Relations* (Winthrop: Cambridge, 2nd edn, 1977).
Ross, G., *The Great Powers and the Decline of the European States System* (Longman: London, 1983).
Rothstein, R., *The Weak in the World of the Strong* (Columbia University Press: New York, 1977).
Ruggie, J. G., 'Continuity and Transformation in the World Polity: Toward a Neorealist Synthesis', *World Politics*, January 1983.
Savigear, P., *Cold War or Detente in the 1980s* (Wheatsheaf Books: Brighton, 1987).
Schelling, T. C., *Arms and Influence* (Yale University Press: New Haven, 1966).
Schlesinger, A., 'Origins of the Cold War', *Foreign Affairs*, October 1967.
Schroeder, P. W., *Austria, Great Britain and the Crimean War: The Destruction of the European Concert* (Cornell University Press: Ithaca, 1972).
  'The 19th-Century International System: Changes in the Structure', *World Politics*, October 1986.
Schwarzenberger, G., *The League of Nations and World Order* (Constable: London, 1936).
  Power Politics (Stevens and Sons: London, 3rd edn, 1964).
Seabury, Paul, 'Practical International Futures', in A. Somit (ed.), *Political Science and the Study of the Future* (Dryden Press: New York, 1974).
Shields, L. P. and Ott, M. C., 'The Environmental Crisis: International and Supranational Approaches', *International Relations*, November 1974.
Shklar, J., *After Utopia: The Decline of Political Faith* (Princeton University Press: Princeton, 1957).
Shue, H., *Basic Rights: Subsistence, Affluence, and US Foreign Policy* (Princeton University Press: Princeton, 1980).
Sims, N. A. (ed.), *Explorations in Ethics and International Relations* (Croom Helm: London, 1981).
Singham, A. W. (ed.), *The Nonaligned Movement in World Politics* (Lawrence Hill: Westport, 1977).
Sked, A. (ed.), *Europe's Balance of Power* (Macmillan: London, 1979).
Smith, M. *et al.* (eds.), *Perspectives on World Politics* (Croom Helm: London, 1981).
Smith, S. (ed.), *International Relations: British and American Perspectives* (Blackwell: Oxford, 1985).
Snyder, G. and Diesing, P., *Conflict Among Nations* (Princeton University Press: Princeton, 1977).
Sofer, S., 'Old and New Diplomacy: a Debate Revisited', *Review of International Studies*, July 1988.
Spero, J. E., *The Politics of International Economic Relations* (Allen and Unwin: London, 2nd edn, 1981).
Stevenson, R. W., *The Rise and Fall of Detente* (Macmillan: London, 1985).

Storry, R., *Japan and the Decline of the West in Asia* (Macmillan: London, 1979).

Strachan, H., *European Armies and the Conduct of War* (Unwin Hyman: London, 1983).

Talbott, S., *Deadly Gambits* (Pan: London, 1985).

Taylor, A. J. P., *The Struggle for Mastery in Europe* (Oxford University Press: Oxford, 1954).

Taylor, P. G., 'International Relations Theory, the Idea of Progress and the Role of the International Civil Servant', *Political Studies*, No. 3, 1972.

Taylor, T. (ed.), *Approaches and Theory in International Relations* (Longman: London, 1978).

Thompson, K., *Political Realism and the Crisis of World Politics* (Princeton University Press: Princeton, 1960).

'Moral Reasoning in American Thought on War and Peace', *Review of Politics*, July 1977.

'Idealism and Realism: Beyond the Great Debate', *British Journal of International Studies*, no. 3, 1977.

Toma, P. and Gyorgy, A. (eds.), *Basic Issues in International Relations* (Allyn and Bacon: Boston, 1967).

Tucker, R., *The Inequality of Nations* (Basic Books: New York, 1977).

Vasquez, J. A., *The Power of Power Politics* (Pinter: London, 1983).

Vincent, R. J., *Nonintervention and International Order* (Princeton University Press: Princeton, 1974).

Human Rights and International Relations (Cambridge University Press: Cambridge, 1986).

'Western Conceptions of a Universal Moral Order', *British Journal of International Studies*, April 1978.

Wagar, W., *Building the City of Man* (Freeman and Company: San Francisco, 1971).

(ed.), *History and the Idea of Mankind* (University of New Mexico Press: Albuquerque, 1971).

Walker, R. B. J. (ed.), *Culture, Ideology, and World Order* (Westview Press: Boulder, 1984).

Wallerstein, I., *The Modern World-System* (Academic Press: New York, 1974).

Waltz, K., *Man, The State and War* (Columbia University Press: New York, 1954).

Theory of International Politics (Addison-Wesley: Reading, 1979).

'Kant, Liberalism and War', *American Political Science Review*, June 1962.

Walzer, M., *Just and Unjust Wars* (Basic Books: New York, 1977).

Watson, A., *Diplomacy: the Dialogue Between States* (Methuen: London, 1982).

Weltman, J., 'On the Obsolescence of War: An Essay in Policy and Theory', *International Studies Quarterly*, December 1974.

White, B., 'The Concept of Detente', *Review of International Studies*, July 1981.

White, J., 'The NIEO: What is it?', *International Affairs*, October 1978.

Wight, M., *Systems of States*, ed., by H. Bull (Leicester University Press: Leicester, 1977).

Power Politics, ed. by H. Bull and C. Holbraad (Penguin: Harmondsworth, 1979).

Williams, P., *Crisis Management* (Martin Robertson: Oxford, 1976).

Wright, M. (ed.), *The Theory and Practice of the Balance of Power* (Dent: London, 1975).

(ed.), *Rights and Obligations in North–South Relations* (Macmillan: London, 1986).

Yergin, D., *Shattered Peace* (Penguin: Harmondsworth, 1980).

Young, O., 'On the Performance of the International Polity', *British Journal of International Studies*, no. 4, 1978.

Zimmerman, W., *Soviet Perspectives on International Relations* (Princeton University Press: Princeton, 1969).

Zimmern, A., *The League of Nations and the Rule of Law* (Macmillan: London, 1936).

Zolberg, A. R., 'Origins of the Modern World System: A Missing Link', *World Politics*, January 1981.

INDEX